IN THE HOUSES OF THE POOR
An exegesis on the latter half
of Saint John's Gospel

IN THE HOUSES OF THE POOR
An exegesis on the latter half
of Saint John's Gospel

Matthew Franklin Cooper

OCABS PRESS
ST PAUL, MINNESOTA 55124
2025

IN THE HOUSES OF THE POOR
An exegesis on the latter half
of Saint John's Gospel

Copyright © 2025 by
Matthew Franklin Cooper

ISBN 978-1-60191-064-6

All rights reserved.

In the houses of the poor
An exegesis on the latter half of Saint John's Gospel

Copyright © 2025 by Matthew Franklin Cooper
All rights reserved.

ISBN 978-1-60191-064-6

Published by OCABS Press, St. Paul, Minnesota.
Printed in the United States of America.

Books are available through OCABS Press at special discounts for bulk purchases in the United States by academic institutions, churches, and other organizations. For more information, please email OCABS Press at press@ocabs.org.

Front cover is from the Russian icon «Воскресение Лазарево» 'The Raising of Lazarus', Novgorod school, 15th century (Novgorod Museum of Art), in the public domain. Rear cover is from a lithograph illustration of the village of El Eizariya from Charles William Meredith van de Velde's *Le Pays d'Israel*, 1857, in the public domain.

*This book is dedicated to the memory of
Erin M. Thayer († 2021).*

May she and all her house receive Allāh's blessings in overabundance.

Introduction

My prior book, *The Lamb before Its Shearers*, is an exploratory lexicographical exegesis of the first ten chapters of the Gospel of Saint John. This book is an attempt at reading the Gospel 'naïvely', and bringing to bear analysis on specific words, tracing their trajectories back through the Septuagint text to their Hebrew roots. It was also a 'companion piece' to a neglected work of fourth-century Antiochian School exegesis: the *Skeireins aiwaggeljons þairh Iohannen*, written in the extinct Gothic language. And it served as a strong commentary on the current events at the time of writing: namely, bearing witness against the ongoing genocide of the Palestinian people of Gaza by the government of Israel.

To summarise that work: I came to several conclusions *from the text* and its allusions backward into the Hebrew scrolls, regarding the pedagogical purposes of the Gospel of Saint John. These conclusions are:

1) *The anti-Hellenistic, anti-philosophical and anti-theological tenor of the text.* Through the themes of light and darkness, blindness and seeing, borrowed through the LXX from the Book of Genesis, Saint John posits the *logos* not as a property of human agents or communities, but instead as the *command* of the Scriptural God which is *embodied* in Jesus's radical, unconditional submission and obedience. Saint John also adopts the critical language of 'measurement' from the book of Job to criticise the entire endeavour of theology.
2) *A broadside against identity politics as such.* The exchange 'at night', in which Nicodemus abortively attempts to

defend the idea of justification through lineage and birthright, ends with Jesus pointing him back to the 'generations of the heavens and the earth' through a baptism in water and spirit uniting us to the entirety of the created order. Later, when answering his Jewish interlocutors, Jesus holds forth that the true children of Abraham are not those claiming blood-descent from Abraham, but instead those who *do what Abraham's God commands.*

3) *A robust response to Gnostic and nascent-Judaistic challenges to the Pauline table-fellowship.* The healing at Bethzatha, the 'farce' at the Feast of Booths and the healing of the man born blind all point semiotically to the *sufficiency* of the *Torah* for its hearers. The teaching is always active in its healing of those who are sick or 'dry', even on the Sabbath (in fact, God's Sabbath—which is meant for man's *instruction*). This kind of double-edged verse is meant to distinguish the Pauline teaching, both from Gnostics who seek to subvert and expunge the *Torah*, and from nascent Judaisers who wish to coopt the *Torah*'s message against the Gentiles in the fellowship. Jesus's healings consistently have the effect of causing *schisms* among His critics: *scattering* the flocks and allowing a new one to form around Him.

4) *Johannine numerology supporting the teaching's universality.* The passage showing the feeding of the multitudes places a significant emphasis on the number 'five', which is actually a 'four-plus-one': indicating the four (Gentile) cardinal directions plus the one (Jewish) centre. The παιδάριον of the passage is actually **Nathanael**. His

In the Houses of the Poor

Semitic name, 'God gives', becomes *functional* in the passage, even as the disciple bearing the name becomes anonymous.

5) *Jesus as the Lamb of God—and as the Able Herdsman.* The text of Saint John's Gospel positions Jesus from the very beginning as the Lamb of God (*seh ha'Elōhîm* שה האלהים) from Genesis 22: the archetypical and thus universally-valid sacrificial offering. He is given on behalf of those human beings who are in darkness (ἐν τῇ σκοτίᾳ) and don't have a clue (οὐ κατέλαβεν). Yet Jesus is also portrayed in a different sacrificial role. He is cast as the Able Herdsman (רעה צאן טוב *Rā'ah Ṣō'n Ṭôb*), an appellation which links Him to Abel and Ishmael from the Book of Genesis. The other kings who came before Jesus, who did not obey the Torah, sacrifice their flock to feed and clothe themselves—and thus they show themselves to be false shepherds. Only the Able Herdsman lays down His own life to spare the sheep.

As I read further in Saint John's Gospel, I continue in the Antiochian vein of Scriptural exegesis inspired by my Gothic kinsman, the author of *Skeireins*. However, this method is bolstered by judicious application of the functionalist literary theory of Prince Nicolas Trubetskoi as exposited by his pupil Roman Jakobson, and also by the Bronze Age economic historiography and Semitic textual analysis of Michael Hudson.

The present book, *In the Houses of the Poor*, addresses more directly the literary-historical context of the Gospel text, and the questions which were facing Saint John when he wrote it. At the outset of the second century the Pauline table-fellowship was beset by crises from all sides. The expulsion of the Paulines from the synagogues was one such. Another was the growth of Hellenising sects following teachers such as Valentinus, Basilides, Cerinthos and Marcion—later grouped together under the label of 'Gnostic'. In reaction, there was a movement to restore the ritual purity codes of the Pentateuch and establish a historicist identity for the Pauline community. And overshadowing it all was the official persecution of the Paulines by the Roman Empire.

Saint John's Gospel is written for hearers with all these crises all firmly in 'earshot'. I agree with Fr Paul Tarazi's thesis, that the Apocalypse written from the author's exile on the island of Patmos was committed to the Pauline communities prior to or contemporaneously with the Gospel text bearing Saint John's name. We know from Saint Irenaios of Lyons, for example, that Saint John himself had at least one personal run-in with Cerinthos, and that he was an avowed enemy of Cerinthos's doctrine. Such Hellenising influences are relevant today in the anti-Scriptural appeal of such resurgent ideologies as Christian nationalism and 'Christian manliness'.

Several relevant literary themes of Saint John's Gospel readily emerge from this context. Jesus's earthly origins are obscured here, as they are in the Gospel according to Saint Mark: He is introduced to us twice as the 'Lamb of God' by John the Baptist. The Davidic lineage of Jesus is deliberately downplayed. Instead, here, Jesus is presented to us as a champion of the impoverished people of Palestine. The feeding of the multitudes and the raising of Lazarus have a definite economic-radical quality that render Him a threat in the eyes of the Roman state.

In the Houses of the Poor

To understand this angle in Saint John's work, it is necessary to turn to the lexicographical and economic-historical work of Dr Michael Hudson, professor of economics at the University of Missouri-Kansas City. Hudson's work correctly characterises Jesus as a populist preacher of Isaiah's 'acceptable year of the Lord' (Luke 4:19), bringing a Levitical debt-relief not only to the sons of Jacob but to all the peoples of the Roman Empire. This reading makes particular sense when one hears that in raising their brother from the dead Jesus saves Mary and Martha 'in the house of the poor' from eviction; and again when Jesus promises a legal 'advocate' to His disciples who will wipe out all debts and correct all measures.

With the raising of Lazarus, however, the question of the kingship of Jesus becomes immediate and urgent. It is directly after the raising of Lazarus that the Judahite authorities plan to have Jesus arrested. The pretext on which Jesus is arrested is that of *regnum appetere*: the same 'desire for tyranny' that *supposedly* afflicted the Gracchi in Rome. Yet Jesus has already refused, even *fled*, from kingship—after the feeding of the multitudes!

The charge against Jesus, a man who has explicitly refused kingship in Chapter 6, of seeking kingship, quickly becomes a stumbling-block for His accusers. Saint John takes what I will, in conscious anachronism, call a 'Marxist' view of this charge. In this Gospel, the charge becomes a mechanism that exposes the contradictory economic and political goals of Rome and of Rome's Judahite clients. Pilate, seeking to show off the absolute authority and might of his Empire, desires that he should *actually* have a king to execute. On the other hand, the Judahite authorities, invested in retaining their own ideological legitimacy, are eager to show Jesus as a Messianic *pretender*, a *false* Davidic claimant. It is precisely these contradictory motives that Saint John exposes at several points: when the Judahites refuse to cross Pilate's threshold; or when Pilate argues with the Judahites (*'Behold, your king!'*); or, most tellingly, when Pilate and the Judahites argue over the wording on the placard under which Jesus is to be executed. Saint John's silence on the question of Jesus's Davidic lineage, in contrast to the genealogies of Saint Matthew and Saint Luke, thus becomes all the more poignant and significant.

Yet even though Saint John is engaging in a 'Marxist' exposure of the material motives behind these two ideological postures, the question of 'whose throne is it?' is actually of extreme, and even overriding, importance. Jesus does not seek the throne for Himself—we saw that in Chapter 6. He points instead, unflaggingly, to the kingship of His Father. Only One gets to sit on the throne—and it isn't Pilate, and it isn't Caiaphas! Yet Jesus, the only One Who gets the message, is also the only One Who is crucified for kingly ambition!

Saint John deploys prophetic language borrowed from Daniel, to show how Jesus's execution in fact places on trial the empty claims of Empire and Temple. But *the family* is also on trial here. Jesus's final request to Mary, His mother, is to *relinquish* her familial claim on Him and be accepted into the house of 'the other disciple'. When she does so, she is free, with him, to stand judgement on her own terms. In the Orthodox Church we call her *Theotokos*. But in Saint John's Gospel, she is *Oxoprospheros*: the one who holds the sour wine which quenches the thirst of a dying man. This is not a belittlement of Jesus's mother at all. Indeed, she is the *only one* who freely submits to God's command to *let go* of her Son, and thus passes His test! She alone extends the hospitality which is God's command, to a man who is no longer family to her.

The place of execution, Golgotha, is linguistically tied to the place where Jesus begins His ministry: Galilee. In fact, Golgotha is a redoubling of the Semitic root *g-l-l* ג-ל-ל from which Galilee is derived. This attests to the *cyclical structure* of the Gospel as a whole, and the *cyclical model* of human history to which the entirety of Scripture attests. God acts in His own time, His own καιρός, amidst human schemes and plans that always follow a pattern of rise, *hubris* and fall. As a species, we do not 'progress'. The choice that faces us is the same choice that our ancestors faced: do we *hear* the teaching and *obey* it; or do we follow our own will along the same cyclical path of construction and destruction?

Thus, we should not expend too much *speculation* on the raising of Lazarus. It is there in the text. It is a literary fact: just as Raskol'nikov's stone is a literary fact for Dostoevsky. Those who ascribe their own 'meaning' to it, in the text, are Pilate and Caiaphas. But the name of Lazarus, who is *lexically* introduced as a son of Aaron (Exo 6:23), points us back to God's *command* to the Levites. Do we forgive the poor their debts? Do we respect the elderly? Do we love the stranger among us as a native? Do we keep just balances and measures? Do we keep all of God's commandments and statutes?

I am only a 'barbarian'. By blood, the tribe who can most closely claim me as their descendant are the Goths: the destroyers of Ephesus in the third century. The second claim upon me goes to the Celts: the Galatians to whom Paul addressed an entire letter rebuking their idolatry. And the third claim upon me goes to the Iranian Scythians: who merit only a passing mention in Colossians. Yet—by God's grace, by His χάρις as Saint Paul uses the term—I am not the first barbarian to read Saint John's Gospel. God has given us another chance, another cycle, within which we may hear His word, and then do it.

—Matthew Franklin Cooper
ᛘᚨᛏϕᚨɪns, snɴns ᚲᚨnϕᚨ
12 April 2025, *Lazarus Saturday*

Table of Contents

Introduction	11
Table of Contents	19
A few notes on the *Skeireins*	21
In the houses of the poor	33
Abuse of the prophetic function	49
Gird them with girdles, bind caps on them	63
A note on authorial self-elision	79
My word, or my words to you?	89
Servants in the vineyard	101
Concerning debt, measures and lawsuits	115
And the Lamb will conquer	141
Plant them on Thy holy mountain	161
The light in the darkness is not overcome	173
Double judgement in the High Priest's house	185
Christ's kingly claim over Pilate	197
They made long their furrows	213
Crucify the messenger	225
A drink at the seventh hour	237
The race is not to the swift	257
Three times 'peace'	269
Full circle, back to Galilee	281
Closing remarks of a Gothic disciple	293
Acknowledgements	311

A few notes on the *Skeireins*

In place of a postscriptum *on* The Lamb before Its Shearers

The *Skeireins aiwaggeljons þairh Ïohannen* is one of two fragmentary extant texts authored in the Gothic language—the other being a translation of the Bible into the Gothic language by the Bishop Wulfila (or Ulfilas)[1]. The Gothic language forms part of the extinct 'Eastern' branch of the Germanic language family[2]: whose 'Western' branch includes English, Dutch and German; and whose 'Northern' branch includes Danish, Norwegian and Swedish. Gothic is purported to be closest in kinship to the languages of other tribes of people who moved into the Eastern Roman Empire around the same time as they: tribes which include Gepids, Vandals, and possibly Old Burgundians[3]. These 'Eastern Germanic' tribes, including the Goths, were semi-nomadic, belligerent even amongst each other, led by tribal kings[4], and

---

[1] Peter Heather and John Matthews, *The Goths in the Fourth Century* (Liverpool University Press, 1991), 145-156.

[2] Robert Dennis Fulk, *A Comparative Grammar of the Early Germanic Languages* (*Studies in Germanic linguistics* series vol. 3, John Benjamins Publishing Company, 2018), 12-14, 19-21.

[3] Fulk, *Grammar*, 19.

[4] Jordanes, *The Origin and Deeds of the Goths*, parallel Latin-English, trans. Charles C. Mierow (Princeton University Press, 1915, *facs.*), 14-15, 23.

A *few notes on the* Skeireins

converted under Roman Imperial influence from a form of Germanic polytheism to Arian Christianity[5].

After being imported into Eastern Rome as *fœderati* (essentially what we would now call 'private military contractors'), economic exploitation and ill-treatment at the hands of their Dacio-Roman military bosses led several of their tribal chiefs, particularly a Christian convert named Fritigern, to stage a revolt which ravaged much of the Thracian countryside (what is now Romanian Dobruja, Bulgaria and European Turkey) between 376 and 382[6]. The Battle of Adrianople, in which the Roman Emperor Valens was killed, was the first victory which presaged a Gothic looting spree across the Roman Empire—with Rome itself being pillaged in 410 by one of Fritigern's successors, Alaric[7].

These Goths would settle and establish kingdoms—one in the west, in Spain and Portugal[8], and one in the east, in Italy[9]. After this, the Iberian settlers would be called 'Western' or Visigoths, and the Italian settlers would be called 'Eastern' or Ostrogoths. Abandoning their traditional nomadic lifestyle would prove

---

[5] Herwig Wolfram, *The History of the Goths*, trans. Thomas J. Dunlap (University of California Press, 1988), 70.

[6] Alessandro Barbero, *The Day of the Barbarians: the Battle that Led to the Fall of the Roman Empire* (Walker & Company, 2005).

[7] Wolfram, *History*, 150-161.

[8] Peter Heather, *The Goths* (*The Peoples of Europe* series vol. 9, Blackwell Publishers, 1996), 187-210.

[9] *Ibid.*, 216-258.

In the Houses of the Poor

fatal for Gothic culture: once they settled down, they adopted Roman habits, Roman clothing, the Roman language, and Roman (that is to say, Nicene) Christianity[10]. Even if the Ostrogothic polity in Italy had not been destroyed by Emperor Justinian and his general Belisarius in a series of wars lasting from 537 to 561[11], and the Visigoths driven out of Iberia by *al-Kalīf* al-Walīd ibn 'Abd al-Malik in 711[12], both Gothic groups were on a self-consigned path to cultural extinction[13].

Their living remnants were largely absorbed by other Germanic kingdoms (Franks, Burgundians, Saxons, Lombards etc.) which had by then taken root in Western Europe. Despite the terror the Goths inflicted on the Western Roman Empire during its twilight years, except for certain place-names and personal names in France, Spain and Portugal, little remains of their cultural legacy[14]. Nowadays, 'Gothic' refers to a style of Western European church architecture[15], and to a post-punk

---

[10] *Ibid.*, 210-215.

[11] *Ibid.*, 263-271.

[12] Wolfram, *History*, 245.

[13] Heather, *Goths*, 297-298.

[14] Despite this, the legacy of the Goths was highly contested during periods of nationalistic fervour! Both the Swedes and the Austrian Habsburgs famously laid disputing claims against each other as the 'true heirs' of the Goths during the 1400s and again during the 1600s. See: Heather, *Goths*, 2, 11; and Wolfram, *History*, 2.

[15] Otto Georg von Simson, *The Gothic Cathedral: Origins of Gothic Architecture and the Medieval Concept of Order* (Princeton University Press, 1964).

A few notes on the Skeireins

artistic and musical subculture which emphasises macabre thematics, dark clothing, body piercings, hair dye, and lots of eye-liner[16].

I should preface this with the caveat that I'm not a medieval historian by training. I'm a teacher and a scholar of economics and *East* Asian languages. But the historical trajectory of this text is still worth exploring in brief. First, it should be noted that *Skeireins aiwaggeljons þairh Ïohannen* is not a title given anywhere in the original text. This was instead a 'native' christening of the text from a later scholar, the Prussian philologist Hans Ferdinand Maßmann, who published it in Berlin in 1834[17].

As to its origins: whether the *Skeireins* is an original work of Gothic exegesis of the Gospel of John, or whether it is a translation into Gothic of the work of a Greek author, is unclear. It seems broadly agreed that Bishop Wulfila is **not** the *Skeireins* author[18]. A number of scholars, following the literary criticism of Friedrichsen, credit the idea that the author of this Gothic document closely follows Greek syntactic and rhetorical

---

[16] Rachel K Fischer, 'The Gothic Aesthetic,' *Reference & User Services Quarterly* 58(3), 2019: 143-148.

[17] William Holmes Bennett, 'Decipherments, editions and critical studies,' in Anonymous, *The Gothic Commentary on the Gospel of John*, trans. William Holmes Bennett (The Modern Language Association of America, 1960), 12-14.

[18] George H McKnight, 'The language of the *Skeireins*,' *Modern Language Notes* 12(4), 1897: 205-209.

conventions [19]. Knut Schäferdiek proposes Theodore of Heraclea—an Antiochian School exegete and ally of Eusebius of Emesa (Ḥimṣ) against Athanasius of Alexandria—as the author of the Greek base text of which *Skeireins* is a translation[20]. This is an intriguing, even plausible hypothesis. To my mind, it's also quite appealing, as it furnishes a solid link between the *Skeireins* text and the Antiochian School of Exegesis. But the attribution of authorship is unfortunately pure conjecture. It is not and cannot be drawn from the text itself! Even granting the rigour of Schäferdiek's analysis and his intuition that it conforms to Bishop Theodore's style, *Skeireins* could equally be the original work of a Gothic student of Theodore, or someone else in his exegetical school with an interest in reaching out to a Gothic-speaking audience.

What remains of the *Skeireins* itself consists of eight folio leaves—palimpsests, sheets of parchment which were scrubbed clean of their original text to make room for a different one. These sheets bear the impress of texts written in multiple hands, in Gothic and in Latin script. Of these, five leaves were included in the *Codex Ambrosianus* E, kept in a library in Milan; and three different leaves were discovered in the *Codex Vaticanus Latinus* 5750[21]. The manuscripts themselves date back

---

[19] G W S Friedrichsen, 'The Gothic "Skeireins" in the Greek original,' *New Testament Studies* 8(1), 1961: 43-56.

[20] Knut Schäferdiek, 'Die Fragmente der "Skeireins" und der Johanneskommentar des Theodor von Herakleia,' *Zeitschrift für deutsches Altertum und deutsche Literatur* 110(3), 1981: 175-193.

[21] Anonymous, *Commentary*, 5.

A few notes on the Skeireins

to the sixth century, with the work itself likely predating even that. The text being written in the Gothic language, it was evidently aimed at an audience *literate in that language*, so an authorship date between 381 (after the completion of the *Wulfila Bible*) and 555 (before the fall of the Ostrogothic Kingdom) seems logically feasible[22]. The scope of the fragments indicates that the *Skeireins* was originally a much longer work, perhaps ten times the eight sheets of parchment that remain.

The *Codex Vaticanus Latinus* 5750 is a document that contains, in addition to the first three Gothic *Skeireins* fragments, an Arian theological tract from the early 500s written in uncial Latin, and also an ancient commentary on the speeches of Cicero (*Scholia in Ciceronis orationes Bobiensia*). This *Codex* was apparently kept quite snugly in a monastery in Bobbio from the seventh century, up until the three sheets of it still there were moved into the Vatican library since 1618[23]. The propinquity of the Gothic text to an Arian document likely shows greater evidence of the Vatican's squeamishness about the storage and physical handling of texts suspected of being doctrinally unsound, than it does of the heretical nature of the text itself.

The fragmentary *Skeireins* text itself contains a number of hints as to its 'positioning', some of which I mention in *The Lamb before Its Shearers*. Here are some of the positions which the exegesis takes, which I believe to have been worth exploring in my first book on the Gospel of John:

---

[22] Wolfram, *History*, 367-371 *tt*.
[23] *Ibid.*, 8-10.

In the Houses of the Poor

1) That Jesus Christ **submits to God**. The Gothic says ᚷᚨᛚᛖᛁᚲᛟᚾ ᛋᛖᛁᚾᚨᛁ ᚠᚱᛟᛞᛖᛁᚾ—'*to imitate His wisdom*' (Bennett more strongly translates this: '*to **conform with** His wisdom*'). Jesus demonstrates the Gospel ᚷᚨᚾᚲᛞᚨᛗ ᚷᚨh ᚷᚨᚾᚲᛋᛏᚣᚨᛗ—'*with words and deeds*' [24]. The Gospel proclaimed by Saint John is not merely an intellectual *assensus*, but an ᚾᛋᛗᛖᛏᛖ: that is to say a 'behaviour', a 'conduct' or a 'comportment'. It's a *praxis*, not merely a *doxa*. It is necessary not only to passively receive the Gospel with the ears, but instead to be provoked into actually **hearing the text** and **living the teaching** that is proclaimed therein.

2) The Gospel teaching ᚨᚾᛞ ᚨᛚᛚᚨᚾᚨ ᛗᛁᛞᚷᚾᚾᚷᚨᚱᛞ ᚷᚨᚠᚨᛁh—it '*thrives into all Middle-Earth*', if I may borrow the bright, green Teutonic song of the original Gothic expression[25]. The baptisms of John and Jesus, the prophet and the teaching, draw all things by **water and spirit** into a **universal kinship**, against which our insistence on states and institutions and ideologies exist in an utterly pathetic rebellion. Unfortunately, in the end, even the Gothic author flinches away from the full functionality of his own language, and retreats

---

[24] Anonymous, *Commentary*, 54 Id.

[25] *Ibid.*, 64 IVb. A brief side-note: this same Gothic language also clearly inspired the pioneering fantasy author J.R.R. Tolkien in his mythopoeic ᛗᛁᛞᚷᚾᚾᚷᚨᚱᛞ or 'Middle-Earth': it was the basis for the Taliska language spoken in Mirkwood far before the events of the *Lord of the Rings*!

A *few notes on the* Skeireins

to speaking of 'all men'. But man is kin even to the animals, to the dust of the earth, as the youngest of the 'generations of the heavens and the earth'.

3) There seems to be an unexamined assumption in much of the *Skeireins* scholarship that the author is on the Arian side of the Christological controversy, simply by virtue of writing in Gothic. This assumption is maintained despite the evidence to our own eyes given by the passage at the end of the fifth leaf, which explicitly refutes the doctrinaire form of Arianism: proclaiming, skulnm nn ἀλλαι... gah ainabanka snnan τφs τφ yisansan τakunnan—'*we all must... recognise the Only Begotten One, the Son of God, to be God*'[26]! Of course, the *Skeireins* author also goes on at length lambasting Sabellius and Marcellus, which was Arius's favoured tactic along with many of his followers. The *Skeireins* author does insist on the **subordination of the Son to the Father**, but as a claim *from the Johannine text*, not as a *theology*[27]. The author uses it in the lead-up to a punchline that refutes Arius in his strongest theological claims!

---

[26] Anonymous, *Commentary*, 69-70 Vc.-d.

[27] If one is interested in that sort of thing, I think one can make a case for the *Skeireins* author taking either a 'homoousian' or a 'homoiousian' stance. But, as I argue in my book, that *isn't the point*. – Auth.

In the Houses of the Poor

4) Once one is no longer tethered to imposing an Arian Christology on the *Skeireins* author, a lot of the 'problems' with the text tend to disappear. The use of the Pauline treatment (following Hebrews) of the 'red heifer' passage of IIIb.-c. is demystified when one no longer needs doubt the *Skeireins* author to be using the same Greek Scripture as the rest of the Antiochian School[28]. My argument in *Lamb* is that, given Arian doctrine's semiotic importance (after 376) for Gothic identity-building and social cohesion, as attested by Peter Heather[29] and other gothicists, this rhetorical manoeuvre amounts to an argument from the text of the Gospel of John, **against Gothic identity politics and nationalism**.

5) The *Skeireins* author insists—against the 'childishness' of the apostles Andrew and Philip in John 6, notably—on the ɣᴀɪʀɸɪðǫs, the **sufficiency of God**[30], who 'happens' (ɣᴀɪʀɸᴀɴ, a doublet of ɣᴀɪʀɸ 'worth'[31]) by

---

[28]James Woodrow Marchand, 'The Gothic intellectual community: the theology of the *Skeireins*,' in *The Making of Christian Communities in Late Antiquity and the Middle Ages*, ed. Mark F. Williams (Anthem Press, 2005), 63-76.

[29] Heather, *Goths*, 313-317.

[30] Anonymous, *Commentary*, 75 VIIa.

[31] One can see such doublets in other Germanic languages, too. In standard German, for example, you have the verb *werden* 'to become, to happen, to occur' alongside its etymological twin *Wert* 'value, worth'.

A few notes on the Skeireins

Himself, without need of any cause or agent or assistance. This language is explicitly borrowed from Paul (ἐν αὐτῷ συνέστηκεν, Col 1:17—God 'stands on His own'), and will later be carried over into the Arabic of the *Qur'ān* (which gives God the title of *aṣ-Ṣamadu* الصمد, 112:2—literally, the 'One Who withstands', by Himself).

I do take *Skeireins* as an inspiration for my work. And, as someone with significant Visigothic and Old Burgundian blood-ancestry, I do honour the *Skeireins* author as my 𐍆𐌰𐌳𐍂𐌴𐌹𐌽 as Scripture encourages me to do. However, it is not my design or purpose to attempt to coopt the *Skeireins* author as a mouthpiece for my own views: I'd like to hope that I maintain a firm and clear line of division between my 𐍆𐌰𐌳𐍂𐌴𐌹𐌽 and myself. This is because by no means do I agree with or endorse everything the exegete says. Indeed, some parts of the work I find shoddy and intellectually objectionable.

The *Skeireins* author's assertion, for example, that Saint John's intention was to 'censure and rebuke' Sabellius of Pentapolis and Marcellus of Ankyra is a mishandling of the Johannine text, for the simple reason that Sabellius and Marcellus were not references for the author of the Gospel! A significant part of my work in *The Lamb before Its Shearers* was thus aimed at re-establishing the historical context of the audience at which Saint John's Gospel was directed: that of emerging Gnostic doctrines and incursions by nascent Judaism within the Pauline community. Thus, I endeavour to make it explicit, that when I speak about modern Palestine or modern Syria or modern Donbass, what I am giving voice to are my views within my context: not the Evangelist's.

In the Houses of the Poor

What the *Skeireins* does do, effectively and well, is that it takes a figurative highlighter to the language of John and points out particular pericopes and lexical choices where special attention is deserved. It thus serves as a particularly helpful 'intermediate reference' with which to approach the Johannine Gospel. The *Skeireins* proved to be remarkably adept in this way. Following where my 𐌽𐌰𐌳𐍂𐌴𐌹𐌽 first trod allowed me to linguistically explicate the Johannine-Evangelical themes of darkness versus light; blindness versus sight; hearing versus unwillingness to hear; sonship by blood versus sonship by 'water and spirit'; and the way of the thief versus the way of the 'able herdsman'.

I presume the noble *Qur'ān* to be correct, that God's reward for work well done is the appointment of successors to that work (24:55). This teaching is no heresy; it is not an innovation of Islām. Rather, it is a deliberate restatement of the Pauline teaching (1 Corinthians 3:3-9). In that spirit, I may hope that the work that I do here, in exegeting the second half of Saint John's Gospel in the same Antiochian-inspired manner, may be counted as a succession to the work of the *Skeireins*: the fruit of a Gothic translator-exegete whose name is lost to time.

It may, after all, be God's will, long after I am dead, that my own name should be forgotten, that all but one-tenth of one of my books should be consigned to oblivion, and that (if anything!) only a handful of scraps of pulpy scrawled-over stock remain of it, a millennium and a half from now—tucked away in some vault away from the eyes of anyone who might pick it up and read it until then. Yet, I would find it an honour far beyond my deserving, if some distant descendant or

A few notes on the Skeireins

relative of mine, in some far-off land whose name I cannot possibly dream of, might find one or two of these scraps worth a stray comment or two. Only if it pleases God to grant it!

To Him alone be given all lordship, and all might, and all shining splendour: from that age, in this age, and unto the ages of ages to come. ᚫᛗᛖᚾ.

In the houses of the poor

A clarification on John 11:6-35

The literary value of 'Bethany'

One habit that (speaking personally here) can be difficult to break for someone who is beginning to hear Scripture, is to hear to the names of Semitic people and places as more than merely collections of sounds. We are confronted with names like Mary, Martha, Lazarus and Bethany (John 11:1). When such a thing happens, we should be primed to hear not just the sounds, but attend to the Semitic functionalities of the names themselves.

The Greek Βηθανία corresponds to the Hebrew *Beit ʻĀnīâ* בית עניה, which can refer to two separate places in Scripture—both of which are in modern-day Palestine. One of these 'houses of the poor' is, at present, al-ʻĪzariyya العيزرية, a densely-packed suburban settlement about five kilometres east-southeast of al-Aqsa Mosque. This place is named after the Biblical Lazarus. The other *Beit ʻĀnīâ* is a stone's-throw north of the confluence of the *Wādī Kelt* with the Jordan River, very close to where, according to local tradition, Christ was baptised.

Yet the physical place is not as interesting, from a Scriptural standpoint, as the name. *Beit ʻĀnīâ* comes from *beit* בית 'house' and *ʻānī* עני 'poor, lowly, humble, afflicted' (or else someone described by such conditions)—hence, 'the House of the Poor'.

There is an additional demand on us to pay particular attention to *location* and *movement*. The author repeatedly

In the houses of the poor

makes note of *where* Jesus is and *where* He is going throughout this chapter, to the point where all these prepositions and movement-verbs seem to crowd in on the 'action'. Similarly to Jesus's appearance at the Feast of Booths, Saint John is not allowing us to lose sight of Jesus or His surroundings, which should draw our attention all the more firmly to the (literary) *setting* of the action.

'He's dead, Jim.'

There are *three* short passages here, between 'the place where [Jesus] was' and the tomb of Lazarus, which in the Greek emphasise Jesus's *position and movement,* and each of them alludes to His movement *three times*: **ἔμεινεν** ἐν ᾧ ἦν τόπῳ '*He **stayed**... in the place where He was*'—**ἄγωμεν** εἰς τὴν Ἰουδαίαν '*Let us **go** into Judaea again*'—καὶ πάλιν **ὑπάγεις** ἐκεῖ '*and are you **going** there again?*', 11:6-8; **ἄγωμεν** πρὸς αὐτόν '*let us **go** to him*'—**ἄγωμεν** καὶ ἡμεῖς '*let us also **go***'—**ἐλθὼν** οὖν '*so when [Jesus] came*', 11:15-17; Ἰησοῦς **ἔρχεται** '*Jesus was **coming***'—κύριε εἰ **ἦς ὧδε** '*Lord, if you **had been here**'*—ὁ εἰς τὸν κόσμον **ἐρχόμενος** '*he who is **coming into** the world*', 11:20-27. Given that this is Saint John writing, we *cannot ignore* his literary use of numbers. 'Three' indicates judgement. And this ninefold allusion to movement—'three' by 'three'—implies that a grand totality, a *summa summarum* of judgement, occurs on the path between 'the place where Jesus was' and the tomb of Lazarus.

Moreover, the body of Lazarus has laid in its tomb for *four days*—that is, '*three plus one*'. Here again there is a numerical attestation of judgement.

In the Houses of the Poor

But *who*, or more correctly *what*, is being judged?

The Hebrew place-name *Beit ʿĀnīâ* links us back directly to the Book of Isaiah, where both *beit* and *ʿānī* appear together in two distinct pericopes:

נצב לריב יהוה ועמד לדין עמים:
יהוה במשפט יבוא עם־זקני עמו ושריו ואתם בערתם הכרם גזלת **העני בבתיכם**:
מה תדכאו עמי ופני עניים תטחנו נאם־אדני יהוה צבאות:

*The LORD has taken his place to contend, he stands to judge his people. The LORD enters into judgment with the elders and princes of his people: 'It is you who have devoured the vineyard, the spoil of the **poor** is in your **houses**. What do you mean by crushing my people, by grinding the face of the poor?' says the Lord GOD of hosts.* (Isa 3:13-15)

And again:

הלוא זה צום אבחרהו פתח חרצבות רשע התר אגדות מוטה ושלח רצוצים חפשים וכל־מוטה תנתקו:
הלוא פרס לרעב לחמך **ועניים** מרודים תביא **בית** כי־תראה ערם וכסיתו ומבשרך לא תתעלם:

*'Is not this the fast that I choose: to loose the bonds of wickedness, to undo the thongs of the yoke, to let the oppressed go free, and to break every yoke? Is it not to share your bread with the hungry, and bring the homeless **poor** into your **house**; when you see the naked, to cover him, and not to hide yourself from your own flesh?'* (Isa 58:6-7)

And, actually, this is where we need to take Lazarus's *name* into careful account. His name is actually a Hellenised form of **Eleazar** אלעזר '*God has helped*', which was the name of the second High Priest after his father Aaron, who was delegated to be in charge of *moving the Tabernacle* which served as *the Lord's*

In the houses of the poor

dwelling in the desert. The name of the man dwelling in the 'House of the Poor' references a High Priest, and one of his sisters—just to drive the point home a little further—shares the name of that High Priest's aunt **Miriam**.

These three textual allusions, taken together, form a remarkable judicial 'case' which is drawn up against certain leaders among the followers of the *Torah*, particularly juxtaposed to the confrontation between Jesus and the *soi-disant* 'seed of Abraham' that took place in the previous chapter! But there is one more piece of evidence that is relevant to the 'case', and that has to do with the question of love.

It says of Jesus that He *'loved'* (John 11:5) Lazarus/Eleazar, as well as his sisters Mary/Miriam and Martha (*mārta'* מרתא, the 'mistress' or 'lady' of the house). The Greek verb is the familiar *agapaō* ἀγαπάω. But so that we are not led astray by idle speculations on the nature of this love (or of love in general!), let us note that the word *agapaō* appears only once in the LXX version of Exodus (where Miriam the sister of Moses and Aaron appears prominently) and only twice in the LXX of the Book of Joshua (where the High Priest Eleazar appears)[32]. In all three cases it corresponds to the Hebrew root *'-h-b* א-ה-ב 'to have affection for, to desire, to cherish, to love'—but more importantly, in two of those cases it is *explicitly linked* to the *action* of keeping the commandments (*miṣôt* מצות) and the

---

[32] This Greek verb does not appear at all in the LXX version of the Book of Numbers.

teaching (*Tôrah* תורה) which God had given (Exo 20:6, Jos 22:5). Jesus's love of this literary avatar of Eleazar, and this literary Miriam, and this literary other 'lady' of the House of the Poor, therefore inescapably *has to do* with the true upholding of the Mosaic Law.

But what is the substance of the judgement?

The text is laying out an *accusation* against the leaders of the community. They *fail* to love God by upholding the Law of Moses regarding mercy towards the sick, and are thus disowned by Aaron, Miriam, the High Priest Eleazar. They are disowned by the all-important *Mārta'*, the 'mistress of the house', that is: the womb of the mother which carries the legitimacy of tribal belonging.

Allow me to back up and explain my reasoning on this point. Jesus *stays* in the place where he is for *two days longer* while Lazarus is ill (John 11:6). The number 'two' does the work here that the *judgement is not complete.* It is only after these 'two' days of Lazarus's illness that Jesus begins to move from the place where He is, towards the poor-house outside Jerusalem.

All this time, 'the Jews', who are so deadly hostile to Jesus and His teachings, are *daily* in the company of the sick man, a point which is emphasised by the disciples (John 11:8). What are they doing all these two days? The Sabbath comes only one day a week—what are the followers of *Tôrah* doing on either one or both of these two days which is *not* the Sabbath? Are they tending to the needs, or caring at all for the sick man in

In the houses of the poor

the poor-house? The text is silent on this point—but it is a damning silence, because Jesus plainly pronounces after the two days are over, that Lazarus is dead[33] (John 11:14). Yet after Lazarus is dead, 'many' of those same followers of *Tôrah* who were nowhere to be found in his sickness, come to condole with his sisters over his death (11:19)!

Fittingly: the pronouncement of the judgement, the *ḥesed*, upon 'the Jews' is placed in the mouth of the 'Mistress' of the Poor-House, the one who textually represents the matrilineal line of descent. 'Lord, if you had been here, my brother would not have died!' (John 11:21) One must recall from the prior chapter that Jesus is the *Rā'ah Ṣō'n Ṭôb*, the Able Herdsman Who leads the sheep *through the door* (that is to say, *the Tôrah*)[34], to understand the depth and weight of this *ḥesed* which shames the targets of this Scriptural polemic. Even though she is directly addressing Jesus here, Martha is accusing her suddenly- and conveniently-sympathetic countrymen of being *without the Law*: if there had been even *one* among these false condolers who would follow the Law to show mercy upon a sick man, then Lazarus would still be alive!

---

[33] As a *Trek* fan, I feel Jesus must have directed this comment specifically to His kinsman James. One presumes that Tiberius was in Rome and thus too far away to hear it. – *Auth.*

[34] Matthew Franklin Cooper, *The Lamb before Its Shearers* (OCABS Press, 2025), 238-243.

In the Houses of the Poor

The vindication of the poor is the one who follows

Yet just before the 'judgement upon judgement' is wrought, ironically within the very words she herself speaks, it is Martha who places her *pistis* πίστις 'trust' in Christ:

ναί κύριε ἐγὼ πε**πίστευ**κα ὅτι σὺ εἶ ὁ Χριστὸς ὁ υἱὸς τοῦ θεοῦ ὁ εἰς τὸν κόσμον ἐρχόμενος

*Yes, Lord; I **believe** that you are the Christ, the Son of God, he who is coming into the world.* (John 11:27)

The question which Jesus put to her, though, concerned the ἀνάστασις, the 'Resurrection'. What the English reader of Scripture will miss if they don't read the Greek original, is that the Greek verb ἀνίστημι 'to rise' (John 11:23, 11:24 and even 11:32—on which more in a bit) is the direct root of this noun, and both are linked through the Septuagint to the Semitic root *q-w-m* ק-ו-ם 'to stand, to arise, to rise up':

לכן חכו־לי נאם־יהוה ליום **קוּמִי** לעד כי משפטי לאסף גוים לקבצי ממלכות
לשפך עליהם זעמי כל חרון אפי כי באש קנאתי תאכל כל־הארץ:
כי־אז אהפך אל־עמים שפה ברורה לקרא כלם בשם יהוה לעבדו שכם אחד:
מעבר לנהרי־כוש עתרי בת־פוצי יובלון מנחתי:
ביום ההוא לא תבושי מכל עלילתיך אשר פשעת בי כי־אז אסיר מקרבך עליזי
גאותך ולא־תוספי לגבהה עוד בהר קדשי:

'Therefore wait for me,' says the LORD, *'for the day **when I arise** as a witness. For my decision is to gather nations, to assemble kingdoms, to pour out upon them my indignation, all the heat of my anger; for in the fire of my jealous wrath all the earth shall be consumed. Yea, at that time I will change the speech of the peoples to a pure speech, that all of them may call on the name of the* LORD *and serve him with one accord. From beyond the rivers of Ethiopia my suppliants, the*

In the houses of the poor

daughter of my dispersed ones, shall bring my offering. On that day you shall not be put to shame because of the deeds by which you have rebelled against me; for then I will remove from your midst your proudly exultant ones, and you shall no longer be haughty in my holy mountain. (Zep 3:8-11)

שָׁמַעְתָּ חֶרְפָּתָם יהוה כָּל־מַחְשְׁבֹתָם עָלָי:
שִׂפְתֵי קָמַי וְהֶגְיוֹנָם עָלַי כָּל־הַיּוֹם:
שִׁבְתָּם **וְקִימָתָם** הַבִּיטָה אֲנִי מַנְגִּינָתָם:
תָּשִׁיב לָהֶם גְּמוּל יהוה כְּמַעֲשֵׂה יְדֵיהֶם:
תִּתֵּן לָהֶם מְגִנַּת־לֵב תַּאֲלָתְךָ לָהֶם:
תִּרְדֹּף בְּאַף וְתַשְׁמִידֵם מִתַּחַת שְׁמֵי יהוה:

Thou hast heard their taunts, O Lord, all their devices against me. The lips and thoughts of my assailants are against me all the day long. Behold their sitting **and their rising**; I am the burden of their songs. Thou wilt requite them, O Lord, according to the work of their hands. Thou wilt give them dullness of heart; thy curse will be on them. Thou wilt pursue them in anger and destroy them from under thy heavens, O Lord. (Lam 3:61-66)

It's intriguing that in one case, God is the one who does the 'rising' and in the other, those doing the 'rising' are those 'assailants' against whom God is being invoked. However, comparing the two, both instances of 'rising' as a noun in Hebrew refer to instances of judgement. The pericope from Zephaniah is of particular interest because of how it mentions those who are judged before the Lord: 'the *proud*' (*ga'awâ* גאוה) and 'the *haughty*' (*gabâ* גבה), both of which are juxtaposed (Psalm 9:23-25) as *antonyms* to 'the *poor*' (*'ānī* עני) against whom they conspire (Psalm 9:30). Both the Lamentations and Zephaniah passages link back to Psalm 9's imprecations against the 'workers of iniquity' who are identified with the rich and

In the Houses of the Poor

powerful. In addition, both passages promise God's ultimate vindication of the cause of the poor man against his wealthy and proud oppressors.

When Jesus first asks Martha about her belief in the Resurrection (ἀνάστασις), it is in response to her *already-professed* belief that her brother will be lifted up on the Last Day (John 11:24). So why would Jesus do this? Is it to draw out from Martha a kind of oath of allegiance, or the sort of intellectual affirmation that modern-day Western evangelical Protestants believe is so important? In a word: no. He is asking Martha to *clarify* the trust that she is placing in Him. In appealing to Zephaniah's prophecy, Jesus is asking whether she trusts, not only that God will lift Lazarus up as though from his seat or as though from a bed where he is sleeping... but also that God will *vindicate* the man who lives *in the Poor-House*.

Martha's response to Christ is the ninth attestation of His movement from 'the place where Jesus was' toward the tomb of her brother: thus, it is the completion of the 'judgement upon judgement'. The importance of Martha's ναί κύριε ἐγὼ πεπίστευκα is not in the 'relationship' she supposedly has with Christ, and not in some intellectual assent to His lordship. Rather, its importance lies in the fact that this *one woman* among these many who claim Abraham as their father and who claim to follow the Law, *is actually willing to follow the Law*, and to place her *trust* in God's *locum tenens*. This is the nature of the *agapē* of Jesus for this woman, in which Saint John is attempting to instruct us.

In the houses of the poor

The prophetic gift of tears

There is a very interesting verb that is used here in John 11: *dakrúō* δακρύω. This is an ἅπαξ λεγόμενον, used only once in the entire Greek New Testament, right here: ἐδάκρυσεν ὁ Ἰησοῦς (John 11:35).

It is a very different verb from the *klaíō* κλαίω 'weeping' which Mary *comes out of the house* to do at her brother's tomb. (The text is actually very insistent on this point, that she *leaves the house* to go to the tomb.) This *klaíō* is a verb which is attested *at length* both in the Greek New Testament and in the Septuagint, where it is often seen conforming to the Semitic root b-k-h ב-כ-ה 'to mourn, to wail, to lament, to weep'. The verb *dakrúō* is used in three different places in the Greek Septuagint where we have extant Hebrew texts, to translate three different verbs—none of which are morphologically related to b-k-h!

1.) The first root which is translated as *dakrúō* in Greek is š-'-g ש-א-ג, used in the word *šə'āgâ* שאגה 'to roar in distress', the way an animal (such as a lion) would do. In such colourful and melodramatic language Job describes his own distress (Job 3:24).
2.) The second root thus translated is r-'-m ר-ע-ם, as in *rā'am* רעם 'to tumble (with a loud sound), to convulse, to roar, to crash, to thunder, to be troubled'. This verb is used to describe the faces of the kings who look upon the wreckage of Tyre in Ezekiel's lament over that city (Eze 27:35).
3.) The third root which is translated by this Greek word is n-ṭ-f נ-ט-ף which is used in the verb *nāṭaf* נטף 'drop,

droplet, tear, to drip, to distil, to prophesy'. The *workers of iniquity* in Micah thus 'drop' a hint to the prophets of their time *not* to prophesy—yet such mockeries are in vain (Mic 2:6).

The third instance is the most intriguing. The RSV translation says that 'Jesus wept', which is most unhelpful: it blurs the original Greek distinction between Mary's *klaíō* and Jesus's *dakrúō*. It could be better said (in English) that 'Jesus roared', or 'Jesus thundered', or 'Jesus shouted'. If the reference is to Micah, the same verb could be interpreted as: 'Jesus dripped (or shed tears)', or even, 'Jesus *prophesied*'.

This three-word phrase ἐδάκρυσεν ὁ Ἰησοῦς is the linchpin of the passage, and not only because it contains an ἅπαξ λεγόμενον. In fact, one could make the argument that this is the central passage of the entire Gospel of John. In terms of its context, this is the *moment* of the 'judgement' at which the 'sentence' is carried out. If you will, in literary terms, this is the moment that Lazarus is restored to life; and it is the moment at which Jesus is irrevocably placed on the road to His death.

The Micah pericope seems to be the most relevant to the passage at hand:

אל־**תּטִּפוּ יַטִּפוּן** לא־**יַטִּפוּ** לאלה לא יסג כלמות:
האמור בית־יעקב הקצר רוח יהוה אם־אלה מעלליו הלוא דברי ייטיבו עם הישר הולך:
ואתמול עמי לאויב יקומם ממול שלמה אדר תפשטון מעברים בטח שובי מלחמה:
נשי עמי תגרשון מ**בית** תענגיה מעל עלליה תקחו הדרי לעולם:

'Do not **preach**'—thus they **preach**—'one should not **preach** of such things; disgrace will not overtake us.' Should this be said, O house of Jacob? Is the Spirit of the LORD impatient? Are these his doings? Do

In the houses of the poor

> *not my words do good to him who walks uprightly? But you rise against my people as an enemy; you strip the robe from the peaceful, from those who pass by trustingly with no thought of war. The women of my people you drive out from their pleasant* **houses**; *from their young children you take away my glory for ever.* (Mic 2:6-9)

Here the fact that Mary and Martha both *left the house* to come to the tomb of their brother becomes relevant again, and the false condolence of their Pharisaical neighbours takes on a sinister shade of meaning. It should be consistently borne in mind that the text of the Gospel of Saint John was being written in the late first or early second century, when the Pauline communities had been *evicted* from table-fellowship with the nascent-Judaistic ones. And here, the pressure is on Mary and Martha to *leave the house*: that is, because the man of the house is no longer living, their neighbours are coming with false condolence—*to foreclose on their house* to satisfy a debt! On the one hand, the raising of Lazarus, the man who was in the Poor-House, is meant to be a message of consolation and strength to the suffering and persecuted members of the Pauline communities in specific, and more broadly to the poor in general. On the other hand, the multilayered Greek verbiage pointing back to the Septuagint text is an indictment against those who claim to follow the laws regarding circumcision and clean and unclean foods, but who neglect the demands of the Law regarding hospitality and care for the sick.

Yet the teaching is that even those who die of neglect, or who are thrown out onto the streets from eviction, are not neglected by God. Jesus comes to the tomb of Lazarus, *drips His tears of prophecy*, and Lazarus is returned to life (John 11:44).

In the Houses of the Poor

And the 'sentence' of the 'judgement' that falls upon the false condolers, those who were absent from Lazarus when he was sick and who died from their neglect, is the same as the judgement that fell upon the disputers with Jesus in Chapter 10, and that fell upon the critics of His healing of the blind man in Chapter 9. There is a *schism* among them. 'Many' of them accept the teaching that they have just witnessed, but others leave to inform the authorities (John 11:45-46).

'It became necessary to destroy the teaching to save it'

Over the course of ten days in late January and early February of 1968, the American armed forces, acting in support of their puppet government in South Vietnam, invaded and levelled the town of Bến Tre on the Mekong Delta, wiping out 5,000 homes, killing over 500 civilians, wounding over 1,000 more and turning 30,000 Vietnamese townspeople into refugees. Reporting for the Associated Press, journalist Peter Arnett flew into the remains of Bến Tre and quoted an anonymous American major about the fighting. The major delivered to him one of the most infamous quotes about the Indochina War, one which became a byword among the anti-war movement for the pithiness with which it expressed Cold War hypocrisy: '*It became necessary to destroy the town to save it.*'[35]

---

[35] Pennsylvania State University Library, 'It became necessary to destroy the town to save it,' Thomas W Benson Political Protest Collection (ca. 1970).

In the houses of the poor

The encounter at Bethany—the House of the Poor—shares a parallel irony. The religious teachers and their followers in this Judaean town are put to shame by Martha's exposure of their inhospitality, and by Jesus's 'dropping' of prophetic tears which raise Lazarus from the grave. What results from this is a schism among the religious community. Obviously, the religious community cannot accept this, and some among them come to see Jesus as a threat. Thus, Caiaphas gives voice to a similarly pithy and infamous quote: ὅτι συμφέρει ὑμῖν ἵνα εἷς ἄνθρωπος ἀποθάνῃ ὑπὲρ τοῦ λαοῦ καὶ μὴ ὅλον τὸ ἔθνος ἀπόληται—'*It is expedient for you that one man should die for the people, and that the whole nation should not perish*' (John 11:50).

What should be obvious to the hearer of Saint John's Gospel, as was obvious to the anti-war protesters during the Indochina War, is the irony in that statement. One of the most basic teachings of the *Tōrah*, the very Law which is the binding glue of the Jewish *ethnos*, is the condemnation against the shedding of innocent blood (Deut 19:7-13). The argument becomes: in order to save the *ethnos*, we must kill the *Tōrah*. To the believers in the God of Abraham living in the late first and early second centuries AD, this passage very much had the savour of the nameless American major's comment on Bến Tre. Saint John is here practically lampooning nascent Jewish theology, which had broken table-fellowship with the Paulines and turned them out of their houses for the sake of upholding the purity of the Law.

It should also be noted that Caiaphas (= *Kefā'* כפא 'rock, stone') is a play on Peter's name, Cephas, which in turn is derived from the same Semitic word. We should not take this resemblance as a historical coincidence, but instead as a deliberate literary allusion. The same judgement that is levelled *externally* at the leadership of the nascent Jewish community, is also (and *a fortiori*) levelled *internally* against Peter's ideological cohort *within* the Pauline community, who were insistent upon maintaining the ritual purity of Jewish dietary laws, in contravention of Paul's teaching on hospitality and table-fellowship. The weaponisation of ritual purity to the neglect of mercy, was by no means solely or even primarily a Jewish failing!

Bringing the setting of this passage, *Beit ʿĀniâ* בית עניה 'the House of the Poor', from the 'background' into the 'foreground' of the Johannine medallion, anchors the story in the Isaian call for justice for the marginalised and the oppressed. At the same time, the rising of Lazarus embodies Zephaniah's promise of God's *vindication*.

Abuse of the prophetic function[36]

The prophetic gift as double-edged sword

A clarification on John 12:1-11

Nick and Dick

In my conversations over coffee with Fr Paul Nadim Tarazi and Fr Marc Boulos, I was struck by the former's insistence that words do not have 'meanings', but rather *functions*. Words are defined not by a dictionary entry, but instead by what role they play in a particular sentence, passage or work. This is not, by the way, a philosophical or a postmodernist idea. I spent a good deal of time investigating the *linguistic functionalism* of **Prince Nicolas Trubetskoi** and his pupil, **Roman Jakobson**.

Trubetskoi's *Notes on Literature* had indeed been sitting on my shelf for several years, but it was Fr Paul Tarazi's lectures which made me go dust the thing off and crack it open again. Trubetskoi analyses different works of Russian literature, from the elegiac medieval *Lay of Igor's Armament* all the way up through Dostoevsky's *Brothers Karamazov*, as well as works of Finnish (the *Kalevala*), traditional Ugric, and Caucasian (the *Nart* sagas) literature and oral tradition.

---

[36] This chapter is adapted and expanded from a Substack post of mine: Matthew Franklin Cooper, 'Abuse of the prophetic function', Substack post, *Skeireins* (26 January 2025).

Gird them with girdles, bind caps on them

I found that his conclusions are remarkably (though coincidentally) similar to those which Fr Paul Tarazi puts forward in his lectures and in *The Rise of Scripture*. A word does not have a fixed 'meaning' bestowed on it by some authority on high; rather, it interacts with other words as part of a dynamic, interrelated *system*. The semantic value of a word is bestowed on it by the other literary-structural elements which *interact with it*[37]. Trubetskoi (and Jakobson after him) pioneered an approach to Russian literature focussed on a close analysis of mechanics and syntax which very closely anticipates Fr Paul Tarazi's approach to Hebrew and Greek Scriptures.

Yet when I asked Fr Paul Tarazi about this, his reply to me was that his research had not been in the direction of Trubetskoi. Instead, he was convinced of the truth of linguistic functionalism by a very different pair of theorists. This pair of fellows is a trifle obscure, and their contributions to the field of comparative linguistics have yet to be recognised, but I do remember their names from our conversation: **Clint Eastwood** and **Richard Burton.**

These two were given starring roles in a war drama in 1968: *Where Eagles Dare*. Fr Paul, watching this film came to a scene late in its run, in which Richard Burton orders one of his prisoners to '*climb down*' a cable onto a tramway gondola[38]. Fr

---

[37] N.S. Trubetzkoy, *Writings on Literature*, trans. Anatoly Liberman (University of Minnesota Press, 1990), xvi-xix, xxii-xxiii.

[38] *Where Eagles Dare*, dir. Brian G. Hutton (Metro-Goldwyn-Mayer, 1968).

Paul tells me he was baffled by hearing this. As a native Arabic speaker who had learned English, he had always presumed that the English verb '*to climb*' had the meaning of '*to go up*' or '*to ascend*', as on a ladder or an incline. It was Burton's order that convinced him that the word doesn't actually carry a meaning at all, but is dependent on its function inside its syntax.

Another example that Fr Paul Tarazi gives is the use of the phrase 'heart of stone' (*leb hā'eben* לֵב הָאֶבֶן) in Ezekiel 36:26. Obviously this is a figurative usage of *'eben*; the author of Ezekiel is not referring to a literal heart chiselled out of a literal rock—it's clearly metaphorical. But the point is that *'eben* is being used in a different functionality here than it is in, say, Genesis 31:46.

Now, I read Prince Trubetskoi's *Notes* before watching Burton's film, so I am compelled to say—which I do by way of affirming my agreement with Fr Paul Tarazi's method and with that of the historical Antiochian School more generally—that I am a follower of Nick, **a devout orthodox Trubetskoian** in my reading of Scripture. For Trubetskoi, the literature and culture of the pre-Tsarist Muscovite states (1263-1547) is the *reference*— the epitome of literary refinement and the height of religious feeling[39]. For me, the *reference* is the original, consonantal Hebrew text that the Greek Septuagint represents in translation. Still, I share with Chomsky's forerunner numerous convictions. Like him, I am convinced that ancient **literature is literature**, not a mere historical artefact of antiquarian

---

[39] Trubetzkoy, *Writings*, xix.

Gird them with girdles, bind caps on them

interest. Like him, I am sceptical of the idea that greater technological sophistication equates to any notion of ethical or aesthetic 'progress'. Like him, I am convinced of the necessity of approaching a literary text firmly in the light of the material and ideological conditions of its **own historical period** and setting. And like him, I hold that there is a **systematic** and **functional** approach that we can take to ascertaining literary fact.

But if you want to call me a '**Burtonian**' instead, I wouldn't take any offense at that. I do have my limits, though. Despite the dangers of duplicity and treachery in the work of studying the Scriptural teaching—a topic of considerable interest to the passage at hand—I maintain (*pace* Eastwood) that we should by no means keep the interpretation of Scripture as '*an all-British operation*'.

Speaking of the British—or rather, the Anglicans...

The Inaugural homily for President Donald Trump's second term was delivered at Washington National Cathedral by the Episcopalian Bishop Mariann Budde on the twenty-second of January this year. The homily caused a bit of a political stir. Trying my best to think about how to understand it, I eventually came (with some help) to the conclusion that it was the *right message*, spoken from the *wrong pulpit*, at the *wrong time*.

What do I mean by this? Well, take a look at what Bishop Budde actually said:

In the Houses of the Poor

> *Millions have put their trust in you and, as you told the nation yesterday, you have felt the providential hand of a loving God. In the name of our God, I ask you to have mercy upon the people in our country who are scared now. There are gay, lesbian, and transgender children in Democratic, Republican and Independent families, some who fear for their lives. And the people, the people who pick our crops and clean our office buildings, who labour in poultry farms and meat packing plants, who wash the dishes after we eat in restaurants and work the night shifts in hospitals. They, they may not be citizens or have the proper documentation, but the vast majority of immigrants are not criminals. They pay taxes and are good neighbours.* [40]

Is there anything doctrinally or ethically *wrong* with any of this? No. Homosexuals and transgender people are people. They deserve to be accorded the same degree of dignity under the law as their straight and cis neighbours. Also, there is nothing wrong, on its face, with calling for the rights of working-class immigrants to be respected. The problem is *who is saying it*, and *where*, and *why*. The Episcopal bishop is *abusing* the literary function of prophecy in an attempt to play it for *institutional power*.

This abuse of the prophetic function happens in Scripture also. In the passage at hand, Judas Iscariot censures Mary the sister of Lazarus for taking her savings and using it to buy a costly fragrant oil, a μύρον, with which to anoint Jesus's feet. Judas chides Mary that the oil should have been sold and the

---

[40] Mariann Edgar Budde, 'Have mercy, Mr. President', *USA Today* (29 January 2025).

Gird them with girdles, bind caps on them

proceeds given to the poor. But *'this he said, not that he cared for the poor but because he was a thief, and as he had the money box he used to take what was put into it'* (John 12:6).

In analogising Budde to Judas, am I thus likening Trump to Jesus? No, *not in the slightest*. Just as I cannot see Joseph Biden without recalling murdered Palestinian children, so too I cannot see Donald Trump without recalling schoolbusses of murdered Yemeni children from the horrid Saudi-led adventure of his first term. Like at least the five presidents prior to him, Mr. Trump has precisely *zero interest* in the authentic teaching—what concerns him is *power*.

Yet we, on the other hand, should have an interest.

How is the prophetic function abused?

Unlike Dostoevsky or the anonymous author of the *Lay of Igor's Armament*, who belong to a different culture and to different epochs, Saint John is not particularly interested in portraying the inner lives or probing the motivations of his characters. Judas Iscariot, just as Lazarus and his sisters in the House of the Poor and Thomas the Twin in the previous chapter, or Nicodemus before that, appears to us entirely in externals. We know he is a thief because Saint John tells us this outright.

Also, because we are already in mind of Isaiah from the prior chapter (specifically Isaiah 58), and because we are *told* that we are *in* the House of the Poor, we should be attuned to what Judas is saying when he appeals to the πτωχοῖς, the *'āniâ* עניה or 'the poor'. Judas is already *stealing*, in the sense that he is trying to *coopt* the theatrical masque, the πρόσωπον, of Isaiah in this scene. When Saint John lets us know directly afterwards that Judas is 'a thief' (κλέπτης, John 12:6), he is doubly alerting us not only to the fact that Judas's motive is greed, but also that he is acting as a ψευδοπροφήτης, a usurper of the prophetic function.

Let's turn our attention to the object of Judas's pseudo-prophetic fury. We see that the μύρον that this literary Miriam is using to anoint Jesus's feet with (John 12:3) is refined from the essence of an exotic plant (νάρδου, 'nard'); that it is 'pure' (πιστικῆς, 'genuine, the real deal'); and that it is 'costly' (πολύτιμος, literally 'of much worth').

There are several trajectories which these roots take. First of all, the easy one: 'nard' is a Chinese and northern Indian plant—in modern Mandarin *gansong* 甘松 (literally, 'sweet pine'), and in Sanskrit *nálada* नलद ('stalky'). The exoticism of this fragrance is doubly attested. First: by the fact that the Hebrew term *nērədə* נרד is a clear loan from the Sanskrit. Secondly: by the fact that this word appears only twice in the Septuagint—both times in the Song of Solomon where its appeal is precisely in its rare, exotic and sensual allure (Sng 1:12; 4:12-14).

The high value placed on woody, fragrant oil-bearing, montane pinelike plants in Asian cultures of antiquity is also attested in the ancient Chinese *Book of Odes* or *Shijing* 《詩經》, coming from the land to which such plants were native. We often see such plants (*song* 松) as images of loftiness and luxury, of fresh scent corresponding to high personal qualities: 山有橋**松**、隰有游龍。 *'On the mountain is the lofty* **pine***; In the*

Gird them with girdles, bind caps on them

marshes is the spreading water-polygonum.' (*Odes*, Odes of Zheng 鄭風, 'Mountain Mulberries' 山有扶蘇 2) Or: 如**松**柏之茂、無不爾或承。 '*Like the luxuriance of the **fir** and the cypress; may such be thy succeeding line!*' (*Odes*, Decade of Deer Call 鹿鳴之什, 'Heaven Protects' 天保 6)[41] The fact that Saint John points to the pervading fragrance of the exotic oil ἐπληρώθη ἐκ τῆς ὀσμῆς 'filling the house', directly parallels the usage of *nērədə* נרד in the Song of Solomon (נרדי נתן ריחו '***my nard** gave forth its fragrance*', Sng 1:12), and also lends a subtly-scandalising, erotic undertone to the episode, to us no less than to Judas.

But we should *not* stop here! This use of the word πιστικῆς 'genuine'—from the same root as πιστεύω 'to believe, to trust, to have faith'—is meant to demonstrate that this literary Miriam, no less than her sister in the prior chapter, is demonstrating her *faith* in the teaching. Her wiping of Jesus's feet with the oil and with her hair is therefore not simply a titillating gesture or one of carnal interest. The use of the word πιστικῆς is meant to show us that the literary Miriam is fulfilling the Law by paying honour to the teacher in her elder sister's house.

And the word πολύτιμος links us back to the Gospel of Matthew—the *mašal* of the merchant who sells all his goods to acquire the pearl 'of great value' (Mat 13:46)—and also forward

---

[41] Unless explicitly otherwise noted, all references to Classical-era texts herein are cited from Donald Sturgeon, *Chinese Text Project: a Dynamic Digital Library of Premodern Chinese* (Digital Scholarship in the Humanities, 2019), https://ctext.org/.

In the Houses of the Poor

to the first epistle attributed to Saint Peter, who commended τῆς **πίστεως πολυτιμότερον** χρυσίου '*the* **preciousness of faith**, *worth more than gold*' (1Pe 1:7). And how does he follow this? '*Without having seen him you love him; though you do not now see him you believe in him*' (1Pe 1:8)!

So Mary—the younger sister in the house—is doing something truly scandalous by getting out this exotic fragrance and using her hair to wipe the teacher's feet with it. But it is her expression of love and trust, of the same sort that her more cerebral elder sister gave voice to in the previous chapter. But Judas, upon seeing this, speaks out that the essential oil can be sold for 'three hundred *denarii*'—that is to say, a year's worth of wages—and given to the poor.

At first it doesn't seem like Judas is saying anything wrong. Caring for the poor, out of one's own substance, is indeed a duty incumbent on God's people (Ps 40:1; Ps 111:6-9). And Jesus's answer to him at first seems baffling: '*The poor you always have with you, but you do not always have me*' (John 12:8). Yet Jesus is in fact making a textual appeal to *the same teaching* as Judas is:

כִּי **לֹא־יֶחְדַּל אֶבְיוֹן** מִקֶּרֶב הָאָרֶץ עַל־כֵּן אָנֹכִי מְצַוְּךָ לֵאמֹר פָּתֹחַ תִּפְתַּח אֶת־יָדְךָ לְאָחִיךָ לַעֲנִיֶּךָ וּלְאֶבְיֹנְךָ בְּאַרְצֶךָ׃

For **the poor will never cease** *out of the land; therefore I command you, You shall open wide your hand to your brother, to the needy and to the poor, in the land.* (Deut 15:11)

Jesus's appeal to Deuteronomy serves the purpose, through the repeated reference to *ha-ereṣ* הָאָרֶץ, of reminding Judas of *where he is*: he is in fact *standing* in the House of the Poor, and

Gird them with girdles, bind caps on them

blaming the younger sister *in that House*, for making a supposed waste of her family's goods! It is not Jesus but *Judas* who is closed-handed to the poor.

Jesus is also, in saying 'you will not always have me' and making reference to His own burial (12:7), alludes to the inevitable plot against His life: the result of His appearance at the Feast of Booths, His healing of the blind man, and His raising of Lazarus. Judas risks no social or physical consequence to himself by throwing the Law at a younger woman who had just been *driven out of her house* by her brother's death. But the fate of the genuine prophet among his own people is necessarily a bleak one, because a true prophet inevitably goes **against the interests of power**.

Fake prophecy is cheap

Judas, even though what he says in John 12 *sounds* correct (it is indeed the teaching of the Scriptures to do justice, and especially to care for the poor), his *use* of the teaching is guided by ulterior motives. He uses the teaching of caring for the poor as a smokescreen for his own self-interested motivations.

So what self-interested motives am I ascribing to Bp. Budde? Well, for one thing, one would do well to examine how she was *fêted* by various news outlets immediately afterwards[42]. They

---

[42] Elizabeth Bruenig, 'Bishop Budde delivered a truly Christian message,' *The Atlantic* (23 January 2025), https://archive.is/lwpBj.

In the Houses of the Poor

were tripping over themselves to declare her a modern-day Saint Thomas à Becket. Yet money isn't the only idol by which people sell out the teaching: reputation, or 'clout', is another. Budde was not only not censured for her sermon, but she was in fact lauded and applauded for it by the same founts of institutional power in the American government and its subservient press that oversaw the Gaza genocide.

Bp. Budde did not speak up at all on the question of that genocide, as was pointed out by the head of *Electronic Intifada*, Ali Abunimah[43]. In fact, she willingly spread the same atrocity propaganda and lies about Gaza that were being peddled about by the Israeli government: in particular, the allegations against Ḥamas fighters of the mass beheading of Israeli children and the mass rape of women that were later shown by international investigators to be lacking valid evidence. Bishop Budde's position on the question of Palestine was the same one of *silence, moral abdication* and *cowardice* that characterised the entire professional-managerial class when Biden was in power. That is because they worship power. If Budde were actually

---

Elizabeth Dias, 'The bishop who pleaded with Trump: "Was anybody going to say anything?",' *The New York Times* (22 January 2025), https://archive.is/eXTzI.

Jack Jenkins, 'After eyebrow-raising sermon to Trump, Bishop Budde beset with criticism and praise,' *The National Catholic Reporter* (23 January 2025), https://archive.is/wiPBv.

[43] Ali Abunimah, 'How the bishop who scolded Trump enabled Gaza genocide,' YouTube, *Electronic Intifada* (24 January 2025), https://www.youtube.com/watch?v=8XJfqtKh6PQ.

Gird them with girdles, bind caps on them

doing her job the way she should be doing—that is to say, if she were in fact obedient to the teaching that she gives voice to and from which she claims authority—she would have castigated *Biden* to his face for sending unlimited amounts of weapons to the Israelis for the purpose of murdering children. She had her bully pulpit then, too. She chose not to use it.

So, then, where are the real prophets?

Prophets have a tendency to get their butts kicked. When Jeremiah or Ezekiel or Isaiah spoke actual truth to actual power, they did so with the full understanding that they were going to suffer for it. Jeremiah and Ezekiel were stoned to death; Isaiah ended up sawn in half. Journalist Gary Webb and historian Iris Chang 'committed suicide'... or so the official story goes, anyway. In both cases, at the very least, powerful political and cultural forces colluded in making their lives miserable to the point where suicide became plausible. Martin Luther King, Jr., Malcolm X and Fred Hampton were assassinated... and none of them were well-liked when they were alive, either. Americans tend to forget that, particularly on the day we set aside to commemorate King—but in fact use it to commemorate ourselves. We don't like it when a mirror gets held up to us and the reflection that we see is ugly. We don't improve ourselves; we attack the guy holding the mirror.

As Fr Marc Boulos puts it:

You can't be the bishop of the national cathedral and remain silent about a holocaust, and then preach about 'mercy' to the next president... You can't cozy up to power. It's fake. It's not prophetic... Prophetic instruction comes at a price.[44]

That's why I have such a high respect for Ta-Nehisi Coates right now, particularly over his latest book, *The Message*. Owing to the high-academic voice and poise and eloquence with which he has advocated for the social-liberal position on racial justice in his previous books (for example, *The Beautiful Struggle* and *Between the World and Me*), Coates managed to attain this position of moral *gravitas* and authority among the *élite* who read *The Atlantic* and *The New York Times*. He would get invited to all the evening-show interviews and national correspondents' dinners.

When he wrote *The Message*, and especially when he started to do publicity for the book, he was faced with the exact same choice that Bp. Budde failed to make correctly. He could choose to continue voicing platitudes and maintaining the institutional privilege accorded to him for saying all the right things to the right people in the right tone... or he could choose to speak up for oppressed people in places like Senegal and Palestine, and suffer for it. Coates knowingly chose the latter. No more talk shows or exclusive dinner invites for him—particularly not after the interview on CBS when he was ambushed with hostile and belittling questions by Tony Dokoupil.

---

[44] Fr Marc Boulos, 'God is not shy', *The Bible as Literature* podcast 550 (YouTube, 25 January 2025), https://www.youtube.com/watch?v=c3tIwFzzx7Y.

Gird them with girdles, bind caps on them

Coates faced a real cost for his prophetic stand. But Coates knows where he comes from: he comes directly out of the Black American prophetic tradition which produced Rev'd Martin Luther King, Jr. and al-Ḥajj Mālik aš-Šabāzz. This tradition is represented in our own Orthodox Church (through the grace of God and not our own deserving!) by Fr Paul Abernathy of Pittsburgh[45], who has been blessedly voluble on the plight of the Palestinians from the beginning.

There are still real prophets today: it's just that they don't speak at Washington National Cathedral, or in the pages of the *Washington Post*. Rather, the prophetic function which comes from the God of Scripture is one which always comes at a cost. And if the prophetic function is no friend of political power, it must also be correctly understood that it is likewise no friend of *institutional* power. Otherwise, that prophetic function is not being exercised on behalf of the *Scriptural* God, but on behalf of *some other god*.

---

[45] I highly recommend Fr Paul Abernathy's book: Paul Abernathy, *The Prayer of a Broken Heart: an Orthodox Christian Reflection on African American Spirituality* (Ancient Faith Press, 2022).

Gird them with girdles, bind caps on them

What is 'biblical manhood' when no man is 'clean'?

A clarification on John 13:2-11

Girded up, with *linteum* in hand

All that is old is new. Ecclesiastes had it right. What has been will be again, and what has been done will be done again. There is no new thing under the sun.

In my post-college days, back when I was still a Protestant, one of the intellectual figures that I was drawn to was the English Victorian clergyman, novelist and socialist Charles Kingsley. He was one of the key leaders of the 'Christian masculinity' movement in Britain. Kingsley was attempting, through his novels and homilies, to establish a Christian religious grounding for things like health education for boys, sport and physical training for bodily health, a patriarchal and 'male headship' model of the nuclear family, as well as a sense of patriotism and service to the British Empire.

It is not at all an accident, though I would learn this far later, that the ideology of 'Christian masculinity' arose in the middle of the nineteenth century amid British Imperial insecurities about its own 'decadence'. The 'Great Game' of the 1850s and 1860s in particular, and the heavy losses inflicted on the British Empire in the Pyrrhic victory against the Russian Tsardom over Crimea (think of the infamous 'Charge of the Light Brigade'), exposed a concern that British men be fit to exercise their dominance over, particularly, the continent of Asia. Christian

A note on authorial self-elision

masculinity shared a heyday with nascent social Darwinist and eugenicist concerns about the virility and physical fitness of the British racial stock.

This is no coincidence. And it should not come as a surprise that the ideology of a consecrated masculinity, of the conflation of spiritual 'holiness' with physical 'haleness' (the result of a peculiarly Germanic confusion, with the Old English *hǣl* 'whole, hale, healthy' and *hǣlig* 'holy' sharing a common lexical root), is recurring in modern America. Back then, of course, 'Christian masculinity' was a largely 'centre-left' social-democratic movement to strengthen the British Imperial project at its prime. In the current American context, it manifests as a 'right' nationalist movement, aimed proximately at shoring up culture against the truly noxious intellectual effects of postmodernity, but more dubiously as a kind of nostalgia-politics for Anglo-American Empire.

A lot of ink—mostly figurative ink, as these present-day evangelical disciples of Charles Kingsley, Thomas Hughes, J.C. Ryle and the like usually write to online audiences or host podcasts—is thus spilled on the articulation of the *masculinity of Jesus*. As though the single most defining feature of the Saviour is a pair of testicles. The reason this comes to mind is because in the thirteenth chapter of the Gospel of Saint John we do, in fact, see a typically and in fact exclusively *masculine* verb being applied to Jesus. Yet the effect of this verb *within the text* is peculiar, and deserves careful explication.

Jesus **διέζωσεν**, 'girded himself up', with a towel (John 13:4). This verb, derived from the Greek **ζώννυμι**, corresponds to the Hebrew roots ḥ-g-r ח-ג-ר 'to gird, to gird on, to bind, to appoint,

In the Houses of the Poor

to restrain, to put on (a belt)' and *'-z-r* א-ז-ר 'to gird, to bind up, to clasp'. The verbal form of this word in the Old Testament *exclusively* applies to *men*, to *male human beings*: whether that's Aaron and his sons in the book of Exodus (Exo 29:9, Lev 8:7-13); or the patriarch Job (Job 38:3, 40:7); or King David (1 Sam 17:39) and the military men under his command (1 Sam 25:31); or the unworthy servant of Elijah the prophet (2 Ki 4:29); or 'the shoot from the stump of Jesse' prophesied by Isaiah (Isa 11:5).

Both in Greek and in Hebrew, this verb is reserved exclusively for grammatically, biologically and culturally *masculine* subjects. God even instructs Job directly: *'Ēzār-nā' kə-geber ḥălāṣêk wə-'ešə'alek wəhôdî'enî* אזר־נא כגבר חלציך ואשאלך והודיעני '**Gird up** your loins **like a man**, I will question you, and you shall declare to me' (Job 38:3). But the original Hebrew doesn't just say 'man', which would be *'îš* איש or *'ādam* אדם—it says *geber* גבר 'mighty man, warrior, hero, giant', which when spoken by God to Job (in his wretched condition) almost takes on the shade of a dare, or a taunt.

In ancient West Asia, it was not the prevailing custom to wear trousers. (Trousers would be introduced much later by my distant ancestors, Iranian-speaking horsemen from the Pontic steppes.) The people who lived in the Two Rivers area and in the Syrian wilderness—both men and women—would wear the long, loose *kûttîna* כותינא 'robe, gown, tunic'. Women would always wear their *kûttînyata* long, below the knee, even when working in the fields. However, when men were called on to do heavy labour or go into battle, they were expected to bundle up the hem of their *kûttîna* between their legs and tie it in front of them. This was called 'girding the loins'.

A note on authorial self-elision

So when the text says that Jesus διέζωσεν, he is doing something that is *specifically and stereotypically male*, even macho or (to use current-day parlance) 'alpha'. In Saint John's context, women did not 'gird themselves up', men did: in preparation for heavy physical exertion or fighting. Given what we have just heard about the plot to kill Jesus, and Judas's role in that plot, the use of this verb hints that Jesus is, in a sense, gearing up for war.

Jesus, girding up His *kûttîna*, does not reach for a weapon to do battle, but instead reaches for a λέντιον. This image abruptly subverts the masculine image of Christ. A Greek term appearing nowhere in the Septuagint, the λέντιον is borrowed from Latin: *linteum*. This term gives three possible references, which I am here listing in order from most to least relevant.

1) The *linteum* can refer to a *household servant's linen kerchief* or *cleaning-towel* which they would use to undertake household chores or other servile labour. In this case the *linteum* would often be associated with household tasks, which would be assigned to slaves or women. This would be the clearest and most obvious function that would rise to mind for a hearer of the original Greek in the first or second century AD.
2) The *linteum* could refer also to the cloth that would be placed on the exposed body of a dead man: that is, a funeral shroud. The usage of *lintea* in the Roman Empire would be especially relevant for a prisoner subject to a public execution. It would be given as a courtesy, to prevent his naked body from being subject to the public gaze, shame and mockery.

In the Houses of the Poor

3) The *linteum* can also refer, as in Livy's *Annales*, to a *linen scroll* on which was contained a history of the Roman people, and stored in the Temple of Juno Moneta in Rome. Only women consecrated to Juno would have been allowed to touch this. Only a very small subset of first- and second-century AD hearers of Scripture, those literate in Latin and familiar with Roman customs, would have been likely to make this connexion. Still, it was a part of that world and should be taken into account.

All three of these functions can be considered as relevant, though not equally, to the text. If we are to interpret it as the '*linen scroll*' of Livy, then the operative reference would be the *Tōrah*. Jesus does not gird Himself up to fight with weapons, but instead with the statutes and instructions of God in hand. Note that the 'seven angels' in Saint John's Apocalypse, who issue forth from the 'tent of witness', are likewise so girded-up, and likewise wear 'clean linen' (Apoc 15:6)! The other material point is that Jesus is not behaving here like a king, but rather like someone under command. The interpretation of the *linteum* as the household servant's kerchief, however, makes much more immediate sense in reference to what He is about to do—that is, to serve His disciples, including the one who is about to betray Him, by washing their feet. But the *linteum* that is given to cover up the body of an executed prisoner is also relevant here as a literary foreshadowing of the Crucifixion.

A note on authorial self-elision

Dr Watson and the clue of the walking feet

Simon Cephas continues to earn his cognomen here, being dumb as a rock. The figure of Saint Peter is addressed in the text, yet from a literary perspective, Peter plays the same role as Dr Watson in the novels of Sir Arthur Conan Doyle. His obtuseness is in fact standing in for the obtuseness *of the hearer*. He does not understand what Jesus is doing—and nor, in fact, do we. The hearer of the Gospel is geared up, from the verb διέζωσεν, to expect Jesus to behave in a manly fashion: to confront, expose and expel the traitor, the evildoer in the disciples' midst, of whom He knows (as do we, having been told several verses before). Yet here He is, acting in a manner unbefitting a teacher of the Law but like a serving-woman or a slave of the household, using a linen cloth to wash the feet of His disciples—including Judas.

The image that should come to our minds here, is of the bath-house in Miyazaki Hayao's 2001 animated film *Sen to Chihiro no Kamikakushi*. Chihiro hires herself out to the boss of the bath-house, the witch Yubāba, to work off her parents' debt. Having done this, Yubāba tasks her with servile duties, such as scrubbing floors and serving bath-house customers (which are in fact *kami* or *yōkai*) by washing them in the bath.

Though Chihiro belongs to an East Asian culture rather than a West Asian one, the function and the expectations are the same. In West Asian cultures, guests would be invited to *wash their feet* as a gesture of hospitality (as Abraham offered to his three guests in Gen 18:4; or Laban to Abraham's steward in Gen 24:32). This was particularly important in desert cultures where walking for long periods of time could be physically

In the Houses of the Poor

strenuous and tiring. The washing of the hands and the feet was also a specific priestly commandment for the sons of Aaron upon entering the Tent of Meeting (Exo 30:17-21)—the same who were commanded to *gird themselves* with priestly girdles and bind themselves with caps (Exo 29:4-9)! This is what Jesus chooses to do for His disciples, knowing that He is about to be betrayed by one of them.

Saint Peter is *flabbergasted*. We see this in his responses: 'Lord, do you wash my feet [too]?' and 'Not once in all this age shall you wash my feet!' Jesus's servility clearly has Peter confused and embarrassed. Perhaps Peter is trying to evade an unseemly accusation that he is placing himself socially higher than his teacher.

Yet when Jesus insists that 'If I do not wash you, you have no part in me,' Peter's immediate *volte-face* is comic. He isn't thinking at all about what his Lord is saying, but rather is grasping immediately at the chance to get in his rabbi's 'good books'. He demands: 'Lord, not my feet only but also my hands and my head!' It's a satirical grimace *a la* Gogol, a savagely-exaggerated *caricature* of obsequy.

If our dear Dr Watson here is so fixated on the 'washing' and the social significance thereof, and chasing himself in these comedic circles trying to please Jesus, then we need to pay attention to the other 'clues'. The foot-washing is *not* a simple exercise in or demonstration of humility—otherwise, Jesus would not have corrected Peter, and Peter would not have *over*corrected in such a comedic way. Peter's obsequious outburst about head and hands is meant to get us, the hearer,

A note on authorial self-elision

to backtrack to the πόδας, the **feet**. Why is Jesus washing the **feet** of the disciples and not any other part of their body?

If a person's *feet* are dirty, and need to be washed, the implication is that *they have been walking*. And this is where the tertiary semiotic of the *linteum* (the 'linen scroll') becomes relevant: a *message* given to a *messenger*. The πόδας puts us immediately in mind of Romans 10:15:

> πῶς δὲ κηρύξωσιν ἐὰν μὴ ἀποσταλῶσιν καθὼς γέγραπται ὡς ὡραῖοι οἱ **πόδες** τῶν εὐαγγελιζομένων τὰ ἀγαθά
>
> *And how can men preach unless they are sent? As it is written, 'How beautiful are the **feet** of those who preach good news!'*

Jesus, who knows that His own time is short, is using the time to prepare His disciples to *go out and walk further* to spread His teaching (cf. Matt 5:41). In that time, of course, before trains or boats, the message had to be delivered on foot, and the apostles (ἀποσταλῶσιν, literally 'those who are sent'—the same linguistic function, by the way, as the Arabic *ar-Rasūl* الرسول) would therefore necessarily be, very literal, *pedestrians*. Saint Paul is, of course, quoting directly from the book of the Prophet Isaiah in this letter:

> מה־נאוו על־ההרים **רגלי** מבשׂר משׁמיע שׁלום מבשׂר טוב משׁמיע ישׁוּעה אמר לציון מלך אלהיך:
>
> *How beautiful upon the mountains are the **feet** of him who brings good tidings, who publishes peace, who brings good tidings of good, who publishes salvation, who says to Zion, 'Your God reigns.'* (Isa 52:7)

In the Houses of the Poor

The honour that Jesus gives to the **feet** of His disciples in preparation of their apostolic function is therefore a deliberate demonstration of the honour that Isaiah gives to the messengers of God in the Old Testament. It is a *pedagogy*, and indeed Jesus Himself explains this to Peter and the others (13:12-17). Note the insistence that Jesus places on their being *sent* (ἀπόστολος) in John 13:16!

Jesus's washing His disciples' feet with the *linteum* thus implies that Jesus is using the '*linen scroll*' (not Livy's Roman history ensconced in the Temple of Juno, but rather the Hebrew *Tōrah*!) to prepare His disciples to *walk* to deliver the teaching unto the Gentiles. His later injunction that His disciples wash one another's feet is an admonition to them to serve the teaching faithfully, and also to bear each other's burdens, to support each other, and to help each other walk to deliver the message. Jesus's διέζωσεν, and use of the λέντιον to wash His disciples' feet, therefore both connect back to the consecration of Aaron and his sons as priests in the Book of Exodus, as well as to the 'men under command' in the first Book of Samuel. The command here, however, is not to reach for the sword, but instead for the scroll.

'You are not all clean'

Jesus then says something rather cryptic. We should examine this saying of His in detail.

> ὁ λελουμένος οὐκ ἔχει χρείαν εἰ μὴ τοὺς πόδας νίψασθαι ἀλλ' ἔστιν καθαρὸς ὅλος καὶ ὑμεῖς καθαροί ἐστε ἀλλ' οὐχὶ πάντες

A note on authorial self-elision

> 'He who has bathed does not need to wash, except for his feet, but he is clean all over; and you are clean, but not every one of you.' (John 13:10)

The RSV rather does us English hearers a disservice here. The ἀλλ' οὐχὶ πάντες in this verse actually carries a double meaning, which is not only repeated but actually *exacerbated* in the following verse: οὐχὶ πάντες καθαροί ἐστε (John 13:11). Where Scripture repeats itself, where it makes an instructional *'āwad* عاود, this is where we need to be paying *closer* attention, not allowing our eyes to glaze over. Saint John says that Jesus says this because 'He knew who was to betray him'. But the double meaning of the Greek is addressed *to Peter*, not to Judas!

The RSV decides on 'but not every one of you', thus favouring one reading of the Greek, but the οὐχὶ πάντες καθαροί ἐστε can mean either 'not every one of you is clean', or *'none* of you is *all* clean'. So even though Saint John aims our 'gaze' at Judas, the traitor in the disciples' midst, Jesus's actual saying is actually far broader and more ambiguous. A better translation which preserves this ambiguity might be, 'you are not all clean'.

But why is this important? This wordplay actually links us back directly to Paul's letter to Titus. **'To the pure all things are pure**, [πάντα καθαρὰ τοῖς καθαροῖς] but to the corrupt and unbelieving nothing is pure; their very minds and consciences are corrupted.' (Tit 1:15) But, as the Book of Proverbs rhetorically asks: 'Who can say, "I have made my heart clean; **I am pure** [Heb. *ṭaharəttî* טהרתי, LXX καθαρὸς εἶναι] *from my sin*"?' And Paul himself affirms this teaching in Romans 3:10. In the eyes of the Lord, *no one is pure*, because *no one is righteous*, and *no one* *understands or seeks God.* Everyone's mind and conscience are corrupt!

Although Judas is the primary target of Jesus's saying here, Jesus is not leaving *anyone* exempt from it, and particularly not Peter. Peter is still thinking in terms of social hierarchies. That's why he keeps chasing himself around in comedic obsequiousness trying to please Jesus during the foot-washing. He is probably still remembering Mary's bathing of Jesus's feet in the fragrant oil and wiping them with her hair (John 12:3). Because his conscience is corrupt, he misses the point of the teaching about the apostolic commission, all the while trying to exempt himself. This satirical jab at Peter is aimed at those in the Pauline community who oppose spreading the message to the Gentiles.

Peter's son: a false construct of Christian masculinity

It is a sad, and telling, characteristic of modern-day Christianity that we flock to no better interpreters of Scripture than this disciple of Carl Jung, this 'son of Peter' named for the river where Christ was baptised. This is because he makes the same mistakes as his patronymic namesake. We Orthodox Christians are not only no exception to this trend, but we may in fact be in *greater danger* of such eisegetical hermeneutics than our Catholic or Protestant brethren.

In the middle of the nineteenth century, Charles Kingsley, Thomas Hughes and J. C. Ryle preached a masculine Christ. But this was *not* in service to the teaching of Saint Paul. They were preaching 'Christian manliness' in the service of duty to an

A note on authorial self-elision

earthly *woman*: Queen Victoria. And they were preaching 'Christian manliness' as part of a drive toward the outright theft of wealth and abuse of power, at the expense of the conquered and subjected peoples of Asia and Africa.

The irony is that in the end, Victorian *machismo* (again, in the service of a woman) effeminises itself. The psychology of the Victorian 'Christian manliness' finds penultimate expression in occult esotericism. British Theosophy and Wicca are both essentially goddess-cults with proxy-Victorias at their centre. These were preceded in Germany by Goethe's religious-philosophical concept of '*das Ewig-Weibliche*', and succeeded in Russia by that grammatical error which snowballed into a private doctrine: Solovyov's and Bulgakov's *Sophianism*.

It is first worth noting what these British fellows managed to get correct. The Gospel of Saint John does not reject healthy masculinity. We can see that clearly from its use of the Greek verb διέζωσεν. Jesus is very much so *a man*, a *Son of Man*. He passed the same test which Job failed, twice, when challenged by God. We know that Jesus is marked out in the Gospel of Saint John as a 'son of Aaron' both by His 'girding up' and by His use of the ritual of foot-washing which was a particular hallmark of the Levite priesthood. And we can see that Jesus is physically exerting Himself to prepare His disciples to become *apostles*, to be *sent out and walk* to spread the teaching, in anticipation of His death. We can plainly see in Jesus, even in this short pericope, the manly attributes of **courage, wisdom, diligence** and **trustworthiness**.

But both Victorian and the present-day preachers of 'Christian masculinity' overstep their mark in egregious ways.

In the Houses of the Poor

They are, for one thing, culturally blind to Scripture's warnings against *builders*. Peterson deliberately mistakes Cain's role in the Old Testament when he points to a generic, 'universal' sibling rivalry as being the basis for his sin of fratricide, and casts Abel as a universal model of 'self-improvement' and Cain as a model of 'envy'. It's impossible to tell where he's getting this stuff, because literally nothing in Scripture shows Abel improving himself. Indeed, Abel (*Hebel* הבל, 'vanity') is a *passing breath*—that is his *function* in Genesis 4. Abel is replaced by Seth. Note that Seth, unlike his fratricidal brother the agriculturalist, *builds nothing* (Gen 5:3-8).

The book of Genesis expresses interest in the division of the sexes into *male and female* (Heb. *zākār ûnqēbâ* זכר ונקבה, Gk. ἄρσεν καὶ θῆλυ; Gen 1:27 via Gal 3:28). But we can see that it isn't concerned, as Peterson is, with the maintenance of culture or the building of civilisations. Its thoughts on the sexes are not man's thoughts, nor its ways our ways (Isa 55:8-9). It suffices to examine Genesis 6, and how the arrogant 'sons of God' (*bənê ha-'Elōhîm* בני האלהים), disobeying their Father, forced themselves on the 'daughters of man' (*bənôt ha-'Ādām* בנות האדם), and 'took to wife of them such as they chose' (Gen 6:2).

The same consonants in *bənôt* בנות 'daughters' can also function in Hebrew as the infinitive-construct form of the verb *bānâ* בנה 'to build'. The result of these unholy unions, the children who are born to the daughters of men are *ha-Gibbōrîm* הגברים 'the mighty men, heroes' (remember God's taunt to Job?), the *'anšê haššēm* אנשי השם 'men of name' (Gen 6:4). Yet the author leaves them, with deliberate irony, anonymous. But

A note on authorial self-elision

these heroes so displease God with their wickedness that God wipes them all out in the Flood.

Note whom God spares. The one righteous man does not 'take' women to wife, rather he has one singular woman spoken and appointed to him by God (Gen 6:18). Righteous manhood is expressed in Scripture by *walking* where God wills (Gen 6:9), and by *doing* His commands (Gen 6:22), particularly to hospitality. Noah makes (at first) only as God instructs. He builds nothing for himself until *after* the Flood (and only brings trouble upon himself and his family as a result).

Peterson, not being a Hebrew scholar, is subject to errors which all flow from the influence of Victorian-era German idealism. In short: he preaches manliness, but he's still a schoolboy. Like his namesake in Scripture, he thinks in terms, not of the divine command, but of human hierarchies and universal archetypes, stemming not from any close or careful analysis the Semitic linguistic framework of Scripture but instead from his psychiatric academic training at the feet of Carl Jung, whose archetype theories were inspired by Goethe! Likewise, not one of the Victorian preachers of 'Christian manliness' was a Hebrew scholar or Semitologist of any note: British Christians were largely fumbling in the dark on that score until Sir Wallis Budge came along. As such, they saw in the Gospel only what they wanted to see: a justification for their own self-interest.

In short, the Orthodox adherents of the *cultus* of Jordan Peterson and the (still mostly evangelical Protestant) adherents of Victorian 'Christian manliness' can see and understand the 'girding up', but they miss the *linteum*. Like

In the Houses of the Poor

Peter in the text itself, they are embarrassed by it. The ideal of manliness in the Gospel is expressed, not in constructing cities or in building monuments, but instead in *hospitality* and *service*, and in *labouring for the teaching*.

In the Gospel of Saint John, the literary character of Peter is constantly eyeing the advantage, trying to get himself into the best position among the disciples of Jesus. As such, he quite mistakes Jesus's approach to such critical matters as purity, wholeness, courage, diligence and the rest. Peter too is a man, but his manhood is darkened by ignorance and self-will. This is why he is so quick to reach for the sword and do violence (John 18:10-11), and also so quick to abandon Jesus when the pressure is on (John 18:15-18, 25-27).

In fact, the American Orthodox Christian penchant for listening to Peterson's Jungian blathering is patently dangerous. We risk building narratives in our mind that run counter to what Saint John is trying to tell us about manhood. Manhood is by no means all 'toxic', by no means an evil. But if we listen to the psychiatrists or to the Victorian empire-builders about what 'masculinity' is, rather than to Saint Paul and his students (including Saint John), then we risk another, different kind of 'arrested development'.

A note on authorial self-elision

A clarification on John 13:23

Certain things have come to light, man...

Saint Matthew is the only one of the four Evangelists who mentions himself, in the Gospel that bears his name, by name (Matt 9:9). The other three Evangelists, including Saint John, take great pains to allude to themselves only elliptically or cryptically, and do not mention themselves by name. For example, in the Gospel of Saint Mark:

καὶ νεανίσκος τις συνηκολούθει αὐτῷ περιβεβλημένος σινδόνα ἐπὶ γυμνοῦ καὶ κρατοῦσιν αὐτόν ὁ δὲ καταλιπὼν τὴν σινδόνα γυμνὸς ἔφυγεν

And a young man followed him, with nothing but a linen cloth about his body; and they seized him, but he left the linen cloth and ran away naked. (Mark 14:51-52)

The νεανίσκος reappears at the end of Mark, sitting on the right side of Jesus's tomb when the myrrh-bearing women come there (16:5). Whether Saint Mark's νεανίσκος 'young man' was a reference to the Evangelist himself is a matter of some debate, though traditionally he has been considered so. The term νεανίσκος links in the LXX to Shechem (Gen 34:19), to Joseph (Gen 41:12), to an unnamed servant of Moses (Num 11:27), and to several hypothetical youths who are of marriageable age or eligible for military service (Deu 32:25, Pro 20:11, Isa 62:5). In the Gospel of Saint Matthew, it links to the 'young man' of great possessions who came to Jesus asking how

My word, or my words to you?

to have eternal life (19:16-22); in the Gospel of Saint Luke, it links to the centurion's servant who was healed by Jesus (7:14). The best indication that the νεανίσκος in Saint Mark is an authorial insertion, comes from his literary function: he is the one who gives the 'good news' to the women at the tomb.

The function of the νεανίσκος as a page or a messenger in Mark 16:5, links him back to the nameless messenger in Numbers, who brought back news to Moses of Eldad and Medad prophesying in the camp. (Note Moses's nonchalant, and even supportive, response to this news!) This is a rich and intriguing parallel, as it suggests Saint Mark is positioning himself as someone *sent* to spread the news of the teaching *among the people*. The people to whom he delivered that message were 'the bitter tower' Miriam of the *Migdol*, the Miriam who is the 'mother of Jacob [= Israel]', and Šlomit or 'Peace' who bears the name of both a great dynastic king and a Herodian princess— and 'they were afraid' (Mark 16:8). The message which Mark bears 'from the camp' is discomfiting to those who would seek refuge in their buildings or their bloodlines or their princes, seeking to eulogise Jesus after His death. Yet they are the ones who are instructed to spread it.

If the νεανίσκος of Mark 14 and Mark 16 is an authorial self-insert, then, the author of the Gospel is saying something both self-effacing (linking himself to a minor character who shows up only once in Numbers), and radically subversive. Eldad and Medad are prophesying in the camp. That is to say: you can kill the messenger of God (Moses/Jesus), but God's teaching is alive and well *in the camp*. 'He is going before you to Galilee; there you will see him, as he told you.' (Mark 16:7)

In the Houses of the Poor

Saint Luke's presence in the writings traditionally ascribed to him is a trickier matter—but it's worth paying attention to all the same. Saint Mark's νεανίσκος-persona has a definite literary value internal to the work. However, because Saint Luke's Gospel is epistolary in format (beginning with an address to one Θεοφίλος—that is to say, literarily, to any 'friend of God'), and because Luke's avowed authorial purpose is quasi-historical, inserting himself into the Gospel narrative becomes a self-defeating exercise. It would undermine his position as an objective observer in events. Rather, the use of ἡμᾶς 'us' in Luke 1:1-4 as a direct address to Theophilos marks the author as narrator. This ἡμᾶς 'us' (inflected in various places as ἡμῖν, ἦμεν, ἡμῶν *etc.*) reappears in several passages of the Book of Acts (16:10-17; 20:5-15; 21:1-18; 27:1-28:16) in reference to himself and Saint Paul. But it deserves pointing out that Saint Luke continues to take meticulous care to avoid mentioning himself by name.

In both of these cases, Mark's νεανίσκος-persona and Luke's use of ἡμᾶς ('I; the *royal* "we", you know, the *editorial*...!'[46]), the indirect self-allusion is a *literary device*, in the same way that a narrator or authorial self-insertion would be in any other work of literature. So when a similar device occurs in the Gospel bearing the name of Saint John, we ought to be prepared to read it in a similar way.

---

[46] Ethan and Joel Coen, *The Big Lebowski* (PolyGram Filmed Entertainment, 1998).

My word, or my words to you?

The voice of the weak disciple

Saint John's technique in authorial self-elision is to refer to himself as εἷς ἐκ τῶν μαθητῶν αὐτοῦ ... ὃν ἠγάπα ὁ Ἰησοῦς 'one out of his disciples... whom Jesus loved' (John 13:23). The Greek word *mathētēs* μαθητής, derived from the verb *manthanō* μανθάνω 'to learn, to understand', is linked through this derivation to the Semitic root *l-m-d* ל-מ-ד 'rod, goad, to beat, to chastise, to be accustomed, to be trained, to be under discipline'. Indeed, in the Syriac *Pəšiṭta* text of the Gospel of Saint John, the word *mathētēs* is retranslated as *talmîda'* ܬܠܡܝܕܐ 'tyro, trainee, cadet, apprentice'—which, by the way, is cognate to the Hebrew word *talmūd* תלמוד 'instruction (for beginners)'. The implication of 'disciple' is not merely a 'student' but someone *under a harsh discipline*: think about a monastic novice, or a student of kung fu or some other martial art.

Now here is where things get interesting. In English we see this phrase 'one out of His disciples... whom Jesus loved'. Because our consciences are corrupt, we automatically think that John is boasting of his privileged position with Christ, his proprietary ownership of the divine message of the Gospel. Who wouldn't want to be the 'beloved pupil', the 'teacher's pet'? But, as Fr Marc Boulos would gleefully tell you: '*it is a lie, ḥabībī!*'[47] This is *not* what Saint John is asserting for himself.

---

[47] Fr Marc Philip Boulos, 'The only one who loves', *The Bible as Literature* podcast 530 (YouTube, 16 August 2024), https://www.youtube.com/watch?v=me64kqn9eEs.

In the Houses of the Poor

True, in the Greek (which for the New Testament, I hasten to add, is original and *authoritative!*), the word used is an inflection of the familiar *agapē* ἀγάπη 'affection, benevolence'. But again looking at the *Pəšiṭta* for a point of comparison, the relevant adjective is not translated as *dəḥabīb* ܢܚܒܒ (the same root as the *ḥabībī* حبيبي that Fr Marc likes to use!) but instead as *dərahem* ܕܪܚܡ. This comes from a common root in the Semitic languages, *r-ḥ-m* ר-ח-ם, having to do with 'the womb' and by extension 'compunction, mercy, pity': ורחמתי את־אשר ארחם '*and [I] will **show mercy** on whom I will **show mercy***' (Exo 33:19). The implication is that this is a *weak* disciple upon whom Jesus showed mercy, or took pity.

This is not a speculative interpretation on the part of the Syriac translator. Note how the text says that John is *reclining* at the Lord's bosom (ἀνακείμενος... ἐν τῷ κόλπῳ). One naturally takes to one's bosom what is weakest or most vulnerable, or in need of protection. We see this in Exodus, where God commands Moses to put his hand to his bosom (*bəḥêqeka* בחיקך, LXX τὸν κόλπον), and it becomes leprous—and to put it back, and it becomes healthy (Exo 4:6-7). In Numbers, the phrase is put, howbeit ironically, into Moses's mouth by God: שאהו בחיקך כאשר ישא האמן את־הינק '*Carry them in your bosom, as the nurse carries her suckling child*' (Num 11:12).

God warns His people in Deuteronomy that should they fail to follow His commands and uphold His law, so great would be the miseries and privations that He would send upon them, that even the tenderest and kindest among them would turn against their nearest of kin and dearest ones, even the 'wife of his bosom' ('*iššâ **ḥêqô*** אשת חיקו, LXX γυναῖκα τὴν ἐν τῷ **κόλπῳ**

My word, or my words to you?

αὐτοῦ) or the 'husband of her bosom' (*'îš ḥêqā* אִישׁ חֵיקָהּ, LXX ἄνδρα αὐτῆς τὸν ἐν τῷ **κόλπῳ**), and leave them to starve (Deu 28:53-57). Naomi takes the newborn Obed to her bosom (*bǝḥêqâ* בְחֵיקָהּ, LXX τὸν **κόλπον** αὐτῆς; Rth 4:13). In the *mašal* of Nathan to David, the poor man's one beloved little ewe-lamb would *sleep at his bosom* (*bǝḥêqô tiškāb* בְחֵיקוֹ תִשְׁכָּב, LXX ἐν τῷ **κόλπῳ** αὐτοῦ ἐκάθευδεν; 2 Sam 12:3). From these examples we can see that this phrase is used with a degree of idiomatic consistency to convey *pathos*. This is true also in the Gospel of Saint Luke, with Lazarus being a pitiable figure who is taken into the **κόλπον** Ἀβραάμ '*bosom of Abraham*', not of his own deserving or meritorious deeds, but because in his lifetime he received '*evil things*' (Luke 16:19-26).

So Saint John's reclining at the Lord's bosom is an admission of his weak and pitiable condition. However, in this instance it also allows him to speak with authority. Peter asks John to relay his questions to the Teacher, and to faithfully report His answers to the other disciples. Being physically closest to the Lord, the 'one of His disciples... whom Jesus loved' is in the best position to relate faithfully the teaching which Jesus imparts. When the author's *persona* in the text is speaking, therefore, we ought to strive our utmost to hear what he is saying and to understand it.

The author, among those in darkness

An overriding theme of the Gospel of Saint John, starting from its Prologue, is *light vs. darkness* (John 1:1-5), to which are notably added *hearing vs. not-hearing* (John 8:12-37) and *seeing vs. blindness* (John 9:1-17)[48]. It is noteworthy, and in fact a note of literary irony, that John bestows his name *not upon himself as the author*, but instead upon the *literary character* of John the Forerunner, who is the '*witness to the light*' by which the men who are in darkness (ἐν τῇ σκοτίᾳ) and who are gormless and stupid (οὐ κατέλαβεν) can see their way (John 1:6-13).

Remember: we are dealing with *literature* here. Let us approach John the same way Trubetskoi does Dostoevsky. It is precisely in *light* of these themes, and in *light* of the author's choice to bestow his own name upon another character rather than himself, that the author's own deliberately-anonymous appearance in the thirteenth chapter should now be regarded. Where does he place himself, what function does he serve, and why?

Jesus has just predicted that one among His disciples will betray Him (John 13:21). Then Peter, seeing that 'one among His disciples… whom Jesus loved' was reclining next to him at the table, even at His bosom, asked that disciple who the traitor was—a question which John faithfully relayed to Jesus (John 13:24-25). Here John's position at Jesus's bosom is advantageous because it allows him to speak with authority. But Jesus then replies that it will be the one to whom He shall give the *psōmion* ψωμίον 'crumb, sop, fragment' when He has dipped it—and then He promptly dips it and gives it to Judas (John 13:26-27).

---

[48] Cooper, *Lamb*, 23-48, 195-231.

My word, or my words to you?

If this were *Crime and Punishment*, the book would be over. Porfiry Petrovich would have *nothing left to do*. The murder would be solved: case closed! Rodion Romanovich would be carted off to Siberia, Petersburg would be down one murderer, and the Head of Investigations can kick up his feet for the rest of the afternoon and collect an easy day's cheque at the end. So that's clearly not the point.

What is happening to Jesus is obvious. That He is going to be betrayed is obvious to us, the hearer. Who is going to betray Him is also clear to us. And He has dropped on us a painfully obvious hint: the one to whom He offered the dipped *psōmion* (as Boaz offered his vinegar-dipped 'morsel' to Ruth; Ruth 2:14) would be the one to betray Him. Yet even as this is happening, τοῦτο δὲ οὐδεὶς ἔγνω τῶν ἀνακειμένων πρὸς τί εἶπεν αὐτῷ '*no one at the table knew why He said this to him*' (John 13:28). It beggars belief. How is that possible? Are they really this blind? Did no one pay attention to what Jesus was saying even seconds after they asked Him? The point that Saint John is making is to show that all of the disciples, *including himself*, were hopelessly 'in the dark'.

The significance of the *fatteh*

We have examined the technique of authorial self-elision, and thus ascertained that Saint John was *not* exalting but instead belittling himself, and gone into some detail on the rôle he plays in this 'scene'. But we're still left with the question: *to what end* is Saint John critiquing himself? And why is he putting in an appearance in his Gospel only now?

In the Houses of the Poor

Other among Jesus's disciples have made their appearance with due symbolic importance. Andrew, the first-called, shares the same lexical and literary functionality as Adam in Genesis (John 1). I have spoken also about the beatific functionality of Nathaniel as the representative of the Jewish 'centre', as the Third of Five and the παιδάριον 'young man' who was made nameless at the feeding of the multitudes (John 6). Nicodemus also plays a role that is strongly symbolic: at times carrying the 'stupid stick' (John 3) and at other times serving as the voice of wisdom (John 7). In order to determine why John is waiting until this point, the turning-point of the Gospel, to make even such an oblique and self-eliding self-reference, we have to return to the context in which his Gospel would be heard. The hint can be found in the setting of this passage.

The use of the word ἀνακείμενος 'to recline, to sit down (at a dinner table)' indicates to us that this entire exchange takes place *at the table*. This is a reference to the κοινωνία 'table-fellowship' of the Pauline community. The betrayal of the κοινωνία was very much at the top of mind for the Pauline community at the time in which Saint John was writing his Gospel. As mentioned earlier, the first and second centuries were a time when the public disputes between the Paulines and nascent Judaism were in full swing, when pro-circumciser and anti-circumciser elements were producing rifts and dissensions *inside* the fellowship, and when esoteric Gnostic doctrines were being introduced to the fellowship in Jesus's name. The disciples asking who the enemy is when the enemy is in fact obvious to us, from a *literary* perspective, shows us that the 'identity' of the κοινωνία's enemy is not the important question here.

My word, or my words to you?

Furthermore, the literary device of the *psōmion* and its explicit tie to the Book of Ruth further cement in the reader's mind the core question of *hospitality*. Boaz offers Ruth (a poor stranger from a despised people, the incestuous children of Lot) bread from his table in the form of a *psōmon* (or *fatta* פת, same as the Levantine Arabic *fatteh* فتة or English via modern Greek *pita*) and furthermore instructs his people not to censure her or give her any trouble. In the Book of Ruth, Boaz's act is a clear indication of his righteousness and his humane treatment of strangers. John is giving us an authoritative recapitulation of Paul's injunction to the Romans to *give bread* (*psōmize* ψώμιζε) even to their enemies (Prov 25:21-22 *via* Rom 12:20). Yet here the guilty party makes the choice, as 'after the morsel, Satan entered into him' (John 13:27), to betray his fellows at the table. Loving one's enemies may not always be the most 'practical' method of dealing with them: Judas's betrayal proves that. But it is nevertheless the method which is *commanded*.

By pointing to himself at such a late time, oblivious to what is happening around him, Saint John could very well be criticising himself for not having spoken up earlier about these issues. It's also possible he is self-critiquing for having remained passive (and 'reclining') while the κοινωνία was being disrupted. Or he may be apologising for not having recognised the betrayal as it was taking place. But at the same time, despite his obliviousness, his authority in speaking up now is clearly derived from the voice of Jesus Himself, at Whose bosom he is reclining. The teaching is being pronounced, authoritatively, to give bread even to the enemies who would betray you.

My word, or my words to you?

The de-ontology of Saint John's teaching

A clarification on John 14:1-15

The rage of the teacher betrayed

Jesus, if we will recall from the last chapter, was ἐταράχθη τῷ πνεύματι *'troubled in spirit'* (John 13:21) when He knew that one among His disciples was preparing to betray Him. This Greek verb, *tarassō* ταράσσω, is *not* a neutral verb, and the RSV translation is almost comically litotic. It's connected emphatically to Joseph's feeling at being betrayed by his brothers (where in the LXX, *tarassō* stands in for the Hebrew *zāʿaf* זָעַף 'to be **enraged**', or *fāʿam* פעם or *bāhal* בהל 'to be disturbed'). In the last chapter, Jesus was seeing the proverbial red when He knew that His own students, His friends, were going to betray Him.

Yet what does He say to them afterward? μὴ **ταρασσέσθω** ὑμῶν ἡ καρδία *'Let not your hearts be **troubled**'* (John 14:1).

In the *Šāhnama*, the tenth-century epic poem by Abolqāsem Ferdowsī, we are treated to a picture of the arrogant young king Kay Kāvus—newly enthroned among his kingdom's opulence, having no limit to his pride, and convinced only the way the very young can be of his own invulnerability. Under the influence of tales of the wealth of the north and of his own greed, Kay Kāvus concocts a plan to invade and plunder Mazandaran. All of his nobles baulk at the notion, which was beyond any of his ancestors' ability to accomplish, and they

My word, or my words to you?

turn to the elder hero Zāl to plead their case against the invasion with the young king.

Zāl is 'deeply troubled' by this. Literally, Ferdowsī says that his soul was *bepīčīd* بپیچید 'wound up', as though in knots or a bundle. He knows full well that his advice will not be heeded. He understands fully that the king is a boy with no experience of the world. He knows that if he goes to Kay Kāvus and pleads against this invasion, he will certainly be spurned and might well lose his own life. But he has no choice, in his heart, but to speak the truth to the arrogant young king. He understands that God and his own conscience demand it. True enough, in the end the king does not listen to him, and he leads Persia's armies to their destruction in the north. Ferdowsī is ruthless to Zāl in his narrative: speaking the truth exposes Zāl to a charge of cowardice, it loses him the trust of the king, and it brings him no solace and no joy—but he also has no choice but to speak it[49].

In this particular instance, Jesus's reaction bears a remarkable similarity to that of the mythological Persian hero Zāl in the *Šāhnama*. He reacts the same way any normal human being would react, to the knowledge that His own friends are going to betray Him. It's the same way that Zāl reacts to Kay Kāvus's moronic plan to invade the Iranian north. He becomes angry, even enraged. But once the moment has passed, He still has the obligation to speak to His disciples, just as Zāl had the

---

[49] Abolqāsem Ferdowsī, *Shahnameh: the Persian Book of Kings*, tr. Dick Davis (Penguin Classics, 2006), 142-147.

obligation to speak to Kay Kāvus. He gets Himself under control, and delivers His ῥήματα *rhēmata* to them, just as Zāl must give his *pand* پند 'counsel, rede, advice' (cognate with the English word '*path*') to the unhearing king.

Obviously, we are dealing with two very different works of literature. Although the *Iliad* and the *Aeneid* were very much elements of Paul's world, the Gospels do not form an epic. There is no 'hero's journey' in any meaningful sense: indeed, *ta Vivlía* as a whole *undermine* any possible claims to the human exaltation of a particular *ethnos*. Jesus is not a heleth of deep Iranian antiquity, clad in shining armour, riding on a steed like a mammoth, swinging a gigantic mace and casting His enemies down before Him in feats that cause the oceans to run red with their blood. But Ferdowsī, despite authoring what is in essence an epic-heroic reimagining of ancient Persian mythology, is nonetheless steeped in the Semitic Scriptures, including the Hebrew scrolls and the *Qur'ān*. The father of Rostam, despite his frightening albinistic appearance and despite some of his occasional heroic excesses, is nonetheless held up *in this instance* as obedient to God and to the demands of truth as a transcendent value.

More to the point, though, Jesus's reaction is simply *human*. Jesus isn't Superman, and He isn't Spock. He feels *rage*. This is something that, speaking as a teacher and as a parent, I feel that *every* teacher (and parent!) goes through at some point, and understands.

We caretakers of young people, of whatever age, can all point to at least one time when we're not listened to, or when our young charges push our buttons, or when they deliberately

My word, or my words to you?

disobey or defy us. And when we go out of our way to make sure they are safe and happy, and our efforts go unrecognised, we are hurt and angry. Modern, 'culturally relevant' pedagogy recognises this in both teachers and students when it talks about amygdala hijacks. The verb *tarassō* should be one which each teacher and parent can relate to in the encounters that they've had with their children.

And children can be different levels of oblivious or wilful. Some of them do push our buttons deliberately; others of them do it without having the least intention. Here, Jesus is being deliberately betrayed by one of His students, one of His friends—*to His death*.

Two Greek verbs 'to go', please

Yet, as every teacher and parent is also aware, venting rage is a luxury we can ill afford, because we care about our kids. We can *feel* rage, but there are hard limits to its expression, because we are in a position of responsibility. There is thus no contradiction in Jesus's being ἐταράχθη in Chapter 13, and His teaching the disciples μὴ ταρασσέσθω ὑμῶ in Chapter 14. It's what human beings who are in a pedagogical position *have to do*: get your own baggage together, get yourself under control (take a five-minute brain break if you have to!), and *teach*.

The contrast between John 13's 'troubled at heart' and John 14's 'do not be troubled' is also, however, what we would now call a 'teaching moment'. The line from John 14:6 which is so often quoted, to use the cliché, 'out of context'—*I am the way, and the truth, and the life; no one comes to the Father, but by me*—

In the Houses of the Poor

has to be heard in the wake of this moment of confusion. Jesus has just been seen by His disciples in a moment of weakness, of out-of-control emotion. How does He teach them after this?

Jesus here uses two *different verbs* here which are both (unhelpfully) glossed in English as 'to go': πορεύω, and ὑπάγω. These Greek terms map in the LXX onto two related Hebrew verbs: *hālak* הלך and *yālak* ילך, respectively. The difference in Hebrew is subtle; they are morphological cousins, a steady walk versus a driven march. The Greek sharpens the contrast: πορεύω is a river flowing downstream in its course (Gen 2:14; see also Gen 5:22-24, 6:9), where ὑπάγω is the sea being *compelled* to retreat (Exo 14:21). The latter, indeed, is often used as an order: *'get gone! scram! beat it!'* (see Matt 4:10, Mark 8:33). So when Jesus shifts from πορεύω to ὑπάγω in John 14:3, His disciples sit up and take notice. So should we.

We see that Saint Thomas, who was introduced to us at the death of Lazarus, has clearly picked upon Jesus's shift in verbiage from πορεύω to ὑπάγω, and is unsuccessfully trying to figure out what Jesus means by it. Why is Jesus saying that He is going, first of His own will, but then switches to saying that He is being *compelled* to depart?

The Gospel of Saint John is *Rabbinic theatre*: when supporting characters such as Thomas appear, they are usually missing the didactic point of the text in one way or another. So when Thomas says κύριε οὐκ οἴδαμεν ποῦ ὑπάγεις πῶς δυνάμεθα τὴν ὁδὸν εἰδέναι 'Lord, we don't know where you are going; how can we know the way?' (14:5), we can be assured that he is missing the point to blackly-comedic effect, similar to Peter's obsequious about-face over the washing of feet in the previous

My word, or my words to you?

chapter. He interprets the shift in language over 'going' as a literal command to take a holiday *somewhere*, and expresses puzzlement over the itinerary and destination.

But to the hearer—assumedly familiar with the foregoing three Gospel texts—the ὁδός 'way' that Jesus is going ought to be clear. Jesus is going *to His death*. The ὁδός is *the Cross*. Because Jesus is speaking words that are *scattering the flock* and *dividing the synagogue*, the combined power of the Sanhedrin and the Roman state are going to see to it that He gets 'cancelled'. It's the same fate that awaited Isaiah and Ezekiel. Jesus started by speaking prophetically, indeed quoting *the very words* of Isaiah, from the beginning of Saint John's Gospel. Yet He is going to end by being betrayed by one of His own, arrested by the *stratiōtēs*, condemned as a blasphemer by the Sanhedrin, dragged through show-trials before Herod *and* Pilate, stripped, beaten, mocked, and ultimately despatched torturously between two bandits. What He started freely, will end in the most painful and humiliating sort of compulsion. His teaching here is that anyone who follows Him is going to suffer similarly.

Consider the audience: shifting from *logos* to *rhēmata*

Because we are already expected to take notice of a rhetorical shift in the Greek here, from πορεύω to ὑπάγω (accentuating the connotative difference between *hālak* הלך and *yālak* ילך in the Old Testament), we should also be attuned to the fact that Jesus makes another rhetorical shift here.

In the Houses of the Poor

Two words are used throughout the Gospel of Saint John for the preaching of Scripture. One of them, λόγος, I spoke about in *The Lamb before Its Shearers*. I argue there that when Saint John uses the word λόγος, it is almost always in reference to a *comprehensive saying or teaching* from Hebrew Scripture, often being a direct quotation from the Pentateuch or from one of the Psalms. My argument was that this term had been mishandled and abused by long centuries of Hellenistic speculation, such that it was made to bear a Platonic-Aristotelian-Stoic value that Saint John not only never intended it to, but in fact criticised and undermined. (The λόγος is the *command*, and thus belongs, like light, to God—whereas man is in the dark and doesn't have a clue about it.)

Now, the non- or even anti-Hellenic usage of λόγος is still at work here. However, the use of a different Greek word shows us that another literary function is being made active. Jesus makes a shift—as He does at several other points in this same Gospel—to ῥήματα. The word ῥήμα, in Greek, also refers to the preaching of the Gospel, but it zooms in the scope even more. It refers to an 'utterance', a 'proclaimed word', a specific verbal address to a specific person. The shift from λόγος to ῥήμα indicates that we ought to consider the addressees of the speech-act in question. Specifically, we need to take into account their *literary* function.

In this context, we need to understand that the two disciples, Saint Thomas and Saint Philip respectively, are being addressed by their teacher after a fit of emotional pique. If this were a school classroom, these two students would be the

My word, or my words to you?

shame-faced ones sitting at the front, whispering to their classmates: *'Hey, guys, stop being so naughty! Mr. Jesus is mad!'*

In terms of his literary function, the name of Thomas (*Ta'wma'* תאומא 'Didymos, the Twin') alludes to two sets of twins in the Book of Genesis. The first is to the sons of Isaac and Rebekah, Esau and Jacob; and the second is to the sons of Judah by Tamar, Perez and Zeraḥ. The term is linked implicitly to struggle. Under the law a woman is held guilty who steps in to defend her husband during a quarrel and grabs her husband's opponent by 'the twins' (LXX διδύμων αὐτοῦ *i.e.* his genitals, Deut 25:11). Likewise, after the conquest of Ai, Joshua's men have the city's king hanged on a 'twinned tree' (LXX ξύλου διδύμου, Josh 8:29). The only instance in the Hebrew Scriptures in which the name of Thomas is not linked to struggle is in the Song, where the beloved's breasts are compared to a pair of twin fawns (Song 4:5, 7:3).

In this case Thomas is being paired, or 'twinned', with the literary character of Philip. The name of Philip (Gk. Φίλιππος = 'friend of horses') is, first and foremost, an obvious historical allusion to Philip of Makedon, the father of Alexander. Philip's name could also refer to the city of Philippoi in Greece founded by the Macedonian king... or to the inhabitants thereof, addressed in Saint Paul's letter to the **Philippians**. The name of the disciple could also be taken to refer to Philip, the brother of Herod (the Roman client-king), or to the city of Caesarea Philippi in Decapolis founded by this latter Philip. In any of these events, though, Philip's name links him indelibly to Hellenism.

In the Houses of the Poor

It seems logical, then—with Thomas's name being Aramaic and linked to Esau and Jacob; and Philip's name being Greek and linked to Philip of Makedon—to hear the ῥῆμα of Jesus addressed to them as being linked to the relations between respective Judaic-leaning and Hellenic-leaning elements within the Pauline community. It is also noteworthy that both Thomas and Philip are asking Jesus rather strange questions. Thomas, picking up the πορεύω-ὑπάγω shift, asks Jesus about where he is going. Philip asks Jesus to δεῖξον ἡμῖν τὸν πατέρα 'show us the Father' (14:8)—a question of where Jesus came from.

The questions themselves show that Thomas and Philip *both* failed to understand the importance of Jesus's appearance at the Feast of Booths, or the idiotic questions the crowds there trying to catch Jesus were asking about Him. Not only that, but Philip's question strikes the hearer at once with its rank arrogance. *No one has seen God at any time* (John 1:18), and Philip wants Jesus to *show him*? As Tevye would put it: 'Unheard of! Absurd!'

Thomas's question of where Jesus is going thus reads as a send-up of nascent Jewish concerns about the fate of the Temple and the political aims of the movement attached to this messianic teaching. And by subsequently taking aim at Philip like this, Saint John once again appears to be critiquing the tendency toward metaphysical speculation among the Pauline community of his own time: the tendency that would come to manifest in Gnosticism.

The Pauline teaching is present here, and John is positioning the Teacher as its *embodiment*. This is not in some mystical or philosophical sense: τὰ ἔργα ἃ ἐγὼ ποιῶ κἀκεῖνος ποιήσει 'he...

My word, or my words to you?

will also do the works that I do' (John 14:12); ἐὰν ἀγαπᾶτέ με τὰς ἐντολὰς τὰς ἐμὰς τηρήσετε 'if you love me, you will keep my commandments' (14:15); ἐάν τις ἀγαπᾷ με τὸν λόγον μου τηρήσει 'if a man loves me, he will keep my teaching' (14:23). Jesus repeats this so often here, and so insistently, that there's *no way we can escape* this being the ῥῆμα that He means to impart. And because it is a ῥῆμα, the addressee is important— or rather, the pair of them. This is where (as Trubetskoi would say) the name of Thomas assumes its literary function and significance.

The commandment to *do the works that Jesus does*, is equally valid for the Semite Thomas, and for the Greek Philip. The historicist Jewish demand from Thomas for the fulfilment in time, for the *destination*, of the Messianic mission to be clarified, is irrelevant. So too is the philosophical Hellenistic demand from Philip, to have shown to his intellectual understanding the true nature of the Father, the Aristotelian 'unmoved mover'. Both demands are gently demonstrated as *non sequitur*. And irrelevant too is our common modern mishandling of John 14:6, which is taken to posit institutional Christianity, demanding mere passive assent, as the exclusive bearer of the 'way' to an eternal salvation. Saint John pre-empts such a mishandling himself, in the text: εἰ δὲ μή **διὰ τὰ ἔργα αὐτὰ** πιστεύετε 'otherwise believe me **for the sake of the works themselves**' (John 14:11). The text itself *de-ontologises* the word. I use this as a pun. John decentralises the historical character of Jesus, and in so doing issues a *command*: Jesus's credentials are to be believed on account of *what He does*, not *Who He is*.

In the Houses of the Poor

And we the hearers are being challenged in the text not merely to confess Jesus with our mouths but to *do the works that we see Him doing.* If Jesus is any kind of 'way' or 'life' (understood not philosophically, but literarily), then the works He does *in the text* are the ῥήματα of supreme importance for us.

Servants in the vineyard[50]

A clarification on John 15:12-22

Who gets to be a γεωργός?

I am overjoyed to report that I did *not* attend the so-called 'Hands Off!' protests against the Trump Administration on 5 April of this year[51]. Quite frankly, I had far better things to do with my time. This is not to say, of course, that I support the Trump presidency. Still less is it to say that I endorse the right-wing nationalist rhetoric which underpins it. Rather, the work in study of the philology of the Gospel of Saint John that I was doing instead on that day will, I believe, stand better witness against that same idolatry in the long run. Certainly better than my attendance at protests which (correctly!) oppose some of Trump's more egregious executive excesses, but which sadly fail to discern or address the roots of those excesses.

The central distinction which Jesus draws in the fifteenth chapter of Saint John's Gospel, after all, is between two kinds of people who are involved in the same *work*. The *mašal*-ic likeness that Jesus continues to borrow here, is that of the Father to a

---

[50] Matthew Franklin Cooper, 'Servants in the vineyard', Substack post, *Skeireins* (13 April 2025).

[51] Staff, '50,000 attend "Hands Off" rally in St Paul, MN', *Fight Back News* (8 April 2025), https://fightbacknews.org/articles/50-000-attend-hands-off-rally-in-st-paul-mn.

Servants in the vineyard

vigneron, a γεωργός (literally, 'ground-worker': a Greek compound noun from which we get the personal name *George*). This is an image we see in several other places—most notably, in Saint Paul's second letter to Saint Timothy! '*A hard-working **farmer** [γεωργός] ought to have the first share of the crops.*' (2 Tim 2:6) That the 'farmer' in this case is God, and not a man, is clarified by Saint James in his epistle: '*Be patient, therefore, brethren, until the coming of the Lord. Behold, the **farmer** [γεωργός] waits for the precious fruit of the earth, being patient over it until it receives the early and the late rain.*' (James 5:7)

The Greek word γεωργός is intimately linked to the Semitic verbal root *n-ṭ-'* נ-ט-ע 'to plant, to set in the ground'[52]. Note that while God is rightfully a γεωργός in this text, this function is almost always pejorative when it is linked to a human! Noah, as soon as he becomes a γεωργός, gets (as we say these days) 'high on his own supply', and blacks out, leading to the incident with his three sons which ends in his cursing of his grandson Canaan (Gen 9:20-27). And wherever human *vignerons* are mentioned in the *Nəbī'im*, the prophetic writings, it is *always* to call down woe upon their heads (Jer 14:4, 51:23; Joel 1:11; Amos 5:16). The only exceptions occur when human *tenants* accept the headship of the singular divine Sovereign *over* them (Jer 31:4-6).

It is God Who is given the privilege, in Genesis, in the Psalms, and in the prophetic writings of Isaiah and Jeremiah, to *nāṭa'*

---

[52] In the first volume of my forthcoming Chinese lexicon *Jiejing Shuowen*, I linked this verbal root to the Chinese words *zai* 在 'at, in, on, present, existing' and its cousin *zai* 栽 'to plant crops, to cultivate'.

נטע whatever people He wills into any given place. God plants the man in the garden (Gen 2:8), and then drives him out (Gen 3:24). He transplants the Hebrew people from Egypt into Canaan (Psalm 80), a privilege which He reserves the power and right to undo at any time (Psalm 44; see also Isa 5:2-6, 27:3; Jer 2:21, 45:4). The first few verses of the fifteenth chapter of John's Gospel are a recapitulation of this teaching from the Hebrew Scriptures. But equally important to note is that all this planting, transplanting, examining of fruits, pruning and discarding is rightfully *His* work—not ours!

The 'Hands Off!' types, therefore, are correct to say that the president should indeed keep his 'hands off' the refugees and migrants who have come within our borders. God has *planted* them here. It is not Trump's job (or any other man's, of any party!) to *transplant* them *en masse* into El Salvadoran prisons, or anywhere else. Those who arrogate that divine prerogative to themselves, so the Hebrew Scriptures teach, only heap curses upon their own progeny.

But that same admonition applies equally to the opposition. The volume in which Democratic administrations also deported migrants from American territory is, of course, relevant—but I am not merely talking about that. From October 2023 to January 2025, the Democrats have been the ones in the position of 'playing God' and deciding, with a startling degree of bigotry, who should get to live in the territory of Palestine and who should not.

Servants in the vineyard

I should give some credit, at least, where credit is due. Although it was largely treated as a side issue to the main protests[53], the 'Hands Off!' protests were not as hostile to the Palestinian cause as I originally suspected they would be, given the Democratic Party's hostility to Arab-American voters during[54] (and after[55]) the 2024 election. Also, hearteningly, quite a few signs were seen at the protests in support of Mahmoud Khalil, the Columbia University activist arrested and threatened with deportation for his support of the Palestinian cause[56].

But the question—the Biblical question—still stands. To whom do you look for vindication against the likes of Donald Trump and Elon Musk and Peter Thiel? Do you look for

---

[53] Lauren Feiner, '"Hands Off": protesters deliver a sweeping message to Trump and Musk at a DC rally', *The Verge* (6 April 2025), https://www.theverge.com/policy/644186/hands-off-washington-dc-protest-musk-trump-doge.

[54] Gal Beckerman, 'Revenge voting over Gaza is a mistake', *The Atlantic* (29 October 2024), https://www.theatlantic.com/politics/archive/2024/10/revenge-voting-over-gaza-is-a-mistake/680446/.

[55] Hannan Adely, '"Don't blame us for Trump," say Arab, Muslim voters in New Jersey', *NorthJersey.com* (18 February 2025), https://www.northjersey.com/story/news/new-jersey/2025/02/18/nj-muslim-arab-trump-policies/78976084007/.

[56] MEE Staff, 'Trump administration's memo on Mahmoud Khalil case "devoid" of facts, lawyers say', *Middle East Eye* (10 April 2025), https://www.middleeasteye.net/news/trump-administration-memo-mahmoud-khalil-case-devoid-facts-his-lawyers-say.

vindication to the God of Ecclesiastes, the only Judge Who lacks nothing, Who can't be corrupted by money or power, and Who can be accounted just? Or do you look to Joe Biden or Kamala Harris or Cory Booker, and the rival billionaire donors that they represent?

This isn't a hypothetical question. We know, or ought to know, the corrupting influence that corporate money has on our political system. Once politicians are bought, there are certain things that they are no longer able to say, commitments they can no longer hold, and injustices to which they have to turn a blind eye.

In order for us to derive any lasting benefit out of these protests, the American people need to start *resisting the impulse to play God* in troubled places of the world, whether they are of either party or no party. That includes, in the Republicans' case: Afghanistan, Yemen, Iraq and Pakistan... as well as Syria and Palestine. And in the Democrats' case: Somalia, Yugoslavia, Libya and Donbass... as well as Syria and Palestine. The call of Saint John's Gospel to μένη ἐν τῇ ἀμπέλῳ '*abide in the Vine*' (15:4) is in fact a call to endure in trust that the true *vigneron*, the true vinedresser, knows what He is doing, and to care for the branches without arrogating to ourselves judgement over the fruits.

So what is our job in the vineyard?

Jesus draws a distinction in the verses which follow, between 'friends' (φίλων, John 15:13; φίλοι, 15:14) and 'servants', or

Servants in the vineyard

even 'slaves' (δούλους, 15:15). What is Saint John trying to get us to hear with this phrasing?

This distinction ought to be at least somewhat familiar to those of us who follow the Orthodox Christian tradition. The hesychastic school which is represented in the *Philokalia*, and given voice especially in the writings attributed to Saint Peter of Damascus, divide human beings along similar lines into 'slaves', 'hirelings' and 'sons'. In the *Philokalia*, the distinction that Saint Peter of Damascus derives is as follows:

> *Men are of three kinds: slaves, hirelings or sons. Slaves do not love the good, but refrain from evil out of fear of punishment; this, as St Dorotheos observes, is a good thing, but not fully in accord with God's will. Hirelings love what is good and hate what is evil, out of hope of reward. But sons, being perfect, refrain from evil, not out of fear of punishment, but because they hate evil violently; and they do what is good, not because they hope for reward, but because they consider it their duty*[57].

Jesus's distinction between 'friends' and 'servants' in the fifteenth chapter of the Gospel of Saint John is of such a similar nature and phrasing that it appears to be, in fact, the source of this hesychastic teaching from the Damascene saint. Indeed, on the surface, there is quite a bit of support for such a reading.

---

[57] Saint Peter of Damascus, 'Book I: a treasury of divine knowledge', in *Philokalia: the Complete Text*, comp. Saint Nikodimos of the Holy Mountain and Saint Makarios of Corinth, eds. G.E. Palmer and Philip Sherrard (Faber & Faber, 1995).

In the Houses of the Poor

The use of the noun φίλος, for example, in the wake of the verb ἀγαπάω, should in fact strike us as significant, particularly given Jack Lewis's well-known and admirable philological distinction of the 'four loves' in the Greek language[58]. The shift from the language of God's selfless and kenotic love to that of brotherly affection does serve a literary function here, and it would seem a logical conclusion to draw that someone who is a φίλος to the Son of God would be a son to God as well, no?

Also, there is the fact to contend with that, at least on the surface, the disciples are being *promoted*! οὐκέτι λέγω ὑμᾶς **δούλους**... ὑμᾶς δὲ εἴρηκα **φίλους** '*No longer do I call you servants... but I have called you friends*' (John 15:15). That's a good thing, right? They've got the golden ticket, the executive membership card! They know the secret handshake! They're 'in' with the righteous, and they're 'down' with God and all His plans, right?

Jack, though his philosophical instincts could occasionally lead him astray, would probably be the first to look askance at this logic. If we examine his *Space* trilogy, and in particular *That hideous strength*, we find that he treats the impulse for cliquishness, the desire to belong, the yearning for the seat at the 'right hand', as a human *passion* that can lead into some very wicked places. This is the impulse that Wither and Frost work on in Mark Studdock at first, for example, leading him deeper and deeper into the demonic inner workings of the

---

[58] Clive Staples Lewis, *The Four Loves* (Geoffrey Bless, 1960).

Servants in the vineyard

N.I.C.E. [59] 'Friendship' is not automatically a positive or desirable thing in Scripture (James 4:4). Conversely, servitude, even being a 'slave', is by no means automatically a detestable thing. Paul—*a Roman citizen!*—introduces himself *to the table-fellowship in Rome* as δοῦλος Χριστοῦ Ἰησοῦ the 'slave' of Christ Jesus (Rom 1:1)!

This reticence of Scripture to indulge such hierarchies tells us that we should call even this spiritual hierarchy in the *Philokalia* into question. Even in its title, the *Philokalia* makes a rather optimistic assumption that the καλός is knowable to men who will thereafter choose to be φίλοι to it. This is not an assumption that is present in Saint John's Gospel. Even from the Prologue (John 1:1-5), the ἀνθρώπων (all of us!) are held to be in darkness and without a clue that we are in darkness. Saint John holds that we have to be *led* out of it by the nose. Or, better-phrased, we have to be *bought* out: hauled out of debt.

So as not to be led astray into thinking in terms of faulty hierarchies, we need to examine Saint John's *verbal language*, to determine *how* he is distinguishing a 'friend' from a 'slave'. The word ἐκλέγομαι, translated in the RSV 'to choose', is linked intimately to the Hebrew verb *bāḥar* בחר 'to select, to appoint, to show preference or favour'. We see it at work here:

ותחת כי אהב את־אבתיך **ויבחר** בזרעו אחריו ויוצאך בפניו בכחו הגדל ממצרים:
להוריש גוים גדלים ועצמים ממך מפניך להביאך לתת־לך את־ארצם נחלה כיום
הזה: וידעת היום והשבת אל־לבבך כי יהוה הוא האלהים בשמים ממעל ועל־הארץ
מתחת אין עוד:

---

[59] Clive Staples Lewis, *That Hideous Strength* (The Bodley Head, 1945).

In the Houses of the Poor

*And because he loved your fathers and **chose** their descendants after them, and brought you out of Egypt with his own presence, by his great power, driving out before you nations greater and mightier than yourselves, to bring you in, to give you their land for an inheritance, as at this day; know therefore this day, and lay it to your heart, that the Lord is God in heaven above and on the earth beneath; there is no other.* (Deut 4:37-39)

God *chooses sons*—that is to say, He *adopts* them—out of servitude, just as He chose to bring the sons of Jacob out of their *slavery* in Egypt in the Pentateuch. Indeed, God uses this very same word to describe Jesus Himself in the Gospel of Luke: οὗτός ἐστιν ὁ υἱός μου ὁ **ἐκλελεγμένος** αὐτοῦ ἀκούετε 'This is my Son, my **Chosen**; listen to him!' (Luke 9:35) By making out of Jesus's disciples brothers for His Son, God indeed ἐξελεξάμην 'chose' to redeem them from slavery to the world (John 15:16 and 15:19). This does not exalt their status. Paul tells us in his first epistle to the Corinthians that God purposefully ἐξελέξατο 'chose' fools to shame the wise, chose the weak to shame the strong, and chose orphans and ne'er-do-wells to shame those who think they amount to something (1 Cor 1:27-28). James tells us that God chose the poor *to be His heirs* (James 2:5).

But note carefully what this means. Just because God has chosen you, does not mean you are suddenly 'free' to do as you please. God frees you from Pharaoh, yes... or from, say, Trump. Being free from them, though, means that you are now *God's slave*. The sons of Jacob were set at liberty from Egypt to be placed under God's instruction. Paul was set at liberty from Caesar to be the δοῦλος Χριστοῦ Ἰησοῦ who taught the Romans. So too becoming a **φίλος**—not merely a 'friend' but a

Servants in the vineyard

foster-brother—of the Son, means something very different from what the disciples expect.

What being a friend to Christ actually entails

The language that John uses here is borrowed directly from Chapter 10. Ὁ Ποιμὴν ὁ Καλός 'the Able Herdsman' is described in *identical Greek terms* to the Φίλος 'friend' of this passage. The Able Herdsman τὴν ψυχὴν αὐτοῦ **τίθησιν** '**lays down** his life' for the sheep (10:11), where the friend here τὴν ψυχὴν αὐτοῦ **θῇ** '**lays down** his life' for his friends (15:13). The same verb τίθημι 'to lay down' is repeated three verses later in the function of God's choosing and appointing these 'friends', these foster-brothers for His Son: ἐγὼ ἐξελεξάμην ὑμᾶς καὶ **ἔθηκα** ὑμᾶς ἵνα ὑμεῖς ὑπάγητε καὶ καρπὸν φέρητε 'I chose you and **appointed** you that you would go and bear fruit' (15:16).

Jesus is therefore speaking twofold about His death. First, in likening himself to Abel (the archetypal Herdsman) laying down his life, He is directly accusing one of His foster-brothers of murdering Him as Cain murdered Abel. The literary irony is that we know which one of them that is, and so does Jesus, but the 'friends' He is addressing do not. But He is also calling His other foster-brothers to follow Him *even in His death*. A loving friend, after all, 'lays down his life' for his friends just as the Able Herdsman 'lays down his life' for the sheep.

The literary image of God dressing the vine is also one of death and burial. In order for a vine to bear fruit, it has to be first *cut off* from the main stock and *planted*, which is to say: buried in the ground. Even the clippings of the good branch

In the Houses of the Poor

must 'die' before they can grow back out of the soil and bear good fruit again.

Being 'chosen' by God as a 'friend' to Jesus thus *directly involves the Cross*. It's not a promotion. It's not a golden ticket. It is a kind of liberation, but not in the sense meant by the *Philokalia*. Being a 'friend' to Jesus still means doing what the Sheikh commands (Heb. ṣāwâ צוה, Gk. ἐντέλλομαι, John 15:14). And being a 'friend' to the Sheikh's Son will still involve the call to martyrdom.

At the beginning of the following chapter, we get another relatively clear literary window-pane into Saint John's historical context, the one which is prompting this discourse on 'friends' and 'servants':

ταῦτα λελάληκα ὑμῖν ἵνα μὴ σκανδαλισθῆτε ἀποσυναγώγους ποιήσουσιν ὑμᾶς ἀλλ' ἔρχεται ὥρα ἵνα πᾶς ὁ ἀποκτείνας ὑμᾶς δόξῃ λατρείαν προσφέρειν τῷ θεῷ καὶ ταῦτα ποιήσουσιν ὅτι οὐκ ἔγνωσαν τὸν πατέρα οὐδὲ ἐμέ ἀλλὰ ταῦτα λελάληκα ὑμῖν ἵνα ὅταν ἔλθῃ ἡ ὥρα αὐτῶν μνημονεύητε αὐτῶν ὅτι ἐγὼ εἶπον ὑμῖν

'I have said all this to you to keep you from falling away. They will put you out of the synagogues; indeed, the hour is coming when whoever kills you will think he is offering service to God. And they will do this because they have not known the Father, nor me. But I have said these things to you, that when their hour comes you may remember that I told you of them.' (John 16:1-4)

There is a reason I have spent so much time and effort in these two commentaries on Saint John's Gospel talking about Palestine. It was indeed the case in the second century AD that

Servants in the vineyard

the early communities of Paul's followers were under persecution. Even though Paul worked within the structure of the Roman family, his teaching of *servitude* to Christ and of *submission* to Christ's Father was directly at odds with what we could call the Roman 'civil religion', even though distinguishing it from the worship of the Roman gods presents considerable problems. To be a Christian in the second century was to be (to borrow a useful Marxist term) a *subaltern*. Embracing Christianity in such a context meant eliminating yourself, *a priori*, from a critically-wide swathe of public rites and practices which guaranteed you honour, a public 'face', a social identity. Failing to recognise the divinity of Caesar meant becoming an apostate from *Romanitas*, and thus a 'public enemy' excluded from the protections of Roman law.

It's difficult for me to read the Gospel of Saint John in the present day and *not* think of the Palestinians. And that isn't just because the Gospel takes place on the historical territory of Palestine! Even pointing to the IDF's wanton destruction of eighteen human lives at Saint Porphyrios Orthodox Church in Gaza[60] and demanding accountability for it, back in October 2023, opened one up to accusations of being a Ḥamas sympathiser and an antisemite[61]. This is how deeply the

---

[60] Office of Public Relations, 'Confirmed: Bombing of St. Porphyrios', *The Order of Saint George the Great Martyr* (19 October 2023), https://orderofsaintgeorge.org/confirmed-bombing-of-st-porphyrios/.

[61] But questioning the worship of the Israeli state clearly *isn't* antisemitic, because the loudest questioners of that worship are

In the Houses of the Poor

worship of the Israeli nationalist project has been embedded in *American* civil religion. And of course we are now beholding people like Mahmoud Khalil and Rumeysa Oztürk being disappeared by our Caesar, for not offering their pinch of incense on that altar.

The Johannine language of Apocalypse, which shows up here briefly but distinctly and recognisably (ἔλθῃ ἡ ὥρα αὐτῶν '*when their hour comes*', 16:4), is meant not to predict an actual cataclysm or warn of a world-historical 'end time'. That is very much so a Victorian-era perversion, meant to bolster Victorian-era British imperialism. Saint John uses this language to address his table-fellows *in their own time*, to recognise and acknowledge the very real dangers they faced from the government *of their own time*, and to reassure them that it wasn't all for nothing. Their slavery to the teaching, their submission to the One God, their friendship with Christ *unto death* would ultimately be acknowledged, by Him, in *His* good time (the hour which none of us knows!).

The distinction between 'slave' and 'friend' in Chapter 15 is not one which highlights a difference of social ranks. It is not even (*pace* Saint Peter of Damascus and the *Philokalia*!) reflective of a real distinction of internal spiritual states. Rather, this distinction is an acknowledgement of the *only* real

---

themselves practising Jews: Dr. Jill Stein, Naomi Klein, Wallace Shawn, Miriam Margolyes, Dr. Norman Finkelstein, Max Blumenthal, Dr. Gabor Maté, Aaron Maté, Katie Halper, Keaton Weiss and Russell Dobular, to name just a few. – *Auth.*

Servants in the vineyard

distinction: God alone is the vinedresser, *and no one else*. Those who don't know it, and don't act accordingly, are slaves to the world, even if they think they are free. Those who *do* know it, and who submit as *labourers* in God's vineyard (not as *vignerons* themselves!), are by comparison closer to 'friendship' with God's Son. Once that framework has been established, it becomes easier to do the real work. We don't agitate for a replacement Caesar, another human claimant who will abuse his human brothers if they fail to mouth the right civil pieties. We proclaim that God alone has the right to plant where He likes, cut where He likes, judge as He likes, and transplant or discard as He likes: because there is none but Him.

Glory to God in the highest.

And, because it follows:

Free Mahmoud Khalil.

Concerning debt, measures and lawsuits

Repaying part of what I owe to Michael Hudson

A clarification on John 16:5-11

Paraclete of the debtors

D r. **Michael Hudson**, Professor of Economics at the University of Missouri-Kansas City, a fellow Minnesotan and one of the finest scholars of ancient economic history living today, is the single greatest and as yet unacknowledged *modern* influence on my work in Semitic studies and Biblical exegesis, alongside **Fr Paul Tarazi** and **Prince Nicolas Trubetskoi**[62]. I would not at all hesitate to call Michael Hudson my 'counsel for the defence'! Indeed, his *function* in the context of modern economic science is to act as the παράκλητος of the global debtor class. In that vein, he has authored and contributed to numerous books on economics of a 'heterodox' bent, such as *Super Imperialism* (1972), *Global Fracture* (1973), and *A Philosophy for a Fair Society* (1994)[63]. And, much like the service of public defenders

---

[62] My antique influences include Saint John Chrysostom; Saint Ephraim the Syrian; Saint Cyril of Jerusalem; Mār Aphraḥaṭ Ḥakkimā; and of course Bishop Theodore of Heraclea and the Gothic author or school responsible for the *Skeireins*.

[63] Michael Hudson, 'Books', *Michael-Hudson.com*, https://michael-hudson.com/books/.

Concerning debt, measures and lawsuits

anywhere else, this is a job that gets nowhere near enough appreciation.

In addition to being an economist, Dr. Hudson also happens to be a Semitologist of considerable intellectual calibre. An academic linguist by training (though that training was originally in Germanic philology), Hudson has done some truly careful and rigorous study of Bronze Age legal texts and inscriptions in Akkadian, in order to cobble together the economic history of Ancient West Asia. He encountered a significant degree of resistance to his work at first, in part because academics of all stripes make an idol of civilisation—and when it came to study of the first civilisation, each group wanted to be able to project back onto it whatever modern values they sought to find there. Hudson's data-based approach, answerable to the texts, was unwelcome because it skewered such philosophical and ideological idols[64].

The palatial-temple system and its collapse

There are several moving parts to Hudson's thesis about the economy at the dawn of Bronze Age West Asian civilisation, arrived at by way of his lexicographical studies of ancient loan agreements written in Akkadian. The first piece of his thesis is

---

[64] Michael Hudson, 'The land belongs to God', speech to the Union Theological Seminary in Columbia, NY (23 January 2017), https://michael-hudson.com/2017/01/the-land-belongs-to-god/.

In the Houses of the Poor

that the temple-trade complex of that age is not as easily untangled as modern-day ideologues want to make it.

It is true that the Two Rivers produced the first merchant class. However, these merchants were connected intimately to the temples and thus were also civil servants. The first merchants of the Sumerian, later Babylonian and Assyrian, city-states were in fact priests, scribes and official functionaries of the temples. And further, these temples can only possibly be considered *public works*. Merchants were tasked with going abroad and selling the surplus crops and goods produced by the city craftsmen to enrich, not themselves, but the temple and the palace whose employees they were, to be used to enhance *public* goods and services like walls, roads, urban housing and workshops[65].

The structure of Bronze Age economies relied on communal land tenure, wherein the means of sustenance on the land under the city-state's jurisdiction was guaranteed for families in exchange for military service and *corvée* labour. Land was set aside for public use in order to sustain people who couldn't work (elderly, widowed mothers, orphaned children) and people (administrators, merchants, scribes) who were employed in non-agrarian pursuits[66].

Economic history thus shows that, without a public administration that had governance roles as well as religious

---

[65] Michael Hudson, G.J. Miller and Kris Feder, *A Philosophy for a Fair Society* (Shepheard-Walwyn, 1994), 38-9.

[66] *Ibid.*, 41-2.

Concerning debt, measures and lawsuits

ones (and the two of these not necessarily being as distinct from each other as we Western moderns want to make them), there could be no mercantile enterprise, no trade going on in any kind of volume requiring official receipts. Contracts and invoices had to be written down, after all. And who was going to do the writing, if not the only people who were literate: the temple scribes? Michael Hudson's careful historiography of Bronze Age economics thus serves to deflate the self-serving Enlightenment-era mythology of the 'state of nature' and the 'social contract', as well as other fables like Hardin's 'tragedy of the commons'[67].

So far, so Karl Polanyi! But the temptation was always there for those given such a trust to abuse it. Even in this communally-managed system, individual merchants or administrators could over time garner enough influence and power to hold farmer-soldiers and their families in debt-bondage. This was both to their own pecuniary advantage, and also worked as a means to political advancement.

The second piece of Michael Hudson's thesis is that such perverse incentives were given broader and broader room for play as the Bronze Age wore on, resulting in the first stages of **privatisation**. Unscrupulous functionaries and creditors were allowed through political and social crises to accrue greater degrees of power over their debtors and over the political structures that produced their wealth. The first such crisis was **warfare**. The creation of large territorial empires along the

---

[67] *Ibid.*, 41-4. Hardin's thesis is mentioned here explicitly.

In the Houses of the Poor

Two Rivers through conquest and expansion led to the delegation of governmental authority downstream from the palace, creating a ready *rentier* class[68].

The second such crisis, linked closely to warfare, was the **alienation of land rights.** In the ancient city-states, personal land rights were paramount to the normal functioning of the palace and temple institutions, for the reasons demonstrated above. Populations needed to be fed, infrastructure needed to be built, and the whole thing needed to be defended. And those called upon to do all of this work were the farmers who doubled as soldiers, and to do that work they needed to be accorded rights in land usufruct. But when wars happened, and farmers were killed or captured, property rights quickly came into dispute[69]. And even in times of peace, when natural disasters happened, farmers were compelled to approach the palace and temple apparatuses for relief. Such instances resulted in the rise of powerful creditors who held land rights *in absentia* over indebted tenants[70].

The third crisis resulting in privatisation was ancillary to this: **spread of sterile interest-bearing land debt.** Absentee landlords and creditors were loath to share the usufruct of 'their' land with the palace and the temple, and leveraged their power in order to claim exemptions from taxation, conscription or the *corvée*. This had the effect of weakening

---

[68] *Ibid.*, 46-8.
[69] *Ibid.*, 48-9.
[70] *Ibid.*, 49.

Concerning debt, measures and lawsuits

public authority and also the strength of a city's armies. Also, when debtors failed to meet their legal obligations to the holders of their debt, the consequence was usually asset forfeiture, eviction and personal debt-bondage[71]. Foreclosures cut into the temple's access to the land's usufruct; and eviction and debt-bondage restricted the temple's access to manpower for public works or for the armed forces. Both aspects of privatisation placed strain on resources and on the labour force needed to maintain public infrastructure.

Declaring a clean slate

On account of this aggrandisement of large creditors in the cities of the Two Rivers region, it was necessary for the rulers in this region to occasionally proclaim a **clean slate**: a restoration of economic order wherein all back taxes and debts would be cancelled; all the alienable land tracts returned to communal management; and all those who had fallen into debt-bondage would be set at liberty and returned to their customary lands. Such **clean slates** were usually declared on the accession of a new ruler to power, or on the thirtieth anniversary of his rule.

Naturally, the clean slate was to the clear benefit of the debtors. Being released from debt-bondage and returned to freedom allowed them to cultivate the land for their own sustenance rather than to service a creditor's desire for power.

---

[71] *Ibid.*, 49-50.

In the Houses of the Poor

But it was also to the *public* benefit of the city-state in question, because it assured that the agrarian usufruct, as well as the *corvée* and conscription policies, served the public rather than private interests. And it was also to the personal benefit of the ruler himself, because it quashed the ambitions of self-aggrandising 'big men' and temple functionaries whose creditor status made them potential rivals to his position.

The clean slate was called, in Akkadian, *andurārum*, and there were equivalent terms in the non-Semitic languages of the peoples of the Two Rivers and their neighbours (Sumerian *amargi*, Hurrian *šudūtu* or *kirenzi*, Hittite *para tarnumar*, etc.)[72]. The cognate term in Biblical Hebrew is the *dərôr* דרור *of* Leviticus 25 and Isaiah 61, which is translated into Greek in the Septuagint text as ἄφεσις. This *dərôr* דרור is the jubilee (*yôbēl* יובל from a triliteral root 'to flow' or 'to carry', also the name of a wind instrument made from a ram's horn) year, the grand release from debts, in which even the land itself is allowed to lie fallow and rest from cultivation.

The Semitic triliteral *d-r-r* ד-ר-ר seen in the Akkadian noun *andurārum* and carried into its cognates (Ugaritic *dirr* 'to gush, to spew forth'; Hebrew *dərôr* דרור 'flowing, running freely, freedom'; Arabic *darra* دَرَّ 'to flow copiously, abundant, to run unhindered'), always carries with it the connotation of a river flowing continuously and naturally without any kind of dryness, stoppage or diversion. It is occasionally used poetically in the Hebrew text, to describe abundant or gushing

---

[72] *Ibid.*, 38.

Concerning debt, measures and lawsuits

flow of some fluid. For example: ואתה קח־לך בשמים ראש מר־**דרור** חמש מאות *'Take the finest spices: of* **liquid** *myrrh five hundred shekels'* (Exo 30:23, RSV).

But by far and away, the more common usage of the term *dərôr* דרור is the legal and economic function which it takes directly from the **clean slate proclamations** of the West Asian Bronze Age rulers. What is called for in Leviticus 25 is precisely a general remission from such debt-bondage, so that debtors could return to their land of cultivation and to their families: ושבתם איש אל־אחזתו ואיש אל־משפחתו תשבו *'Each of you shall return to his property and each of you shall return to his family'* (Lev 25:10, RSV).

The same function is seen in the prophetic writings, where the same *dərôr* דרור is much more starkly set forth as being meant for the legal and economic liberation of those in debt. We see it in Isaiah:

רוח אדני יהוה עלי יען משח יהוה אתי לבשר ענוים שלחני לחבש לנשברי־לב לקרא לשבוים **דרור** ולאסורים פקח־קוח לקרא שנת־רצון ליהוה ויום נקם לאלהינו

The Spirit of the Lord God is upon me; because the Lord hath anointed me to preach good tidings unto the meek; he hath sent me to bind up the brokenhearted, to proclaim **liberty** *to the captives, and the opening of the prison to them that are bound; to proclaim the acceptable year of the Lord, and the day of vengeance of our God.* (Isa 61:1-2)

This language isn't just flowery metaphor. The legal functionality is inescapable, because this verse contains a mass of language linking to the rites of kingship and kingly

In the Houses of the Poor

accession. The *šənat-raṣôn* שנת־רצון 'acceptable year' and the *yôm nāqām* יום נקם 'day of vengeance' are both references to the timing of the *andurārum* by Akkadian kings, being respectively the generational *anniversary* of a king's rule and the *day* of a king's accession to the throne, when clean slate proclamations were customarily made[73]. The use of the verb *māsaḥ* משח 'to anoint' is another clear allusion to a kingly accession.

There follows a succession of verbiage which is associated with the royal proclamations of a new king. The verb *bāśśar* בשר (incidentally, the same as the personal name of the prior President of Syria, *Baššār* بشار 'bringer of good tidings') is a function accorded to a *royal herald* or a *military envoy* whose job is to report the king's victories. This is the source of the familiar Roman Imperial function of εὐαγγελίζω 'to bear good news, to preach the Gospel'. The verb *haboš* חבש functions in four ways: it can mean 'to saddle up' a horse or a donkey (*i.e.* Jdg 19:10); it can mean 'to bind up' a wound (Eze 30:10); it can mean 'to invest' an official with the symbol of his office, like a capuchon (Exo 29:9) or a girdle (Eze 16:10); or, by extension, simply 'to govern' (Job 34:17). And, of course, the doubled verb *fəqaḥ-qôaḥ* פקח־קוח refers to a privilege that only kings enjoyed, to 'open the prisons' in pardon. These verbs are applied to, respectively, *'anāwîm* ענוים 'the poor' (see Chapter 2 of this

---

[73] Hudson comes to a similar conclusion himself, linking Isaiah 61 by the Qumran corpus to the figure of Malkî-ṣedeq ('the king is just') from Genesis 14 and Psalm 109. Michael Hudson, *... And Forgive Them Their Debts* (ISLET, 2018), 11-15.

Concerning debt, measures and lawsuits

book, on John 11), *nišbərê-lēb* נשברי־לב 'the broken-hearted' (cf. Psa 33:19, 50:19, in both cases referring to despairing people long deprived of justice), and *'asûrîm* אסורים 'those in (penal) bondage' (cf. Gen 39:20, the casting of Joseph into his Egyptian prison). With all of this language in its immediate presence, can the *dərôr* דרור of this passage be anything other than a clean slate proclaimed for those *šəbûyim* שבוים in 'bondage' to debt?

The instances of *dərôr* דרור in Jeremiah and Ezekiel both likewise also pertain to a legal-economic function of remission of land-based debts and the return of the people to their communal rights in the land. Jeremiah 34:6-22 declaims a judgement against King Ṣidqîyâ ('God is righteous') and his *insincere* clean slate proclamation which freed all Hebrew slaves, male and female, only for him to renege on his promise of freeing the slaves afterward. Jeremiah promises Ṣidqîyâ God's vengeance for this cruel duplicity: that God will likewise 'liberate' his kingdom to the sword and disease and hunger, and the king himself into the hands of the Babylonians[74]. And the passage in Ezekiel speaks specifically to the *dərôr* דרור being used to restore the public property (of the prince), while also warning the prince not to alienate the property of any of the people, למען אשר לא־יפצו עמי איש מאחזתו '*so that none of my people shall be dispossessed*' (lit. 'scattered away from their rightful land', Eze 46:18).

Michael Hudson's contribution was not only to show how the Bronze Age economic structure functioned, and how in some

---

[74] *Ibid.*, 9-10.

In the Houses of the Poor

ways the temple-palace complex in West Asian Bronze Age cities was a much more functional (howbeit inegalitarian!) 'public sphere' than ours is in the present day. He also showed how the system was eventually exhausted, compromised from without and within, resulting in a state of permanent economic disorder by the time of the Roman Empire. Unscrupulous administrators, absentee landlords and other big creditors figured out ways of getting around the clean slate proclamations and have their land-holdings derived from foreclosure exempted from their scope.

The occurrence of *dərôr* דרור in Ezekiel 46 criticises, and in so doing shows us, one legal loophole by which creditors could defend their expropriations against clean slate proclamations. This was by making themselves the adoptive 'heirs' of their debtors, whether through marriage, through loan contracts with sonship and inheritance rights serving as collateral, or through more blatant forms of extortion. (One is reminded of Jacob selling Esau a mess of pottage in exchange for his birthright as the eldest son, in Genesis!) The dispossession of debtor families' natural sons from the land through these fictive forms of adoption, and the resulting accumulation of land titles in the hands of their 'adopted' creditor-sons, was one of the prime catalysts for the formation of a **landed aristocracy** in the Two Rivers region[75]. The Ezekelian passage explicitly closes this loophole, stating that the rights of one adopted under such circumstances cannot extend past the year

---

[75] Hudson, Miller and Feder, *Philosophy*, 52-4.

Concerning debt, measures and lawsuits

of liberation, and that the property must revert to the natural sons of the proprietor. But wealthy proprietors must not abuse this right to dispossess the people, who should be able to return to *their* land!

But what does all this have to do with John's Gospel?

Plenty, as it turns out.

Remember, the topic at hand was Jesus's prediction of His followers' *dispossession* from the synagogues (John 16:1-4), on the very eve of His capture! Jesus is leaving, and the disciples have no one to turn to.

Jesus then promises to send them a παράκλητος 'counsellor, advocate, defence attorney' (16:7). This term does surface in the Septuagint text, in Job 16:2, where it serves as a translation of the non-legalistic Hebrew *mənaḥāmî* מנחמי 'comforters', but the function here is different. In the Book of Job, the term is pejorative: Job is belittling those who come to give him unsolicited advice. Here, however, the term is clearly genuine. And in a Roman context, the term παράκλητος functions as an adaptation of the Latin *advocātus*, a legal counsel for a defendant in a lawsuit.

The legal functionality of this term is made instantly clear from what follows. The παράκλητος promised by Jesus will come to ἐλέγξει! This interesting Greek verb should be familiar to students of philosophy: He will deliver an *elenchus*; that is, a logical refutation of the prosecution's case against the accused. And what will this refutation entail? It will concern (περὶ):

a.) ἁμαρτίας 'sin, offence, transgression, misstep';
b.) δικαιοσύνης 'right, justice, integrity, virtue'; and
c.) κρίσεως 'judgement, opinion, condemnation'.

The first of these concerns, that of ἁμαρτίας 'sin', is intimately linked to clean slate proclamations. The language of *remission of sins*—ἄφεσις ἁμαρτιῶν—comes from Paul's epistles, but it is intrinsically linked *at the lexical level* with the *dərōr* דרור of Leviticus 25. Thirty-nine of the occurrences of ἄφεσις in the Greek Septuagint text refer to clean slate policies: including all of those in Leviticus, Numbers and Deuteronomy, as well as those in the books of Esther, Isaiah, Jeremiah and Ezekiel. One of them (Exo 18:2) has to do with the marital separation of Moses from Ṣifōrâ; and four others (2 Sam 22:16; Lam 3:48; Joel 1:20, 3:18) are poetic, having to do with flowing rivers or liquids that act like flowing rivers. Thus, logically, when Paul is describing the ἄφεσις ἁμαρτιῶν—the *remission of sins*—to the Hebrews, the Ephesians or the Colossians, he is clearly drawing on the *legal* terminology of clean slate proclamations in the book of Leviticus.

Here, Jesus promises an *advocātus*, a defence attorney, who comes to offer an *elenchus* (or refutation) concerning 'sins'. This is a functional parallel to the Pauline language of ἄφεσις ἁμαρτιῶν. Thus, this promised *advocātus* this can be no one other than the legally-empowered emissary of a king who has come to proclaim—as was done in the book of Isaiah—a **clean slate**. In this case, the promised *advocātus* is an agent acting on behalf of the Father against those who did not believe the Son (John 16:9) when He stood up in the synagogue and proclaimed the remission of debts from Isaiah 61 (Luke 4:16-21)!

Concerning debt, measures and lawsuits

What is equally interesting is that the other two Greek words that Jesus uses to describe the mission of the *advocātus*, both have *economic* functions! The term δικαιοσύνη or 'justice', for example, when applied to people, is generally taken to refer to the virtue or character trait of even-handedness, fair-mindedness, willingness to hear both sides and make an impartial decision. But in the *Torah*, this term (a correlate of ṣedeq צדק), could also refer to the *measures* in commerce or in financial transactions! Justice was using *one* set of measures, rather than a light one for loans and a heavy one for repayment[76]. מאזני **צדק** אבני־**צדק** איפת **צדק** והין **צדק** יהיה לכם אני יהוה אלהיכם אשר־הוצאתי אתכם מארץ מצרים 'You shall have **just** balances, **just** weights, a **just** ephah, and a **just** hin: I am the Lord your God, who brought you out of the land of Egypt.' (Lev 19:36) And again: אבן שלמה **וצדק** יהיה־לך איפה שלמה **וצדק** יהיה־לך למען יאריכו ימיך על האדמה אשר־יהוה אלהיך נתן לך 'A full and **just** weight you shall have, a full and **just** measure you shall have; that your days may be prolonged in the land which the Lord your God gives you.' (Deut 25:15)

Clean slate proclamations were almost always couched in the language of exactly *this* concept of justice themselves, of balancing the scales, of returning to a harmonious *status quo ante*. The clean-slate Edict of Ammi-Ṣaduqa (1646 – 1626 BC), for example, introduces itself as a (return to) *mīšarum* 'balance,

---

[76] See Hudson, *Forgive*, 22.

equity, justice'[77]. The direct Biblical Hebrew cognate of Akkadian *mīšarum* is *yāšar* ישר 'level, even, smooth, just, righteous, to make straight, to be pleasing', which is functionally equivalent to and even in some cases interchangeable with *ṣedeq* צדק (and thus, via the LXX, δικαιοσύνη) very notably in Isaiah: אנכי העירתהו **בצדק** וכל־דרכיו **אישר** הוא־יבנה עירי וגלותי ישלח לא במחיר ולא בשחד אמר יהוה צבאות *'I have aroused him in **righteousness**, and I will **make straight** all his ways; he shall build my city and set my exiles free, not for price or reward," says the Lord of hosts.'* (Isa 45:13) It is also so in Proverbs: **צדקת** תמים **תישר** דרכו וברשעתו יפל רשע *'The **righteousness** of the perfect shall **direct** his way: but the wicked shall fall by his own wickedness.'* (Prov 11:5)

Yet John's use of δικαιοσύνη is not straightforward. In the Septuagint text, the Greek term almost always maps to an approbative connotation: referring either to God's justice, or to someone who stands blameless before God (or to that impossibility). So why, here in John 16, would the *advocātus* arrive to *refute* this 'justice', just as he arrives to refute 'sin'? Here we have to turn to Michael Hudson's work on the *oligarchical turn* which underpins Paul's context, and the ideological means by which the Roman Republic in particular turned the Bronze Age understanding of *mīšarum* upside-down and inside-out.

---

[77] Ammi-Ṣaduqa I, trans. J.J. Finkelstein, 'The edict of Ammiṣaduqa: a new text' (*Revue d'Assyriologie et d'archéologie orientale* 63/1, 1969), 47, 49. See also: Hudson, *Forgive*, 131-132.

Concerning debt, measures and lawsuits

This part of Hudson's thesis is most deftly and explicitly demonstrated in his 2023 book *The Collapse of Antiquity*. Hudson demonstrates convincingly from the primary sources that interest-bearing debt and monetary instruments were imports into the Hellenic world of early antiquity, arriving in the 8th century BC from West Asia by way of Phoenicia and Syria[78]. What unfortunately didn't make the transition from West Asia into southern coastal Europe was a *strong public sector* capable of centrally managing credit. In the Hellenic, and later Roman, contexts, credit was managed privately, through independent usurers. Even more quickly and more dramatically than in West Asia, this lack of central debt management led to the emergence of an unchecked profiteering and racketeering oligarchical elite, whom Ramsey MacMullin describes, with a flourish of colourful anachronism, as '*mafiosi*' [79]. The development of Greco-Roman political life, more so than the Bronze Age West Asian palatial cities, created a permanent financial polarisation between a small citizen-patrician class, and a much broader plebeian class, which often resorted to rallying behind kings and 'tyrants' to make their voices heard and their complaints known[80].

As Hudson tells it, the same Greco-Roman context also crafted a clever inversion of the Bronze Age understanding of *mīšarum* to suit creditor interests rather than the overall public

---

[78] Michael Hudson, *The Collapse of Antiquity* (ISLET, 2023), 31-39.
[79] *Ibid.*, 11.
[80] *Ibid.*, 40-41.

good. The *mīšarum* was an attempt to *balance* creditors' and debtors' justice by treating forgiveness of debts as sacred. Creditors' justice came to be the sole standard of the Roman *iūstitia*, asserting instead the sacred nature of debt itself, and the outright responsibility of the debtors to pay in full what they were lent, along with whatever conditions or rates of interest they agreed to (or were compelled into) at the time of lending. This view of justice was expressed openly in, for example, the first century BC oratory of Cicero[81].

This history is very much worth bearing in mind when approaching the Pauline and Johannine texts when they speak of δικαιοσύνη. The Psalms speak repeatedly of God's righteousness, for example, and only obliquely or hypothetically of human righteousness. But remember: it is in Paul's letter **to the Romans** wherein he makes the clearest and sharpest distinction between *human* 'law' and *God's* law, *human* 'righteousness' and *God's* righteousness. (And remember that 'sin' is the exact same thing as financial debt, only to a far higher Creditor!) Indeed, he hammers on this point over and over and over again to his Roman hearers (Rom 3:3-5, 3:21-26, 4:3-13, 6:16-20). One can almost hear Paul's Italian deacons nodding in exasperation: 'I *think* I *get* the *point*.' But of course Paul's answer all throughout his letter is Judge Chamberlain Haller's: 'No—*I don't think you do!*'[82]

---

[81] *Ibid.*, 421, 424-5.

[82] Jonathan Lynn, *My Cousin Vinny* (20th Century Fox, 1992).

Concerning debt, measures and lawsuits

John's later contributions ought to be considered in the same light. What I have just put forward from Michael Hudson's economic history of the Greco-Roman world is *not the text*; rather, it forms part of John's *context* and thus ought to be considered as such. Still, the possibility exists, and it is a strong possibility, that the δικαιοσύνη which Jesus's promised *advocātus* comes to refute in Chapter 16 is precisely the self-serving creditor's *iūstitia* of Cicero. It is the same oligarchical system of *iūstitia* that will destroy His life and attempt to bury Him out of all men's sight (John 16:10).

Judgement and economic 'crisis'

And the same goes for John's usage of κρίσεως in 16:8. This term is used in the LXX as a Greek translation of the Hebrew words *mišfāṭ* משפט, *rîb* ריב and *dîn* דין. It refers, in the broad sense, to a 'lawsuit' (Deut 17:8), though depending on the Hebrew referent indicated, κρίσις can also function either as the act of *bringing* the lawsuit (as in Exo 23:6 – לא תטה משפט אבינך **בריבו** 'You shall not pervert the justice due to the poor in his **suit**.') or as the act of *deciding* it (as in Lev 19:35 – לא־תעשׂוּ עול **במשפט** במדה במשקל ובמשׂוּרה 'You shall do no wrong **in judgement**, in measures of length or weight or quantity.')

Regardless of which function of κρίσις from the *Torah* is at work here, the result is the same. According to Jesus's promise, the *advocātus* comes to refute ὁ ἄρχων τοῦ κόσμου 'the ruler of the world'. Regardless of whether this prince (literally, this *archon*) is the *bringer* of the κρίσις or the self-appointed judge who decides it, Jesus promises a drastic role-reversal for him.

This archon will suddenly be neither the plaintiff in the case nor the judge who decides the verdict, but instead the *one who is judged* (τούτου κέκριται, John 16:11).

We should pay particular attention to how Paul uses this language. In his first letter to the Corinthians, he *specifically* refers to the *human* (ἀνθρώπων) *rulers* who had Jesus put to death (1 Cor 2:5-9). Paul's explicit usage of a title that was used for *city magistrates* or *co-rulers* from Hellenic antiquity (ancient Athens, for example, had a ruling council that consisted of three ἄρχοντες elected from and by the city's aristocracy[83]) indicates that he is referring in the first instance to the *Roman* magistrate and his state apparatus who decided and presided over Jesus's execution. It's common for modern Orthodox Christians to leap to the inference that the archon in this text, 'the ruler of the world', is a reference to Satan[84], and this isn't wrong. But the 'Satan' against whom the *advocātus* brings his suit is Caesar: the *false* creditor who lays an unjust claim to the world and its people. Jesus represents the only true Creditor.

It would be fitting at this point to offer a word on the Greek word κρίσις itself. As explained above, the Greek word refers in its broadest sense to a 'judgement'. The descended Modern Greek word κρίση still carries this function of 'judgement,

---

[83] Aristotle, *The Athenian Constitution*, tr. and ed. Sir Frederic G. Kenyon (Public domain, 1920), III.

[84] To give one modest example: Fr Jonathan H. Cholcher, 'Demonology' (St. Mark Orthodox Church of Bradenton, 2023), https://bradentonorthodox.org/demonology/.

Concerning debt, measures and lawsuits

opinion, verdict', although it has been influenced by semantic backdrift from French and English to refer to 'an emergency, a volatile situation, a dramatic turning-point'.

In my exploration of Russian economist Ruslan Dzarasov's insightful and innovative blend of world-systems and post-Keynesian thought as applied to the broad historical trend of predatory financialisation, I explicitly credited Michael Hudson as one of the few people in American academic economic circles who was able to predict and accurately describe the *2007-2008 financial crisis* in the United States[85]. I find it significant that we refer to this event as a *crisis*, but I do not think most Americans think deeply or take seriously *what that word actually signifies*.

Hudson points to the fact that modern economies have no mechanism for redressing endemic social problems that come out of having a massive disenfranchised debtor class, as the main root which underlies their tendency to suffer regular, massive and painful upheavals. In Bronze Age West Asia, such systemic upheavals were averted by the palatial-temple system deliberately 'rebooting' the economy with clean slates: wiping out all non-commercial, and especially land-based, debts. As we can see from the law code of Ḥammu-Rāpi and the proclamation of his descendant Ammi-Ṣaquda I, in enacting clean slates they explicitly believed themselves to be following

---

[85] Matthew Franklin Cooper, *Akhmatova's Acolytes* (Wabasha Street Books, 2024), 205-6.

the will of Anu and Enlil, respectively, for the purposes of averting disaster and promoting general prosperity.

It is clear from the language used in Leviticus and in the prophetic writings that their authors adopt and approve this logic from their Bronze Age predecessors. The innovative difference is that it defers judgement not to any culture-heroic ancestral figure or to any idol fashioned to human ends, but instead to an *unseen* and thus completely unswayable 'Elōhîm, who is the only actual Creditor and the only real Proprietor of the land. The conceit of Leviticus is that we are all, in an ultimate sense, His tenants—and temporary ones, at that[86].

Michael Hudson views Scripture through a historicist rather than a literary lens, and so gives voice to the depreciated documentary hypothesis in some places[87]. This is not a surprise. Hudson is an economist first, a linguist second, and a textual scholar third: such is the intellectual autobiography he lays out in the foreword to ... *And Forgive Them Their Debts*[88]. However, when he applies himself to careful lexicological treatment of the relevant texts, and to respectful handling of Semitic terminology, his intellectual honesty shines through and his craft is sterling. And, more to the point, it's very hard

---

[86] Hudson, *Forgive*, 204.

[87] *i.e.* Hudson, *Forgive*, 181, 194, 204-5. But in spite of that, please note that he does come to some very Tarazi- and Abou Chaar-esque conclusions about Scripture's anti-kingly and 'shepherdist' political tenor! – *Auth.*

[88] *Ibid.*, xvii-xviii.

Concerning debt, measures and lawsuits

to *refute* him when he notes the unfortunate consequences of the turn which Christianity took in the late fourth and early fifth centuries. In his telling, it went from being a Semitic, text-referential, pro-debtor doctrine of the clean slate, to being either an oligarchic pro-creditor doctrine in the West (under the pernicious influence of Augustine of Hippo), or a quietist mystical doctrine of otherworldly salvation in the East (under that of Cyril of Alexandria)[89]. How else, indeed, are we to explain the utter divorce from Pauline teachings on debt and forgiveness, from the actual structure of Western economies and the way they crush debtors?

And how else are we to explain the fact that we can talk about economic 'crises' like the ones we seem to be having every decade, without considering the possibility that *our system is under God's judgement*? Even a modern Greek would be able to make that connexion without even thinking about it, but we speakers of English can't seem to do it. Speaking for myself, from an etymological perspective, I blame the Norman French... but naturally that's the radical Midwestern German in me talking.

---

[89] Michael Hudson, 'The arc of time: pro-creditor history', interview with Ben Norton (Geopolitical Economy Report, 25 May 2023), https://michael-hudson.com/2023/05/the-arc-of-time-pro-creditor-history/.

In the Houses of the Poor

The earth as place of judgement

In Michael Hudson's treatment of the proximate causes for the collapse of Old Babylonia in the 17th century BC, he explicitly links the weakening of the king's power over creditors to an *ecological* crisis: '*over-cultivation and over-irrigation of the land, silting up of the canals, and abandonment of alternate fallow seasons*'[90]. In Hudson's reading of Babylon's economic history, the concentration of debt and the emergence of a landed aristocracy in Old Babylonia led directly to the overstressing of the land, both at the hands of an increasingly-stressed tenant farmer class and through the creation of a permanent underclass of landless paupers and debt-slaves. The same thing happened in Assyria in the 13th century BC[91].

Here I believe Hudson's careful, and correct, ecological reading when approaching the textual record of these ancient Two Rivers civilisations could be mutually enriched with Fr Paul Tarazi's reading of the Levitical laws regarding *dərôr*. The Hebrew literature is, after all, *likewise* ecologically concerned—very likely on account of the remembrance of such ecological disasters as occurred in the Bronze Age civilisations of the Two Rivers! In Tarazi's reading, the three major feasts established in the books of the Law—the feast of weeks, the day of atonement, and the sabbatical and jubilee years—serve the same purpose as the *Sanzheng* 三正 or 'Three Commencements' in the Chinese

---

[90] Hudson, *Forgive*, 160.
[91] *Ibid.*, 174.

Concerning debt, measures and lawsuits

Book of Documents. That is, they *protect the natural order* from overexploitation!

> *These [sabbatical and jubilee] directives actually protect the earth from the children of Israel along the same lines as those pertaining to the Day of Atonement. The concentration on the earth per se during the sabbatical year is not so much to protect it from the human beings' sins as to protect it from being overworked by them. This 'liberation' of the earth from those who assume that they own it allows it to be a 'mother' for the vegetation, animals and human beings that live on it*[92].

He goes on to show how the primacy of place in Leviticus 25 in the sabbatical year is given to the unharvested field and the undressed vine, and also to the cattle and the beasts who are made to labour for their human masters. The beneficiaries of the sabbatical year are *ha'ereṣ* הארץ 'the ground, the earth' and the *kol-ṣəbā'ām* כל־צבאם 'all the hosts' of creatures that live in it (Gen 2:1)!

And this too ties to John 16. The Septuagint text translates *ha'ereṣ w-kol-ṣəbā'ām* הארץ וכל־צבאם as, literally, ἡ γῆ καὶ πᾶς ὁ **κόσμος** αὐτῶν '*the earth and all its **cosmos***'! And it is the ruler of the world who is under judgement. The *advocātus* of John 16 comes to deliver a refutation which *exonerates* God—I will talk about this typically Johannine language later—in front of all the nations. This exoneration *concerns* God's ruling on debts

---

[92] Paul Nadim Tarazi, *Land and Covenant* (OCABS Press, 2009), 107-108.

(Leviticus 25), measures (Leviticus 19) and lawsuits (also Leviticus 19) as detailed above. Michael Hudson, good *advocātus* that he is, has delivered a remarkable *amicus* brief on God's behalf in his written works on Bronze Age economy.

Yet the τὸν κόσμον of John 16 is not only the human debtors who are set free by the *elenchus* of Jesus's promised advocate. It is also *the land itself*, and the creatures thereof, which humans tend to use *as debtors*, or *as subjects*, as though they owe us everything.

It's radical, sociopolitical literature

Michael Hudson's work in Semitic lexicography is of inestimable value to any student of either the Hebrew or the Greek Scriptures. His lens is economic-historical rather than literary: that's his training, and he brings that training with exquisite scrupulosity to the text. His analysis of the relevant texts and, more importantly, the *historical* trajectory *in antiquity* of the *andurārum* and its influence on the Hebrew of Leviticus, however, is *vital* to students of the Hebrew scrolls as literature.

When it comes to studying the Gospel of Saint John, too, Hudson's work is deeply relevant. Our mindset in approaching the Greek text has been contorted by the *mafioso* 'pay what you owe' eisegesis of the Latin Fathers, and by the spiritualised malappropriation of the language of debt and measurement at the hands of the Alexandrian Fathers. We therefore cannot but *mishear* the *advocātus* of John 16, who comes to bear judgement against the one who falsely claims rulership over this world.

Concerning debt, measures and lawsuits

Hudson in his scholarship on ancient West Asia and its economic language thus serves, *functionally*, as the Holy Spirit to our generation. His multi-volume study on the Bronze Age Two Rivers city-kingdoms and the workings of their palace-temple complexes serves as an invaluable grounding in the historical world of the authors. And his contextualisation of Jesus in the world of debt-driven Roman agrarian displacement and settlement, and of Pharisaical acquiescence to the 'spirit of the times' in the *prosbul* loophole to the Levitical *dərôr*, leads us to the inescapable conclusion of what the Pauline corpus is. It's *radical, sociopolitical* literature!

And the Lamb will conquer[93]

A clarification on John 16:31-33

The place of Victory Day in modern Russian literature

The ninth of May is a secular commemoration that is the closest the Russian-speaking world comes to *qōdeš* קדש. I say 'secular', but only in reference to its origin: it is also an official commemoration of the Russian Orthodox Church. It is a 'set-aside' day, a day of deeply emotional significance for Russian people. It symbolises both the feat of halting fascist ideology in its eastward tracks, and also the immeasurable losses, deep wounds and scars that came from achieving that feat.

The Second World War had the largest human impact on the Soviet Union and on China. Over the course of the war the Soviets lost nearly nine million soldiers, and over thirteen million civilians. Of these, two-thirds of the military dead, and just over half of the civilian dead, were ethnic Russians; all constituent peoples of the Soviet Union suffered loss. This is a horrific level of trauma on a whole-societal scale, one that far outpaces anything that English-speaking countries suffered in the same war (the Blitz and Pearl Harbor notwithstanding). It goes without saying that the Second World War left a deep and

---

[93] Matthew Franklin Cooper, 'And the Lamb will conquer', Substack post, *Skeireins* (8 May 2025).

And the Lamb will conquer

lasting mark on contemporary Russian literature, whose importance is hard to overstate.

The most emblematic and seminal work is perhaps *They Fought for Their Country* (*Они сражались за Родину*, 1943) by Michael Sholokhov, who followed it up with the short story *The Fate of a Man* (*Судьба человека*, 1956), though numerous authors contributed to the genre. Constantine Simonov's *The Living and the Dead* trilogy (*Живые и мертвые*, 1959-1971) and Boris Polevoi's *The Story of a Real Man* (*Побесть о настоящем человеке*, 1947) are two other high-profile examples of the direct literary impact of the war in prose.

And in the world of Russian verse we find the same depth of impact. While Anna Akhmatova is better known earlier for her love poetry, and later for her scathing lyrical indictment of Stalin's repressions in 'Requiem', she nevertheless also penned war pieces like 'The First Long-Range Artillery Shell in Leningrad' («Первый дальнобойный в Ленинграде», 1941[94]) which weeps over the loss of her child to that same shell. Olga Bergholz, another female poet of this era who worked in broadcasting during the war, wrote prolifically about the siege of Leningrad, her hometown: including, poignantly, 'Return' («Возвращение», 1944[95]), which is a lament to the loneliness of

---

[94] Anna Akhmatova, tr. Lyn Coffin, *Poems* (W.W. Norton, 1983), 62. Original Russian version at *RuVerses.com*, https://ruverses.com/anna-akhmatova/the-first-bombardment-of-leningrad/.

[95] Olga Bergholz, tr. Vladimir Markov and Merrill Sparks, 'Return', at *RuVerses.com*, https://ruverses.com/olga-bergholz/return/.

coming back to a city in which not only the gardeners but the gardens, and even the birds and the streams, are lost irrevocably. Boris Slutsky, a Russian-Jewish poet of Slavyansk, gave voice to the grim inhumanity of the ideology they were facing at the time, in 'How Did They Kill My Grandmother?' («Как убивали мою бабку?», 1947[96]).

Later contributions to the genre, such as those by June Morits in the 1970s and 1980s, were able to dare the political disapprobation of the Soviet authorities to call into question the selective retelling of events, the creation of a collective hero-myth, the rationalisation and flattening of the raw human emotions of deprival into a sanitised ritual of national 'remembering'. Morits's poem '9 May 1945' («Девятое мая сорок пятого года»[97]) adroitly juxtaposes the 'Immortal' pageantry of state memory with the intimate void left by her older sister, who was working at a munitions plant when she was killed at the age of 19. Morits's line of critique runs parallel to that by Kurt Vonnegut of how Armistice Day, a sacred day of remembrance specifically set aside ($q\bar{o}de\check{s}$[98]) for the military casualties of WWI and the horrors they lived through, was

---

[96] Boris Slutsky, tr. Daniel Weissbort, 'How They Killed My Grandmother', at *RuVerses.com*, https://ruverses.com/boris-slutsky/how-did-they-kill-my-grandmother/9869/.

[97] June Petrovna Morits, 'Девятое мая сорок пятого года', *Owl.ru*, http://www.owl.ru/morits/stih/off-records2262.htm.

[98] My interpretation, not Vonnegut's. – *Auth.*

And the Lamb will conquer

diluted into the more politically-palatable Veterans' Day, stripping individual suffering from collective remembrance[99].

Today, the tension between memory and myth has taken on additional layers. The Ukrainian military's indiscriminate shelling of the Donbass since 2014—targetting schools, hospitals and residential areas—constituted a brutal policy of collective punishment against a population already alienated by Kiev's language policies. These actions, extensively documented by the OSCE and UN-affiliated human rights groups, created a fertile ground on which a reckless disproportionate escalation, such as we saw in February 2022 from Russia, could be justified.

The tragedy lies in how history has been manipulated to figleaf action and inaction on both sides. The rehabilitation of odious far-right nationalist figures like Bandera and Shukhevych—whose followers engaged in ethnic cleansing campaigns against Poles and Jews—by the Ukrainian government, has left it open to the charge of Nazi sympathies, providing cover for a Russian goal of 'denazification'. In Donbass itself, such actions have likewise obtained a local political significance in a region where the memory of the Second World War has a particularly strong purchase, and have steeled the population to embrace armed resistance. This was a

---

[99] Kurt Vonnegut, Jr., *Breakfast of Champions* (Delacorte Press, 1973).

resistance which the rest of the Russian world was remarkably slow to join[100].

This politicisation and ideological polarisation of memory has even impacted the rest of Europe. The vice-president of the European Commission has threatened national leaders such as Slovakia's Róbert Fico and Serbia's Aleksandar Vučić with political consequences. Both leaders have chosen to accept invitations to the upcoming octogintennial Victory Day celebrations in Moscow[101]. The Slovak and Serbian heads of state, in making their choices, cite their own historical memory of the Second World War and their deeply-felt obligation to the Red Army for their own liberation.

Nikē and the Johannine corpus

The Russian term *побeдa* 'victory, vanquishment', which as we can see now carries such a heavy (geo)political weight around it, is derived from a Proto-Slavic perfective or prepositional prefix *no-* 'at, on, by, after' and abstract noun *бѣдa* 'trouble, misfortune, adversity, calamity, poverty, want'. What does this Slavic term connote? Is the implication that victory is that which comes 'after' one has weathered 'adversity'? Or is it that one can inflict 'misfortune' 'on' the

---

[100] Cooper, *Acolytes*, 337-42.
[101] Eldar Mamedov, "'It's 2025 not 1939!" EU threats over Russia Victory Day draw backlash', *Responsible Statecraft* (17 April 2025), https://responsiblestatecraft.org/eu-threats-victory-day/.

And the Lamb will conquer

other guy after vanquishing him? From our twenty-first century vantage point, looking backwards through fragmentary texts, it's hard to tell. Rather, one must see here some of the guesswork and ambiguities of reconstruction that necessarily goes into etymology.

I do have a bone to pick with the, I suppose they must be Bulgarian or Pannonian or Moravian, ninth-century translators of Scripture into Slavonic after Saints Cyril and Methodius. It isn't that they got the basic denotation wrong at all! Rather, they missed a brilliant opportunity to showcase the potential flexibility and double-edged beauty of their own language—something that the Semitic authors of the Old Testament seldom wasted an opportunity to do. The Slavs translate the 'trouble, misfortune, adversity' in John 16 not as *бѣда* but instead as *скорбни*, though they keep Jesus as saying He has *побѣдихъ міръ*. Again, not *wrong*: just a bit of a let-down.

But we can already see how Saint John's Gospel is playing around, lexically, with *suffering* and *victory* in this way. The juxtaposition is already there in the Greek! ἐν τῷ κόσμῳ **θλῖψιν** ἔχετε ἀλλὰ θαρσεῖτε ἐγὼ **νενίκηκα** τὸν κόσμον '*In the world you have **tribulation**; but be of good cheer, I have **overcome** the world.*' (John 16:33) One thing that is immediately noticeable about this verbiage is how *specific* it is to John. He can't be said to have invented it whole cloth, but he is *noticeably* fonder of using the Greek word for 'victory', νίκη, than either the Septuagint translators, or Paul, or Luke. It's worth investigating where he is getting it, and what function it serves here.

In the Houses of the Poor

In Saint Paul's epistle to the Romans, he is clearly not only invoking but quoting *verbatim* that best-beloved among the Orthodox Christians, Psalm 50: למען תצדק בדברך **תזכה** בשפטך 'that thou mightest be justified in thy sayings, and mightest **overcome** when thou art judged.' (Psa 50:6, Brenton's English LXX, Romans 3:4) Notably, the word νικήσῃς 'overcome' is used in the LXX to translate *tizkê* תזכה 'to be in the clear, to purify, to be justified'. That Hebrew term almost automatically tells us we are dealing with a *trial*, with an *exoneration* or *legal* victory rather than one of military combat: in which case *lāḥam* לחם would be used instead, along with a different Greek word in translation (like πολιορκέω).

In Romans 3, Paul is speaking with regard to the 'trial' of the Hebrew *Torah* before a Gentile audience. Sadly, many interpret Romans as a *repudiation* of Hebrew Law, when it is in fact a *vindication* of that Law even though those to whom the Law was given—the followers of Scripture, who were then beginning to be called Ἰουδαίους 'Jews'—had fallen short of its expectations. The God of the Hebrew Scriptures is ever faithful, and His promises will pass every trial to be vindicated in the end, particularly before those who did *not* keep up their end of the bargain. So when Saint John adopts this verbiage of *vindication* in his own Gospel, we ought to bear in mind that *this* was the trajectory it took to get there: Psalm 50 as it appeared in the Septuagint text, by way of Saint Paul's letter to the Romans.

The language of θλῖψις 'trouble, misfortune, adversity' also occurs in Romans as part of this exact same rhetorical framing, of Jewish (lack of) faithfulness to the Law as compared to that of the Gentile (Rom 2:9). Here, θλῖψις is the consequence which faces anyone, Jew or Greek, who *does not obey* the Law, but instead serves ἐριθεία (the self-serving interests of a faction, or what we would now call a 'special interest group')! So we have a doubly clear literary trajectory through Romans for this fairly rare word (in Scripture) νίκη, particularly in conjunction with θλῖψις. Whenever John uses it in his first letter or his Apocalypse or his Gospel, it *refers back* to the *legal vindication* of God's promises against the cases brought by *both* the Jews *and* the Gentiles.

'You will be scattered, and leave me alone'

When one hears νίκη as legal vindication or acquittal as through Psalm 50, and when one hears it as being God's acquittal against the charges brought against Him by both His chosen people (the Jews) and His 'other flocks' (the Gentiles), the preceding verses, to use SZA's turn of phrase, 'hit different'.

> ἄρτι πιστεύετε ἰδοὺ ἔρχεται ὥρα καὶ ἐλήλυθεν ἵνα σκορπισθῆτε ἕκαστος εἰς τὰ ἴδια κἀμὲ μόνον ἀφῆτε καὶ οὐκ εἰμὶ μόνος ὅτι ὁ πατὴρ μετ' ἐμοῦ ἐστιν
>
> *Do you now believe? The hour is coming, indeed it has come, when you will be scattered, every man to his home, and will leave me alone; yet I am not alone, for the Father is with me.* (John 16:31-32, RSV)

The RSV actually inserts that *'home'*. It isn't an irrational or egregious supposition, but it's a supposition; it's not there in the original Greek text. The Greek reads εἰς τὰ ἴδια—'each to *his* own'. When we hear the Pauline verbiage drawn from Romans 2

In the Houses of the Poor

and 3, this preceding εἰς τὰ ἴδια is heard as a σκορπισθῆτε, a 'scattering', of the people away from the Law and back to their own prior *identities* as 'Jews' and 'Greeks'.

Identity politics is a perennial human reaction to distress or misfortune. In the wake of the economically-punitive post-war conditions set down on the German people at the Treaty of Versailles, and *particularly* in the wake of the Great Depression of 1929, no small contingent of middle-class Germans in the Weimar Republic turned to a particularly nasty form of identity politics in response to their woes. John Maynard, Lord Keynes, prophesied in 1919 that under such conditions of distress, Germans would listen *'to whatever instruction of hope, illusion, or revenge is carried to them in the air'*[102].

And so they did. And that revenge took them to the city limits of Leningrad and Stalingrad. And it took Jews and many others, by the trainful, to their deaths.

The problem is that θλῖψις is irreducibly, and painfully, personal. Despite her unhappy inclination to Hellenism, Simone Weil put it remarkably well in her *Lectures on philosophy*: 'Human beings are so made that the ones who do the crushing feel nothing; it is the person crushed who feels what is happening.'[103] No one understands Jesus of Nazareth's suffering 'alone' (16:32), not even His mother, because no one

---

[102] John Maynard Keynes, *The Economic Consequences of the Peace* (Macmillan, 1920), 235.

[103] Simone Weil, *Lectures on Philosophy* (Cambridge University Press, 1978), 139.

And the Lamb will conquer

else *is* Jesus of Nazareth. Just as none of us is anyone else. Each of us is scattered 'to his own'.

But let's come back down to reality for a moment; I'm already in danger of Hellenising this question too far. The material point is that when we suffer, which we do *by necessity* alone, we psychologically take refuge in groups. We seek others out who share, or at least empathise with, our grievances. We are scattered in suffering but we don't stay scattered. We form our own groups which then seek to justify, explain, excuse and lay blame for our suffering. Hitler was as successful as he was in mobilising the Germans in their economic and political suffering—or at least enough of them to make him politically dominant—because he made himself an expert at the latter.

And this is exactly what both the Hellenisers and the Judaisers did in response to their dispossession and persecution in John's own time. Rather than return to Leviticus and the pro-debtor teachings of Paul, they adopted two different kinds of identity politics. Some of them (*e.g.* the Ebionites) took refuge in a rigorist reading of the dietary and cleanliness laws of Leviticus, and attempted to expel the 'unclean' Gentiles from their midst. Others of them withdrew into secret sects and posited an esoteric teaching that attempted to harmonise the teachings of Jesus with nascent neo-Platonism, separating those 'in the know' (γινώσκει) from the mass of ignorant and unenlightened letter-followers. Those caught in the middle of these two factions were 'left alone' by themselves. (Now go read Romans 2 again!)

The Jesus of Saint John's Gospel is thus shown as the literary proxy of those who hewed to the 'middle road' in the early years of persecution, who became neither Ebionites nor Gnostics but stuck to the table-fellowship, and continued to suffer (θλίβω) as a result. Jesus's vindication (νίκη) is offered as a word of comfort, a word of 'peace' to the 'mid-roaders' of John's time, just as it is in Saint John's first letter and in the Apocalypse. But even that word of comfort contains within itself a note of caution. And to explain that caution, I turn to the Soviet-era poets for a present-day analogy.

The misleading advantage of Marxism

From a Pauline perspective, no ideology is justified. But the Soviet ideology has a decisive advantage over German fascism and American liberalism. Allow me to explain.

German *Nationalsozialismus* elevates the *Herrenvolk*, and justifies the grievances of Germans against Jew, Slav and Gypsy by way of appeal to the magic of blood and ancestry. Ironically—and Soviet-exile philosopher Nicolas Berdyaev was very quick to pick up on precisely this irony[104]—the German obsession with blood-purity and justification through ancestry was a contorted, violently-twisted mirror of the ideology of Rabbinical Judaism. The claim of hereditary inheritance-rights, of blood-ties to Abraham, Isaac and Jacob formed the basis of Judaism's ideological appeals to antiquity, as set forth in the works of Flavius Josephus among other later commentators

---

[104] Nicolas Berdyaev, tr. Donald Lowrie, *The Fate of Man in the Modern World* (Hesperides Press, 2012, digital edition), 6.32-6.33.

and apologists. The appeal of Nazism to the *Volksgemeinschaft* is precisely the appeal that Jesus's proto-Rabbinical critics made against Him and His followers in John 8:33: '*We are the descendants of Abraham*'.

On the other hand, the logic of American liberalism is a barely warmed-over Hellenism. The world-embracing, universe-striding Hellenic ideology under Alexander was an assimilationist one. In the Alexandrian ideology, it doesn't matter what tribe your parents are from, what your lineage is, or in what area of the world you were born. If you speak Greek, eat like a Greek, dress like a Greek, walk like a Greek, shit like a Greek, *think* like a Greek—then you're a Greek [105]. It's exceptionally difficult for an American to consider this ideology and not think of the 'melting pot'!

In its explicit form, the ideology of the 'melting pot' closely follows America's victory in the Spanish-American War[106]. America's belief in its own moral and military superiority made attractive to the empire-builders the progressive prospect of immersing, educating and inculturating recent European immigrants into Taylorist industrial capitalism and the American Way. There were some limits to this assimilationist

---

[105] Christos Zerefos and Marianna Vardinoyannis, eds., *Hellenistic Alexandria: Celebrating 24 Centuries* (Archaeopress, 2018), xviii.

[106] The Pluralism Project, 'God's melting pot' (Harvard, 2020). https://pluralism.org/gods-melting-pot. The first explicit mention of the 'melting pot' is dated to 1908.

mindset, but the mindset itself was steeped in Hellenistic thinking.

Hellenism is stamped all over our political system and our national *mythos*. The *E pluribus unum* which was used to justify the 'melting pot' ideology[107] is taken from the oratory of Cicero, in a paraphrase of the Greek philosopher Herakleitos. And both the *Annuit cœptis* and the *Novus ordo seclorum* found on our money, used first to bless our territorial expansions westward and afterward our imperial acquisitions abroad, are derived from the poetry of Virgil in homage of Homer! The former is taken from a prayer to Jupiter (Zeus) in Book IX of the *Aeneid*; and the latter is in reference to the oracles of the Temple of Apollo in the *Bucolics*[108]. The American project—particularly after 1898, though there were hints of it before—was very much conceived of as the creation of a new Macedonian Empire or a new Rome. The desire to take in subject peoples and immigrants and remake them in our image, precisely the desire of Alexander and the Seleucids, was perfectly mirrored in the creation of our own *New Colossus*—as inscribed at the base of the Statue of Liberty in 1903[109].

---

[107] *Ibid.*

[108] Ralph Mohr, 'Dollar words come from Virgil poems', *The World* (17 August 2002). https://theworldlink.com/dollar-words-come-from-virgil-poems/article_d3696e47-fb09-5aa5-9904-7ec8f9a80367.html.

[109] National Park Service, 'The Statue of Liberty' *NPS.gov*. https://home.nps.gov/stli/learn/historyculture/colossus.htm.

And the Lamb will conquer

But why do I say that from a Pauline view, the Soviet ideology has an 'advantage'? The interpretation of Marx's doctrines by Lenin, and the subsequent reinterpretation of both by Stalin, may strike one as being deeply at odds with Pauline teachings. This for the very understandable reason that Lenin in particular was violently hostile to every manifestation of Christianity in the lands which he governed! Yet Berdyaev was one, and not the only one, to recognise the close kinship of Soviet communism with the κοινωνία, and not merely for the communal pooling and sharing of goods shown in Acts 4:32-35[110]!

But Marx's economic analyses represented a real attempt, howbeit fatally hampered by his reliance on Hegel (and thus Plato), to break free of the two traps of biological-historical necessity and escapist idealism. The Soviets, many of whom had a Jewish background and who were steeped in the Hebrew language and Scriptures, understood and acted on this in a way that Marx's Gentile, Western European disciples did not.

Marx correctly rejected both idealism and biological determinism as forms of 'false consciousness', just as Saint John rejects both the Greek speculation about Jesus's mission (John 7:35) and the Jewish preoccupation with wombs (3:4) and bloodlines (8:33) as irrelevant. Instead, Saint John continues to insist on *deeds* which follow the Law of a God concerned with how one treats one's neighbour. Indeed, Marx follows precisely

---

[110] Nicolas Berdyaev, *The Russian Revolution* (University of Michigan Press, 1961).

In the Houses of the Poor

the stress Saint John lays on 'doing', on πρᾶξις (John 5:29), who in turn follows Saint Paul (Rom 8:13, 12:4; Col 3:9). Yet Marx—and the Soviets who followed him—stumbles over the *most important point*, over the *one thing needful* (Luke 10:42).

Hegel proves to be Marx's *Untergang*, and that mostly through his student Feuerbach. Removing the unseen God as the *reference*, means that Marx places his *trust* not in the deferred judgement of the only possible impartial Judge, but instead the immediate judgement of all-humanity, of humanity in the abstract. But how can all-humanity, an abstract humanity, be a judge over itself? Plato's shadow comes limping back through the doorway, like Barney after Moe throws him out of the bar. An all-humanity cannot vindicate itself (νικᾷ) over *any* human, because all humans suffer (θλίβονται) alone.

Immortality has no 'yesterday'

The poetry of June Morits, and I'm sure this is not accidental, holds the Johannine key to the riddle Marx fails to solve. In her poem '9 May 1945', she *repeats* the phrase '*У бессмертия нет "вчера"*'—'Immortality has no "yesterday"'—in the second and third stanzas[111]. Here, as in the modernist poetry of Wen Yiduo in the poem 'I wanted to come back' from his anthology *Stagnant water*, written on the occasion of his daughter's death for which he was absent[112], the technique of repetition carries a

---

[111] Morits, 'Девятое'.
[112] Wen Yiduo, tr. TT Sanders, *Red Candle* (Cape Editions, 1972), 37.

tone of irrepressible *grief*. It carries the tenor of a phrase repeated to oneself to help shake off the feeling of loss.

We are first arrested by the fact that Morits's poem is written entirely in the *present tense*. There is not a single была or былы to be found, yet the poem's time-frame is entirely past-oriented: the Great Patriotic War was a long time ago, and we are meant to understand that she is not writing this poem as an eight-year-old girl. She uses the official language of the Victory—*Победа*—paid for with the lives of the Immortal Regiment—*Жизней Полка Бессмертного*. Yet immortality knows no 'yesterday', just as this poem knows no past tense! Immediately we *hear* something that rings false about this use of the official terminology.

And she goes on to describe her sister, killed in the siege of Leningrad, as though she is still a nineteen-year-old young lady, present and speaking and dreaming of becoming an architect after working to help liberate her people in the munitions plant. This present-tense description of her lost sister drives the point home with the force of a stab to the heart. Even though her sister agrees *on the surface* with the official vocabulary, the victory hoopla and fireworks and accordions, we still are made to feel that there is something that this misses.

The Immortal Regiment is *frozen in time*. It is *fixed* in an eternal (and artificial!) present. It is not accessible to grief or true remembrance. Yet June Morits's sister, a breathing, living, dreaming, working, believing part of that Regiment, is in a *different* present, a *parallel* present, one in which June Morits is allowed to express her grief in other than official terms. It is only with a different repeated phrase, '*Все для Господа живы*', that this tension is allowed to break. 'Everyone is alive for the Lord.' It is the Lord Who makes space for June's deeply personal grief in a way that the fireworks and accordions and parade do not: for the remembrance in the present tense.

John 16:32-33 plays counterintuitively with verb tenses to showcase exactly the point that Morits is making. The grief, the θλῖψις, is in the present tense ('The hour is approaching'—'you have tribulation') and so is the relief ('but be of good cheer!'), yet it is all framed in reference to events which clearly *have already been set in motion*, for which the aorist tense is used. And for the legal acquittal represented by Jesus's Resurrection—*which is yet to come!*—the perfective tense is used ('I have overcome the world').

Morits's attitude towards the Great Patriotic War is unambivalent: she clearly holds the Victory as a good and worthy thing, and the Soviet cause as justified in its battle against fascist race-hatred. And Saint John would agree: the Germans had mired themselves in an 'eternal perfect', their racial identity frozen in a mythic past. Little better in Saint John's view is America's 'eternal aorist': the repetition of Alexander's expansions without reference to memory or concrete hope.

But it's clear Morits sees something deeply false with the Soviet version of an 'eternal present' corporate remembrance that has to whitewash the personal stories, that leaves no space for tears over what might have been, had a piece of shrapnel fallen somewhere else. Soviet commemoration is an aorist *sans* perfect: it worthily praises the victory, but offers no account of

And the Lamb will conquer

the suffering. On the other hand, if 'everyone is alive for the Lord', then a true νίκη—a true acquittal, a true vindication—becomes possible for June's sister, and for every other in the Immortal Regiment. A qualitatively different kind of 'eternal present' opens to view.

And the Lamb has conquered

The foregoing, I should note, is not an attempt to set Russian lexicography and grammar on an equal footing with Biblical Greek or Biblical Hebrew, or to claim that the Slavs have a unique insight into the logic of Scripture that is closed to Americans or Germans. To make such an assertion would be to fall into a distinctly Hegelian trap!

My Czech-Jewish relatives suffered in the *Shoah*. Those who were fortunate were liberated by the Red Army, along with the vast majority of the others on the Eastern Front. The ninth of May is thus deeply relevant to me. Yet I have struggled with the ramifications of Victory Day in a way similar to June Morits here. The American and German memory-holing of the ninth of May, and specifically the Russians' role in it, in response to current events in Ukraine, I personally find to be a hateful and repugnant bit of (geo)politicking. I react *viscerally* to the attempts by fellow Americans to downplay or airbrush the Immortal Regiment from the history-books.

Yet I find myself slightly discomforted with the patriotic fervour which, in a few hours' time, will be on full display at the commemoration in Moscow's streets. Perhaps it is *because* I am American by culture? Perhaps it is *because* I am habituated to my nation's 'melting-pot' ideology and capitalist individualism? And yet, if a Russian Jew like June Morits feels the same way as I (an American Orthodox Christian) do about it, our shared reaction rules out an explanation reliant on differences in ideology or religious identity or culture. Something else is at work.

The real crime of Byzantium with regard to Paul's message wasn't Saint Constantine himself. It was his *co-optation* of the νίκη of Christ as a *symbol*—his daubing of the Cross upon the Imperial standard to justify *military conquest.* But the legal acquittal of the One God and His judgement before all nations and all times *cannot* be used as propaganda. This is why Morits's poem is so hauntingly effective: her 'all are alive before the Lord' reveals a sharp delineation of the human need for the *one perspective* from *one eternal present.* If all deeds are held to the light before such, then no human being, let alone any human nation, can withstand it unscathed! *Only One* can overcome the cosmos: it isn't me, and it isn't you. And that is reason for 'good cheer'.

С днем великой победы!

Plant them on Thy holy mountain

A clarification on John 17:1-12

The operation of glory in Scripture

John 17 is sometimes termed the 'High Priestly Prayer'. It contains the longest of Jesus's prayers in the New Testament. The beginning of the prayer is dotted with the familiar Greek lexeme δόξα 'glory', the same from which we get the terms 'doxology' and also, incidentally, 'Orthodox'. The lexeme appears in both verbal and nominal form, as Jesus asks the Father to glorify (δόξασόν) His Son that the Son may *glorify* (δοξάσῃ) Him (17:1), having *glorified* (ἐδόξασα) God on earth through that which He accomplished (17:4), to *glorify* (δόξασόν) Him with the *glory* (δόξῃ) that He had before the world came to be (17:5).

One sees a similar repeated insistence on *glory* in Saint Paul's letter to the Ephesians (1:12-18). Those who first heard the Gospel, as those in Ephesus are so called, are destined to live for Christ's glory just as Christ was destined to live for the Father's. The mechanism expounded in Ephesians does indeed place Christ in the function of a priest after the Levite tradition. It also places the Ephesians themselves in a priestly function for the transmission of Christ's Gospel. The Father in Heaven is the source of all glory, utterly sufficient to Himself. The glory is given to Christ His Son and *locum tenens*, and subsequently given to and magnified through Paul, who gives it to the Ephesians to spread to the world. The apparent exclusivity seen in John 17:9 (*'I am not praying for the world but*

Plant them on Thy holy mountain

for those whom thou hast given me') is to be understood according to this literary 'hierarchy' which is shown in the opening of Paul's letter to Ephesus.

Fr Paul Tarazi and Fr Marc Boulos both explain the importance of the city of Ephesus to the Christian mission. It is set up as a counter-metropole, both to the Caesar in Rome, and to the Sanhedrin in Jerusalem. But the point is not to exalt the institutional Μητρόπολις Εφέσου, presently under the ὠμοφόριον of the Ecumenical Patriarchate, over all other Orthodox Churches! No. The sordid game of Popes and Patriarchs, wrangling over political and spiritual supremacy over the Church since the 800s, is clearly not what Paul has in mind. The geography of the physical city is *literally* important to the Pauline corpus because it stands *over-against* the Temples of Solomon and Herod (both travesties of the true Temple, which is in fact a desert tent!), and *over-against* the Forum Romanum (a travesty of the true Proprietorship of the unseen God). The setting-apart of the Ephesians as those to whom the Gospel was first preached is a primacy of witness, not a primacy of worldly honour or institutional power.

The city of Ephesus is also of particular historical importance to the Johannine literature. There are textual indications that Saint John belonged to the place himself: most notably in the Apocalypse, which Saint John self-avowedly wrote from exile in Patmos (Apoc 1:9), an island about fifty miles offshore. He also addresses Ephesus first among the churches of Asia, in warm terms, advising them to return to their first love and to put away the works of the Νικολαΐτης (Apoc 2:1-7). In the Patristic writings, Saint Irenaios (the student of Saint Polycarp, himself a student of Saint John), writing in the second century AD, makes reference to John residing in Ephesus and refusing to bathe in a bath-house patronised by a certain Kērinthos, a leader among the Hellenisers[113].

Fun little historical aside: in the year 269 AD, my ancestors landed in Ephesus, sacked and looted the place, and burned the Temple to Artemis to the ground[114]. The *glory* of Ephesus never recovered. Sorry about that. It's a nasty little habit we Teutonic barbarians have. But we got our comeuppance: the Moors sent us packing out of Hispania in the eighth century, ending *our* kingdom's glory. On the plus side, my ᚠᚪᚦᚱᛖᛁᚾ did leave behind an exegetical fragment on the Gospel of Saint John as inspiration for this book. Such is the way history goes.

But glory (δόξα) in Scripture does *not* operate this way. If the glory of a place is in its palaces and temples and monuments, then all glory is 'passing away' (1 Cor 7:31). The Temple to Artemis was one of the ancient world's seven wonders. Now that site is a quiet field, a grassy plain with a few pillar-bases and scattered stones. Fr Marc Boulos visited that site during his trip to Türkiye. He tells me that if he hadn't been told where he was, he never would have known he was standing in the middle of it. Likewise, the only lasting traces of Gothic settlement on

---

[113] Saint Irenaios of Lyons, *Against Heresies* (Veritatis Splendor, 2012), III.iii.4.

[114] Wolfram, *History*, 53.

Plant them on Thy holy mountain

the Iberian Peninsula are archaeological: like the necropolis[115] at Sarrià de Ter in Catalonia, where my sixth-century Visigothic kinswomen lie buried.

This is why the culture-warriors, the defenders of 'Western civilisation', the religious nationalists of various stripes, the advocates of 'Christian manliness' and so on, the sorts who have Romanesque busts as profile pics on their social media accounts, are all (at best) barking up the wrong tree. The goal of the δόξα of Scripture is not to glorify a man, a monument or a civilisation. It is to glorify the One God *through teaching*.

Ephesus as a neo-Levite training-ground

The litany of δόξα 'glory' in Saint Paul's letter to the Ephesians is a direct and conscious echo of a similar litany in the Book of Exodus—specifically, the 'song of Israel' in Exodus 15. Δόξα translates, in this instance in the Septuagint text, the Hebrew words *gəʾôn* גאון and *gaʾâ* גאה from the triliteral *g-ʾ-h* ג-א-ה 'to rise up, to grow, to triumph, (to be) exalted'; and in the following chapter, it translates *kābôd* כבוד 'honour', from the root *k-b-d* כ-ב-ד 'to weigh, to be heavy'. There is an irony in this dual usage of the Greek term δόξα which we will get to later. But this song is in fact a song specific to the *Levites*, as it is sung

---

[115] '*It feels like… I'm living… inside a dre—e—eam…!*' 'Necropolis', track 2 on Manilla Road, *Crystal Logic* (Roadster, 1983). This song was, fittingly enough, covered by Utah power metal band Visigoth on *The Revenant King* in 2015.

not only by Moses but also by Miriam, cited as the sister of Aaron (15:20), who leads the house of Levi.

Thus the repetition of δόξα in Jesus's high-priestly prayer in John 17 serves as an indirect literary 'callback' to the scene of Lazarus's death in Bethany in John 11. The names of Lazarus, Mary and Martha are a direct reference to the Levite priesthood. Recall that *there*, Jesus put the question to Martha, 'the mistress (of the house)', about whether she trusted in the *rising* (ἀνάστασις) of the Lord. Recall also that the active textual reference in John 11 (Psalm 9) is a rising of that Lord in judgement against *ga'awâ* גאוה 'the proud'!

Embedded in this repetition of δόξα, then, are:

1.) **Jesus, the new Moses.** The repetition of *gā'â* גאה 'glory' promises and presages the overthrow of the 'ruler of this world', just as Pharaoh's riders were overthrown into the sea (Exo 15:1), by the One Who has 'power over all flesh' (John 17:2).

2.) **Levite priestly duties upon the disciples.** The citation of the 'song of Israel' (Exo 15:20) in Jesus's blessing of the disciples makes it clear that *they* (the literary proxies of the Pauline table-fellowship) are the new Levites. Priestly authority devolves onto them (John 17:6-8).

3.) **Declaration of a counter-metropole.** The citation of the Philistines, the Moabites, the Edomites and the Canaanites in the 'song of Israel' (Exo 15:14-15) mirrors similar declarations of West Asian kings and temple priests over subject peoples. Jesus makes a similar declaration, having glorified God 'on the earth' (John

17:4) and established His disciples as a counter-empire 'in the world' (17:11).

The hierarchical 'weight' of Christ in God, and the disciples in Christ, and the world in the disciples, is precisely the mechanism that Paul sets up in Ephesus. It mirrors both the Levite priesthood *and* the hierarchical structure of the Roman household. But the purpose of distributing the 'weight' this way is not for the *construction* of a new Jerusalem—as though it were a repeat of the Maccabean revolt which established the fallen Hasmonean Kingdom! (Where is all the 'weight' of the Temple of Artemis now?)

Rather, Ephesus is a training-ground for the disciples. It's a camp, just as the Hebrews lived in a camp in the wilderness to be tutored in God's Law. The disciples are not meant to *stay* in Ephesus, let alone build monuments! Ephesus is a 'base camp' where students are trained. They are then *sent out* from there with the message.

'... On earth, having accomplished the work...'

In *The Lamb before Its Shearers*, I devoted one chapter to discussing the operation of the word ἔργον 'work' in John, in the Pauline writings, and in the Septuagint[116]. The context there was the healing of the man born blind.

---

[116] Cooper, *Lamb*, 213-231.

In the Houses of the Poor

To briefly sum up my clarification on John 9 from *Lamb*: the functionality of 'work' was a double jab. Firstly, it was aimed against the disciples' question of *theodicy*. They were wondering what sin the man or his parents had committed to be born blind. Jesus tells them that isn't the point. The point is *doing the work* so that God's will for them can be *shown*. If you see someone suffering, you don't ask how they got there: you aid and comfort them. The day of judgement is the day on which all works will be *shown* for what they are—whether they are the works which God has commanded, or whether they are not. The works which God has commanded will be rewarded with their exposure and completion; those which have not, will be punished with their exposure and undoing.

Secondly, it was aimed at distinguishing the work proper to God from the work proper to man. God's work is creative and self-motivated; the work of man is *commanded* and *sent* to him. This distinction is carried inside the Hebrew verbiage associated with work. The term *'ābad* עבד 'to (do servile) work' is never used for that work done by God, only by man. The work done by God is *'āsâ* עשה 'to do, to make' or *lā'ak* לאך 'to craft, to occupy oneself' or, more rarely, *fā'al* פעל 'to fashion, to sculpt'. This distinction was set in place and made operative in John 9 to warn man from *taking on the job* of the One Who created him. The clay doesn't get to question what the potter is doing (Isa 29:16, 45:9), because, in the literary terms Saint John uses, the very eyes of man are made with the clay that He has fashioned them from.

Because John 17 has already made reference through its use of 'glory' to the song of Israel in Exodus 15, that is where we

Plant them on Thy holy mountain

ought to look for an answer to the question of what sense this 'work' is meant. We see in Exodus 15 that *'āsâ* עשה (15:11) and *fā'al* פעל (15:17) are *both* used. In the former verse, it is in reference to the *fala'* פלא 'wonders' which God has done. And in the latter verse, it is in reference to the *har* הר 'mountain', the *makôn* מכון 'place' which God has fashioned with His hands—and where He planted His people, in order to hear His Law.

As Captain Kirk once asked: *'What does God need with a starship?'* [117] Scripture's answer is resounding: *nothing*. God doesn't *need* any kind of temple built by human hands. God doesn't need any kind of palace. God doesn't need any kind of chariot, or palanquin, or ship (capable of warp speed or not!). He fashions His dwelling-place with His own hands. It is *human beings* who need these things. It is out of God's condescension to the Hebrews' need for a visible place of worship, that He comes to rest in a Tabernacle—a *tent* which can be moved!

John 17 must be read precisely in this light. We know Jesus was a craftsman's son—but what did He *build*? Nothing. The *works* which He accomplished up to this point in the Gospel of Saint John, in order, are:

1.) making wine out of water (John 2:11);

2.) driving the moneychangers out of the Temple (2:15);

3.) healing the son of the βασιλικός (4:50);

---

[117] William Shatner, *Star Trek V: The Final Frontier* (Paramount Pictures, 1989).

In the Houses of the Poor

4.) healing the lame man in the Sheep Gate (5:9);

5.) feeding the 5,000 (6:11);

6.) walking on water (6:19);

7.) evading arrest at the Feast of Booths (7:30);

8.) saving the woman caught in adultery (8:9);

9.) healing the man born blind (9:6-7);

10.) raising Lazarus from the dead (11:44);

11.) washing the disciples' feet (13:5).

Jesus follows each of these his acts with a *teaching* drawn from the *Torah*. Each one of these works is *creative*, an act of *poesis*, but not one of these *works* is an act of building. Jesus erects no kind of edifice or structure of any kind! Rather, His work, his 'weight-lifting', is *demonstrative* and *pedagogical* in nature. Jesus's work is to reveal the *Torah* through His *praxis*.

To give a few examples: the turning of the water into wine is two-pronged. It explicates the expected code of desert hospitality to strangers and also demonstrates Jesus's obedience to His mother. The driving of the moneychangers out of the Temple is an act of direct civil disobedience against the debt policies of the Sanhedrin and the proclamation of the Levitical *dərôr*. The healing of the son of the high-ranking official is a demonstration of the proper treatment of foreigners.

This is where the irony in the double meaning of δόξα kicks in. The sort of ἔργον 'work'—hospitality, liberation, healing and pedagogy—that brings the ὀρθὴ δόξα 'proper glory' or 'correct

Plant them on Thy holy mountain

weight' to the One God Who brought the Hebrews for worship to a place which He fashioned with His own hands, is *not* the work of building 'weighty' monuments of wood and stone. Paul's **Orthodoxy** has nothing to do with Justinianic propaganda! It's the sort of 'weight' that the moths and rust don't eat away (Matt 6:19). If God has no need for a starship, then He certainly has no need for a physical bastion in Ephesus that the likes of my thieving Therving forefathers could pillage and raze to the ground.

Paul's logic, and John's logic, is the logic of Ansar Allāh. The American empire can't bully and beat you with its navy, if you don't have any physical infrastructure to destroy. They can strafe your festivals and take out a tent or two with air strikes. But if you hide out in the hills like your shepherd ancestors, and carry out hit-and-run attacks, you'll eventually outlast even the fighter jets on the USS *Truman*! With due apologies to Dave Chappelle: *modern problems require ancient solutions.*

The 'weight' of the weapons of Saint Paul and Saint John, though, are not like the weight of Samad-3 drones and Chinese Toufan missiles[118]. Their weapon is merely the message of the

---

[118] I clarify that my reference to Ansar Allāh is *analogical*, not evaluative. Like the Pauline κοινωνία, their movement originated in the 90s as a nonviolent civil disobedience movement, Ḥizb al-Ḥaqq حزب الحق. That was before repression forced the movement to adopt militant tactics. As a disciple of Tarazi, I note Ḥusayn al-Ḥūtī's textual focus with particular interest and sympathy, even as my own focus remains on Paul's *Torah* hermeneutic of liberation. – *Auth.*

In the Houses of the Poor

Torah—the only king, judge and proprietor is God—but updated for the age of Roman supremacy. In an age when the spirit was to confess '*no king but Caesar*', Paul is teaching that '*there is no Caesar but God*'! And God's glory—though hierarchically distributed to Paul, to the disciples in Ephesus, and thereafter to the world—is the glory of a *tizkê* תזכה, a *legal exoneration*, rather than a triumph of arms (*lāḥam* לחם). Yet even this message was subversive enough that the servitors of Caesar and the defenders of his divinity had to suppress it, whether by persecuting those who taught it, or by (eventually) coopting it and moulding it into a tamed symbol, a tool of Roman ideology.

Jesus's 'high priestly prayer', investing His disciples with the duties of the tribe of Levi in the Book of Exodus, is thus also a placement of the disciples on His holy mountain. The Sinai to which Jesus alludes here, which in Exodus stands over-against the city of Pharaoh, is a literary reference to the Pauline 'base of operations' in Ephesus. The disciples' job is not to stay there, and not to build anything there. They are instead there so that they may learn to 'be one' in the teaching, just as Jesus and the Father 'are one' in that He accomplishes the work the Father has appointed to Him (John 17:4, 11), and to be 'sent... into the world' (17:18). That way they can take up the 'weight' of the Gospel and carry it... anywhere.

The light in the darkness is not overcome

A clarification on John 18:1-11

Water, civilisation and a wash of many names

In East Jerusalem, there is a valley called the *Wādī al-Jūz* وادي الجوز 'the Wash that Passes Through'[119], running between the Temple Mount and the Mount of Olives. Elsewhere, this same *wādī* is called *Wādī an-Nār* وادي النار 'Fire Wash' and *Wādī ar-Rāhib* وادي الراهب 'Monks' Wash', particularly around the *Dayr Mār Sābā* دير مار سابا Orthodox monastery founded by Saint Sabbas the Sanctified. The Palestinian naming of this wash, different names for different drainage areas, should not strike one as odd.

The practise of giving different names to different sections of the same river is a longstanding Indigenous practice. It mirrors the Ojibwe toponymy of the Mississippi River—which is a name we white folks took from the Ojibwe language, Anishinaabemowin. Between the headwaters and Lake Bemidji, the river is called *Omashkoozo-ziibi* 'Elk River'. Between Lake

---

[119] Another translation of this name is 'Valley of the Walnuts', and this translation also works. But the triliteral root *j-w-z* ج و ز pertains to the 'middle, main part' of something, or else 'to cross, to pass through' the middle of two places. The Persian *gōz* گوز 'walnut' is actually interfunctional with this root, because what is the part of the nut that you eat? It's the *middle part* enclosed within the two halves of the hull. – Auth.

The light in the darkness is not overcome

Bemidji and Lake Cass, the river is called *Bemijigamaag-ziibi* 'Running Between Lakes River', appropriately. Between Lakes Cass and Winnibigoshish, the river is *Gaa-miskwaawaakokaag-ziibi* 'Flourishing Red Cedar River'. Downstream of Lake Winnibigoshish, it's called *Wiinibiigoonzhish-ziibi* 'Little Stagnant Murky River'. After the Leech Lake River joins it, it's called *Gichi-ziibi* 'Big River'. And after the Crow Wing River joins it, it's called *Misi-ziibi* 'Great River'[120].

To Palestinians in the *Wādī*, or to Anishinaabemowin-speaking nations in northern Minnesota, different names for different stretches of river is just good sense. Once different water flows into a confluence, or once it stalls through a lake with its own ecosystem dependent on the stiller water, the character of the river changes. It becomes a different river. As you can see from the Ojibwe toponymy, the names are descriptive and precise. They name the river based on the character of the water, or on the plants and animals that can be found on its banks.

The people who would insist on a single name for a river with different characteristics, or who give it a name that's merely sounds strung together without semantic content, are those who would want to *control* the river in its downward flow. Reading Hudson's book on Bronze Age West Asia, most of the

---

[120] Jordan Engel, 'The headwaters of the Mississippi River in Ojibwe', *The Decolonial Atlas* (12 January 2015), https://decolonialatlas.wordpress.com/2015/01/12/the-headwaters-of-the-mississippi-river-in-ojibwe/.

violent conflict between the earliest civilisations was over communal *water access rights*[121]. If you control the river from a point upstream, you can control irrigation, navigation, trade—essentially, you control what other people eat and how much they have. Contentions over water control were actually the main driving force for cities to build larger walls and stronger fortifications, and maintain larger armies.

It's the same as what Israel is still doing to the Palestinians. Those who control all the fresh water, can turn it off at will and let the people whose land they occupy die of thirst and starvation. *Don't call it barbarism!* Barbarians don't stoop that low. Nomadic tribes could, and did, burn villages to the ground and slaughter everyone in sight. But as a rule they didn't dam up their enemies' water to watch them die of thirst. That kind of lingering cruelty requires 'civilised values'.

Why am I talking about riparian control in the context of Bronze Age warfare, in a commentary on the Gospel of Saint John, though? Because Jesus is about to be crucified. And He is passing through the *Wādī al-Jūz* into Gethsemane.

The 'Dusky Wash' in the *Kətubîm*

This particular place, the stretch of the *Wādī al-Jūz* between the Temple Mount and the Mount of Olives, has considerable importance in the Hebrew *Kətubîm*. It is called the *Naḥal Qidrôn*

---

[121] Hudson, *Forgive*, 70.

The light in the darkness is not overcome

נחל קדרון, the 'Gloomy', 'Mournful', or 'Dusky Wash'. It is, in terms of literary semiotics, the boundary between the city of Jerusalem and *hamMidbār* המדבר 'the wilderness' beyond. When King David is forced to flee Jerusalem and abandon it to the advancing armies of his son Absalom (*'Abi Šalōm* אבי שלום = 'my father is peace'; how's that for irony?), he and his followers flee the city amid the loud wails of his people, into the wilderness by the way of the 'Dusky Wash' (2 Sam 15:23).

While he is doing so, a cousin of the previous king Saul named Šim'î (שמעי = 'famous', from the same root as the son of Noah, Šēm שם 'name') throws rocks and mocks and curses David in his flight (2 Sam 16:5-13). Eventually, he returns to David and falls before him, begging amnesty (2 Sam 19:16-23). Later he is held under house-arrest by David's heir Solomon, forbidden on pain of death from leaving Jerusalem by crossing the *wādī*. Yet he disobeys this command and crosses the *wādī* in pursuit of two of his runaway slaves. Then Solomon has Šim'î put to death, after reminding his court of the insults he'd hurled at David in *his* flight from Jerusalem (1 Kgs 2:36-46).

Later, the *wādī* gained literary significance as a disposal site for ritually-unclean objects, like idols and altars made for the Canaanite gods Ba'al and 'Ašērâ (1 Kgs 15:13; 2 Kgs 23:4-12; 2 Par 15:16, 29:16, 30:14). Here such objects were burned and committed to the wash as ashes. Yet it was also the boundary of the *qōdeš* set aside by the Lord in the prophetic book of Jeremiah (31:40).

Which of these references is functional in the Gospel of John, though? The clearest reference appears to be to the passage from 2 Kings: David's forced flight from Jerusalem and the saga

In the Houses of the Poor

of šimʿî. That Jesus ἐξῆλθεν 'went out' with His disciples into Qidrôn (John 18:1) directly mirrors how David *yēṣē'* יצא 'went out' (LXX ἐξῆλθεν) from Jerusalem (2 Kgs 15:17). Likewise, that Judas παραδιδοὺς 'betrays' Jesus is a literary parallel to the betrayal of David to Absalom by Aḥitofel (*'Aḥî Tōfel* אחי תפל = 'my brother is false', 'my brother lacks in taste') in the following chapter of 2 Kings.

The actual *name* of Qidrôn, too, ties back to the Prologue: καὶ τὸ φῶς ἐν τῇ σκοτίᾳ φαίνει καὶ ἡ σκοτία αὐτὸ οὐ κατέλαβεν *'The light shines in the darkness, and the darkness has not overcome it'* (John 1:5, RSV). The name of the *wādī* in Biblical Hebrew, *Naḥal Qidrôn* נהל קדרון 'Dusky Wash', makes it a literary place of darkness. It is semiotically linked to the darkness of the human condition which Saint John's Prologue sets out.

Thus, we are placed in a setting in John 18 where the literary irony of the text is given full space to play out. The backdrop is set up to reenact the betrayal of King David by his own friend and his own son. Only this time, even the *concept of kingship* is being unwittingly fatally undermined by the idiots who are sent to capture Jesus at Judas's behest!

Mind your step in the dark!

Later in the second book of Samuel, David exclaims: כי־אתה **נירי** יהוה ויהוה יגיה חשכי *'Yea, thou art my **lamp**, O Lord, and my God lightens my darkness'* (2 Sam 22:29, see also Psa 17:29). There is no indication that Jesus and His disciples need any kind of light in the Dusky Wash. Yet we are told that the soldiers that Judas

The light in the darkness is not overcome

leads there bring with them φανῶν καὶ λαμπάδων 'torches and lanterns' (John 18:3).

I refer the reader back to my first chapter in *The Lamb before Its Shearers*, on the Johannine Prologue. The Hellenist mindset predominant in Saint John's world, following Plato and Aristotle, held the λόγος 'word, speech' to be the property of man. The saying attributed to Socrates at the core of this belief, is ὁ δὲ ἀνεξέταστος βίος οὐ βιωτὸς ἀνθρώπῳ *'the life which is not inquired into, is not the life [worthy] of a man'*. Saint John thoroughly deconstructs this Socratic belief and turns it inside out, as a dare to the entire philosophical mindset. The λόγος of Saint John's Prologue is, *pace* Aristotle, *not* the property of man, but of God—and so are ζωὴ 'life' and φῶς 'light', which are only *bestowed* on man *by* God.

Yet the ἀνθρώπων 'men' insist on being their own little light-bearers. *'This little light of mine'* is still a popular church camp song—in English, but as Fr Marc Boulos points out in his commentary on Luke 8:16, the *logic* of this 'Christian' church-camp boilerplate is in fact of *Antichrist*[122]. Fr Marc demonstrates through his tracing of the Greek roots back through the Septuagint into the Hebrew text, that Luke 8:16 is in fact a witness *against* the human ownership of the light, because it is not the human being's, in the first place, to cover or hold or set apart for himself. Saint John is saying the same thing that Saint Luke is.

---

[122] Fr Marc Boulos, 'God is the Light', *The Bible as Literature* podcast 551 (YouTube, 1 Feb 2025).

In the Houses of the Poor

In the Johannine Prologue, the properties of λόγος 'speech' and ζωὴ 'life' and φῶς 'light' are paired *structurally, chiastically* (when compared against Genesis 1, from which this terminology is drawn) with θεός God. Saint John then goes on to chiastically pair ἀνθρώπων 'men' with σκοτία 'gloom, darkness'. And now here we are in the Dusky Wash, and the soldiers and officials led by Judas are coming, bearing torches and lanterns (and probably singing, *'This little light of mine...'*)!

The purpose of light shining in darkness is to help you make things out that you can't see otherwise, and more importantly tell where to put your feet so you don't stumble or fall down (Psa 118:105). Saint John, in this Gospel verse, takes care to mention that Judas is εἱστήκει 'standing' with the men he brought to the Dusky Wash when Jesus appears (18:5). Yet the men are at first unable to identify Jesus, and when He reveals Himself to them, they ἀπῆλθον εἰς τὰ ὀπίσω 'drew back' and ἔπεσαν χαμαί 'fell to the ground' (18:6).

The irony here is delicious... and damning. The arresting posse arrives with their torches and lanterns, but they can't recognise Him until He identifies Himself—*twice!* And when He does so, they *rear backwards* like spooked horses, and *collapse*. The scene is Monty Python, it's slapstick farce; but there's also a serious warning to it. If there truly is 'a lamp to your feet' as in Psalm 118, your feet will be sure. But if you trust in *your own* 'little light', the actual Light is going to dazzle you and trip you up.

The torches in the Dusky Wash aren't just stage-props. They're emblems of futility. David, *fleeing through this same wash*, needed no lamp. Jesus needed no 'papers'. Yet the

The light in the darkness is not overcome

soldiers, the officials and Judas, relying on the human light of Hellenistic reason, hear Jesus's self-identification as the *Teaching*, they are startled and stumble.

The temple slave's name is 'King'

The other reference to the 'historical' *Kətubîm* which deserves mention, is the temple slave whose ear is cut off by Saint Peter. This pericope is usually cited in Christian commentaries which emphasise Jesus's nonviolent approach to His arrest. But if that were the only point, Saint John would not feel the need to point out the name of the slave whose ear was wounded.

First, note the deliberate echo in John 18:10, of the saga of Šimʿî in the *Kətubîm*. Šimʿî is a kinsman of King Saul who hurls stones at David after he flees this *wādī* and curses and mocks him in his misfortune, flinging dust and rocks at his retreating army, volubly remembering the Judahite usurpation of the Benjaminite ruling line and delighting in his enemy's downfall (2 Sam 16:5-14). After David triumphs over Absalom and is restored in kingship, Šimʿî is shown throwing himself at David's feet and begging for mercy, which David grants (2 Sam 19:16-23). Later, he is shown pursuing two of his slaves across this same *wādī* and being subsequently put to death when King Solomon, the builder of the first Temple, finds out about it (1 Kgs 2:36-46).

Now we can properly account for the irony in the slave's name: *Malchos* (Μάλχος = *Melek* מלך 'king')!

In the Houses of the Poor

On the surface, there is an obvious and clear functional value to giving the Temple slave the name of 'King'. In a classical context, calling anyone in a position of power a 'slave' is a clear diss. And it is a diss aimed at Pilate, as well as Pilate's boss Augustus. Saint John is tagging Augustus as the puppet of the Temple authorities, conned or browbeaten into doing their bidding.

The act of naming the slave as 'King' is an open act of subversion that belittles Caesar. But that isn't all that's going on here. John 18 is a three-way typological role-reversal, a midrāšic reinterpretation of the 'Šimʿî arc' from Second Samuel and First Kings. The Šimʿî of the *Kətubîm* pursued two slaves across Wādī al-Jūz in an act of disobedience to King Solomon. Now, the new Šimʿî (Judas) pursues Solomon's rightful heir across the same *wādī*, in the company of a slave bearing the name of 'king'!

Furthermore, Saint Peter is placed in the role of Bənāyâ, the captain of David's (and later Solomon's) guard. Yet it is not Judas Peter attacks, but instead the slave named 'King': and, significantly, he *cuts off his ear*, the organ of hearing. Remember that the Hebrew root *šəmāʿ* שמע 'to hear' refers not only to the somatic physical sense, but also to the faculty of *judgement*, the ability to 'hear' a case in a court of law! The wounding of Malchos is thus a literary allusion to the Temple's *failure of judgement* in their arrest of Jesus. Yet ironically, Peter has also not *heard* the teaching correctly, and Jesus has to rebuke him for his act and tell him to stay his hand (John 18:11).

The light in the darkness is not overcome

Keep your feet on the ground

The use of the word χαμαί 'on the ground, to the ground' here, isn't just a stray prepositional phrase. It has a *function*. When the soldiers fall 'to the ground', they demonstrate what happens when Jesus's warning, *'Walk while you have the light'*, goes unheeded: *'he who walks in the darkness does not know where he goes'* (John 12:35). Their own human-lit lights, their *'lanterns and torches'* (18:3), are inadequate to comprehend or overtake the true Light... and so they stumble in the dark.

Yet we risk missing the more important point, if we hold to a spiritualised, allegorical reading of this passage. The same χῶμα 'earth' with which Jesus heals one man's sight (John 9:6), now stands witness to the blindness of those who seek to arrest Jesus (18:6). The earth is God's possession. Those who seek to control and master it as princes delude themselves.

This is why the names (in the plural) of the *Wādī al-Jūz, in Arabic*, are so important. These names are not imposed by kings or imperial administrators, but by the people who walk there and do not stumble, because they walk while they have light to see by! Just as with the Ojibwe naming *Omashkoozo-ziibi* after the elk that drink there, or *Gaa-miskwaawaakokaag-ziibi* after the red cedars growing on its banks, the names the Palestinians gave to this *wādī* are *functional*. They are based on what can be seen there, from ground level, in broad daylight.

Here it's the wash that 'passes through' or 'passes between' the Temple Mount and the Mount of Olives. Over there, it's the wash 'of monks' because that's where Saint Sabbas the Sanctified withdrew to his lonely cave back in the fifth century, and established the community of desert ascetics that's still there to this day. And over there, it's called the wash 'of fire' because of its treacherous roads and because of the stunning views that can be seen from it in twilight.

We're accustomed to 'seeing' these places, in the colour plates of our English-language Bibles perhaps, as dots or lines on a map... like a game of Risk or a Paradox Interactive turn-based strategy title. These maps are marked with artificial colours that represent no actual physical features, but instead *political* delineations, showing which king ruled where. We are accustomed, in other words, to *seeing* these places, and *thinking* of them, the way that kings and administrators saw them... not in the way that the people who live there see them. When we 'see' the land itself through the eyes of human artifice—which is exactly what political maps are, make no mistake—then we are 'seeing' the way Caesar 'sees', the way Pilate 'sees', and the way Judas in this passage 'sees'. We are not giving a lamp *to our feet* (2 Sam 22:26) so that our steps may be sure. All of us fall 'to the ground', and return to it, in the end. The hope is in walking in the *instruction* of the One Who walks in the earth (Gen 3:8) as only One Who cares for it can.

Double judgement in the High Priest's house

A clarification on John 18:15-24

Known to the High Priest

One of the consistent themes to which I have called attention in my writings on the Gospel of Saint John in the footsteps of the *Skeireins*, both here and in *The Lamb before Its Shearers*, has been the consistent emphasis I've placed on the anti-Hellenistic 'edge' in Saint John's writing. Of course, his work is also aimed against the pro-circumcision clique, and also internally against the Pauline disciples who are tempted to betray the teaching of Christ in favour of pet theories of their own. Here, though, at the beginning of Jesus's trial in Saint John's Gospel, that 'edge' is shown in all its keenness, and it is shown in the use of a single phrase.

Saint John accompanies Jesus, alongside Simon Peter, to the home of Annas, the High Priest's father-in-law. Again, Saint John uses the technique of authorial self-elision (Chapter 5) to refer to himself in the third person, in this case as ἄλλος μαθητής 'another disciple'. But then he says something interesting—one that exposes to the light the entire conflict of Saint John's social context. He says that this other disciple was **γνωστὸς τῷ ἀρχιερεῖ** '*known to the High Priest*'! Peter could only be let into the courtyard of the High Priest with John's say-so to the maid at the door (John 18:15-16).

Saint John's positioning of these two words together, γνωστὸς 'known' and ἀρχιερεῖ 'High Priest', serves an interesting function. The Greek word γνωστός, derived from

Double judgement in the High Priest's house

γινώσκω 'to know', is in the same family of Greek lexemes that includes γνῶσις 'gnosis, (secret) knowledge', the like of which was promised by several neo-Platonist-adjacent, Hellenising schools which insinuated themselves and recruited among the early Pauline table-fellowship. And, of course, the ἀρχιερεῖ refers to the *Kohen* כהן who presided over the Sanhedrin in Herod's Temple. With this phrase, John is literarily setting the stage for a confrontation between the two contending tendencies in the Pauline community.

Again, because our consciences are corrupt, when we modern readers see a phrase like γνωστὸς τῷ ἀρχιερεῖ, we think John is boasting, flaunting his status over Peter. In the scene of the Last Supper (Chapter 5), John's 'closeness' to his Teacher was not necessarily a good thing, or a reason for boasting. Again, think about it like a school of taekwondo or kung fu. The μαθητής who is physically close to his teacher is the one who needs extra support and attention: the weaker of the tyros, or one who is slower to grasp the forms and stances.

Here, John's 'closeness' to the High Priest is even *less* of a grounds for boasting than his closeness to Jesus. The High Priest's father-in-law is very much so a figure of ignorance and corruption in the present scene. And John, in owning up to a close connexion between himself and that figure representing Temple authority and the Pharisee faction within it, may be making a confession of sorts. Perhaps John had been close to the Judaising tendencies within the Pauline community. And if he had been closer to them even than Saint Peter, who was rebuked by Saint Paul precisely over his failure to invite uncircumcised Gentiles into the table-fellowship, that would be a damning self-indictment indeed!

The names and accusations of Annas and Caiaphas

The name 'Annas', belonging to the High Priest's father-in-law, provides a further point of connexion between this character and the author of the Gospel in which he appears. The Greek Ἄννας is a rendering of the Hebrew dithematic theophoric name *Ḥānanyâ* חנניה 'God is gracious, God favours'. This figure's name is literally interesting because it is a reversal of John's own name *Yôḥānan* יוחנן 'God has graced'. It would be like two Germans with the names Waldbert and Bertwald appearing in the same work.

At the same time, a similar kind of wordplay is going on between the characters of Caiaphas (*Kefā'* כפא 'stone, depression in a rock face') and Cephas, which we are told in the text (John 1:42) is the Aramaic synonym for Peter (Πέτρος = *Kêf* כף 'rock'). Given that both of these characters appear in the present pericope, the similarity of these names is functional, and we are meant to take note of it.

The question is, *why* this wordplay with names?

I would draw attention, with this wordplay in mind, to the fact that there is a *charcoal fire* burning in the courtyard, which the slaves and the officers had lit because it was cold (John 18:18). The repetition of δοῦλοι 'slaves' and ὑπηρέται 'officers' shows us that we are dealing with the same themes as in earlier in the chapter, when Judas brought the ὑπηρέτας 'officers' and the ἀρχιερέως δοῦλον 'High Priest's slave' named Malchos (=

Double judgement in the High Priest's house

'King') to arrest Jesus (Chapter 11), and they had brought *lanterns and torches*. The use of man-made lights and torches earlier in the chapter was shown, farcically, to be insufficient to identify Jesus or even for the officers to keep on their feet in the dark! This is a repetition of the theme of the Prologue, in which humankind in general is described as ἐν τῇ σκοτίᾳ 'in the dark' and οὐ κατέλαβεν 'clueless' (John 1:5).

Here, a man-made light reappears: the ἀνθρακιὰν 'charcoal fire' (same Greek root as the English word 'anthracite'!). And here, the 'slaves' and 'officers' also reappear. And here, Peter reappears. Literarily, then, we may take it as given that John isn't done with the theme of God's light vs. man's darkness. But an extra layer of textual allusion is added. The term ἄνθραξ 'coal' is used in the Septuagint to refer both to live burning coals (*gaḥalê* גחלי) in the censer of the priest (Lev 16:12) and also to a certain type of gemstone, possibly a turquoise (*nōfek* נפך) in the High Priest's breastplate (Exo 28:18). Either way, the fact that it is a *charcoal* fire, and the fact that the characters around it are the same categories of officials and servitors who came to the *Wādī* to arrest Jesus, links Peter *threefold* to the High Priest. The disciple with the High Priest's name is warming himself by the High Priest's fire in the company of the High Priest's servants!

The imagery is clear. The threefold linkage of Peter with the High Priest (through his name, company and proximity to the artificial fire) accompanies Peter's threefold verbal denial of Christ (John 18:17, 25, 27). There is here a clear criticism of the pro-circumcision tendency within the Pauline table-fellowship of whom Saint Peter is the key representative. Peter's action of drawing near the man-made fire tended by the 'slaves' and 'officers' rather than accompanying his Lord to the trial, is a literary mirror of his political closeness to the Judaising faction within the table-fellowship. It was for this closeness that Saint Paul openly rebuked Peter *by his Aramaic name Kêf* in Galatians 2:11-14.

The teaching, abandoned on all sides

Yet the main 'action' of the scene is taking place inside the High Priest's house where Jesus is being interrogated by Annas and his son-in-law. Here is where the question of γνῶσις is being put to the test. Annas is interrogating Jesus precisely about his διδαχῆς—his 'didacticism', his 'teaching'. The purpose of this interrogation is clear. The High Priest and his father-in-law are attempting to make, or fabricate, a case against Jesus that He has betrayed the *Torah*, or that he has somehow falsified it or introduced occultic teachings from the Greek philosophical schools or mystery cults. Yet Jesus's response to them is a *flat renunciation* of any such secret teaching.

> ἐγὼ παρρησίᾳ λελάληκα τῷ κόσμῳ ἐγὼ πάντοτε ἐδίδαξα ἐν συναγωγῇ καὶ ἐν τῷ ἱερῷ ὅπου πάντες οἱ Ἰουδαῖοι συνέρχονται καὶ ἐν κρυπτῷ ἐλάλησα οὐδέν τί με ἐρωτᾷς ἐρώτησον τοὺς ἀκηκοότας τί ἐλάλησα αὐτοῖς ἴδε οὗτοι οἴδασιν ἃ εἶπον ἐγώ

> '*I have spoken openly to the world; I have always taught in synagogues and in the temple, where all Jews come together; I have said nothing secretly. Why do you ask me? Ask those who have heard me, what I said to them; they know what I said.*' (John 18:20-21)

Double judgement in the High Priest's house

Jesus makes a threefold affirmation of the *Torah* here! The teaching Jesus taught was *out in the open*, in the public places where Jews gather for worship and for the reading of the Text.

Jesus is, literally, *inside the gate*. Semiotically this is an important fact: He is in the place where the most occult secrets are revealed to initiates. He is being subject to interrogation. The innermost of His doctrines are being (as we say these days) 'unpacked', questioned and scrutinised. Yet He defends His teaching before the High Priest by appealing to His *public* works and words, where Jews gather for prayer and study. In these two verses Jesus *disowns* the Gnostics by speaking up that He has taught *Torah*, the whole *Torah* and nothing but *Torah*—so help Him Dad!

Yet the response to this by Annas—quite possibly a self-critical reflection of John himself, on account of the links between the names—is to have Jesus struck on the face for His appeal to the audience. Jesus appeals to the *Torah*, and to His accordance with it in all His public preaching. However, in answer, Annas appeals to the temporal power and authority of the priesthood. The officer who strikes Jesus says: οὕτως ἀποκρίνῃ τῷ ἀρχιερεῖ '*Is that how you answer the High Priest?*' (John 18:22)

Jesus is the one being questioned in the High Priest's house, but in actuality it's the contemporary doctrines of the Judaisers and the Gnostics that are on trial! The teaching of the Pauline community, for which Jesus is the literary stand-in, was one in which the teaching of the *Torah*, particularly in its aspects of debt-forgiveness and the renunciation of Caesar's godhood, was made public and open to all people—not only to those claiming blood descent from Jacob. Yet this teaching stands rejected, both by those who claim an occultic interpretation of Jesus's sayings, and by those who claimed an authority parallel to the followers of Hillel the Elder in adjudicating the boundaries of the table-fellowship.

Remember that these *literary characters*, even if they correspond to actual historical figures, are nonetheless πρόσωπα, theatrical masques! The fact that Annas's name is a dithematic inversion of John's, along with the fact that John confesses himself to be 'known to the High Priest' (and who knows the High Priest better than his father-in-law?), shows us that we are dealing with a kind of indirect, literary self-accusation and confession. If Saint John had indeed been close to the Ebionites, this may well be his way of fessing up to, and making amends for, his own betrayal of the teaching.

The double judgement

Peter's behaviour in the courtyard of the High Priest's house contrasts comically with his attack on Malchos earlier in the chapter. His earlier bravado which resulted in the loss of an ear, is now completely gone. When under pressure from the maid, from the servants around the fire and from Malchos's kinsman, Peter buckles. He denies Christ three times. He is evidently afraid of the consequences if he follows Jesus into the house.

Saint Peter often gets hit with the literary 'stupid stick' in the Gospels. That is on account of his highly-public spat with Saint Paul over the treatment of Gentiles in the table

Double judgement in the High Priest's house

fellowship. But Saint John is making an important point here when showing Jesus under trial. This is turning point of the Gospel. This is where everything comes to a head, where it is tried. Jesus's teaching is shown, under investigation, to be nothing more and nothing less than the *Torah*. The *Torah* is the didactic teaching delivered to all nations, through the human sins demonstrated in the stories of the literary Hebrew people. That is why it doesn't matter whether Annas or Caiaphas are literal historical people, or literary masques of John and Peter respectively. The teaching is anti-historical and anti-philosophical. Jesus is slapped in the face and accused of talking back to the High Priest, by someone who is trying to secure a position of the High Priest *in history*, that is, history as written by the Romans.

That's the whole point. The Judaisers were trying to take the Law and the Prophets and make these *instructional* texts into a *history* of their people. They were trying to make themselves the protagonists. That was the entire project of Flavius Josephus.

Of course a teacher of *Torah*, particularly that about redeeming the land and delivering the people from their debts, would incur the hostility of such a historicising sect. The High Priest and his father-in-law are cross-examining Jesus, precisely because the *Torah* does not justify the historicist claims of their particular nation.

But once the Judaisers' cross-examination is finished, what is shown to them is that Jesus has no secret γνῶσις. He has discovered no hidden truth. There is no occult doctrine. The inner chamber is empty… except for the scroll that He read from in Luke 4. '*Why do you ask me?*' He says. '*Ask those who have heard me.*'

The Teacher is teaching the same syllabus that was set out three hundred years earlier, even helpfully translated in Septuagint Greek. The syllabus was never hidden from the class; it's just that the class *doesn't want to read it*. Ask any teacher nowadays! The wealthy don't want to be told that their riches were wrung sinfully from the backs of the poor. The officers don't want to be told that the Caesar who pays their bills is a shmuck. The 'chosen people' don't want to be told that they failed to keep up their end of each and every one of the covenants that their own God made with them. The nations don't want to be told that their 'values' are vanity, that their 'freedom' is in fact slavery, and that the stories they tell about their 'civilisation' are self-serving lies that cover up the brutalisation of their Indigenous neighbours.

But rather than deal with the *Torah* teaching, those same students invent secret teachings for themselves. They don't want to listen to the Teacher's lectures. They would rather live in an abstracted realm of pure ideation, a fantasy-world. In that fantasy-world, they can make themselves out to be their own private gods, and they can justify themselves any way they like. To slightly misquote Kyle Reese: 'That's what Hellenism does. That's all Hellenism does.'[123]

---

[123] James Cameron, *The Terminator* (Orion Pictures, 1984).

Double judgement in the High Priest's house

The teaching, alone

The interrogation of Jesus Christ before Annas shows, in this Gospel as well as in the 'synoptic' ones, how utterly alone Jesus is. Jesus is the Lamb of God—His singularity and aloneness are as significant as His silence. I noted in my previous book that the lone sheep in the *Torah* is usually considered as bound for sacrifice or for destruction in the wilderness[124]. Here again we see Jesus, alone, without a word to say in His own defence except for the words He has already said.

In J.R.R. Tolkien's book, Elrond of Rivendell tells Frodo Baggins that 'this task is appointed for you... if you do not find a way, no one will'[125]. Jesus, I hasten to add, is not Frodo. *Ta Vivlía* contain no 'hero's journey', unlike Tolkien's books. But the burden of teaching them is very much like the burden of bearing a ring of power. Once you have that burden, you can't put it aside. Or rather, you can choose to put it aside, but once you do, it will be *'a burning fire shut up in [your] bones'* (Jer 20:9). And to actually teach *ta Vivlía* (as opposed to abusing *ta Vivlía*, as is so commonly done here, as a prop for nationalism or democratism or 'Judaeo-Christianism' or the curation and marketing of a church 'brand') is a very lonely thing... if you're doing it properly.

---

[124] Cooper, *Lamb*, 58-9, 69.
[125] J.R.R. Tolkien, *The Fellowship of the Ring* (Ballantine Books, 1973), 354.

In the Houses of the Poor

Frodo exclaims to Gandalf that 'I wish it need not have happened in my time,' to which Gandalf replies: 'So do I, and so do all who live to see such times. But that is not for them to decide. All we have to decide is what to do with the time that is given us.' [126] And surely Tolkien, being a nice Catholic schoolboy, was well aware that he was placing upon Gandalf's tongue the language of another wanderer, Paul: *'Make the most of the time, for the days are evil'* (Eph 5:16).

As Michael Hudson aptly points out, Isaiah, and later Ezekiel and Jeremiah, were children of privilege. They were (at least initially) all wealthy men, and they all served as advisors to the Hebrew kings[127]. Yet each one of them was driven to speak out on behalf of the land, on behalf of foreigners, on behalf of those who were in debt, or on behalf of those who were in positions of social and legal vulnerability. In short, they were driven to teach the law of 'Elōhîm. And all of them suffered for it. Isaiah knew full well that his message would be rejected (Isa 6:9-13). Jeremiah also speaks with the understanding that his people will not listen (Jer 7:27-29). And God warns Ezekiel up front that his rebellious house will refuse to hear him (Eze 2:4-8).

Jesus, Who is both the Lamb of God and the Able Herdsman, is placed in much the same position that they were. Like them, He is utterly alone. Like the *Nəbî'* Ezekiel, He is given only God's words to speak. He Himself is mute. That's the reason He offers no defence of His own.

---

[126] *Ibid.*, 82.
[127] Hudson, *Forgive*, 184.

Double judgement in the High Priest's house

Those who build an identity around a tribe or a bloodline or a priestly caste, will make the choice to slap Jesus in the face for 'talking back' to us. But to those who would clothe themselves in allegorical abstractions and esotericism, Jesus offers no comfort either. This is the pattern of the rediscovery of the teaching: when men go seeking power and secrets, what they find is only the scroll. In the *Kətubîm*, when Ḥilqiyâ the *Kohen* כהן goes into the destroyed and deserted inner chamber of Solomon's Temple and finds the scroll of the *Torah* in the ruins, and King Josiah hears about it, he tears his clothes in fear of the Lord's wrath (2 Kgs 22:8-13)! The inner chamber is empty. There is no secret knowledge. There is no hereditary privilege. There is only the scroll, waiting to be heard afresh.

Here again, John's text offers us a binary choice. We can build an identity—whether that identity is around blood and soil and kinship and flags, or around a set of ideas. Or we can follow the voice of the Able Herdsman. The witnesses of Christ are those who hear the voice of the mute Lamb: the unvoiced consonantal text of *Torah*.

Christ's kingly claim over Pilate

A clarification on John 18:33-40

Why *all* Americans get 'render unto Caesar' wrong

One fascinating feature of Saint John's Gospel is the fact that the term ἀλήθεια 'truth, verity, candour', which is the negation (ἄ-) of the verb λανθάνω 'to be hidden, to be unaware'[128]. This term appears more often in Saint John's Gospel than in any of the other three. Therefore, when one of the characters in that Gospel, even though it is Pilate, asks us τί ἐστιν ἀλήθεια, 'What is truth?' it is worth exploring precisely that question. But we should do so *analytically* and *literarily*, by appealing *to the text*, and not by contriving imaginary castles of our own words in the Aristophanean clouds.

First, it's worth taking note of the fact that the other three Gospel authors, Matthew and Mark and Luke, tend to drench this term in **literary irony.** One 'synoptic' passage or pericope that appears in all three of the other Gospels occurs in the twenty-second chapter of Matthew's, the twelfth of Mark's, and the twentieth of Luke's. It is not without significance that the term ἀλήθεια occurs particularly with regard to the question of *tribute to Caesar*. Because it concerns Caesar, this pericope pertains to the present discussion of John 18, in which Jesus is

---

[128] The **lanthanide** series of 'rare-earth' metals were so named by Swiss chemist V. M. Goldschmidt in 1925, precisely because they tended to 'hide' themselves among other minerals. – *Auth.*

Christ's kingly claim over Pilate

hauled before Caesar's representative in Judaea, Pontius Pilate. I shall pay due honour to my saintly patron here and use Matthew as the example:

> τότε πορευθέντες οἱ Φαρισαῖοι συμβούλιον ἔλαβον ὅπως αὐτὸν παγιδεύσωσιν ἐν λόγῳ καὶ ἀποστέλλουσιν αὐτῷ τοὺς μαθητὰς αὐτῶν μετὰ τῶν Ἡρῳδιανῶν λέγοντες διδάσκαλε οἴδαμεν ὅτι **ἀληθὴς** εἶ καὶ τὴν ὁδὸν τοῦ θεοῦ ἐν **ἀληθείᾳ** διδάσκεις καὶ οὐ μέλει σοι περὶ οὐδενός οὐ γὰρ βλέπεις εἰς πρόσωπον ἀνθρώπων εἰπὲ οὖν ἡμῖν τί σοι δοκεῖ ἔξεστιν δοῦναι κῆνσον Καίσαρι ἢ οὔ
>
> *Then the Pharisees went and took counsel how to entangle him in his talk. And they sent their disciples to him, along with the Herodians, saying, 'Teacher, we know that you are **true**, and teach the way of God **truthfully**, and care for no man; for you do not regard the position of men. Tell us, then, what you think. Is it lawful to pay taxes to Caesar, or not?'* (Matt 22:15-17)

Note that the use of the term 'truth' in the mouths of the Pharisees is anything but sincere! They are specifically trying to catch Christ in an *elenchus*, to refute Christ by ensnaring Him in a dilemma. If Jesus answered that Caesar had a right to collect taxes on the people of Judaea, He could thereupon be attacked in the synagogues as a hypocrite, having earlier proclaimed a general release from debts. On the other hand, if He answered that Caesar had no such right, His saying would be related to the Roman governors, and He could be arrested as an insurrectionist, an enemy of the Roman state.

Jesus's answer to this inveigling question is famous, but its importance is often abused or misinterpreted for political purposes. He first demands that one of His questioners show

Him the money to be paid in tax. He then asks that the inscription and bust on the coin be identified, and so it is: as Caesar's. And thereupon He says: ἀπόδοτε οὖν τὰ Καίσαρος Καίσαρι καὶ τὰ τοῦ θεοῦ τῷ θεῷ *'Render therefore to Caesar the things that are Caesar's, and to God the things that are God's.'* (Matt 22:21)

Christians of different political orientations have different motivated readings of Jesus's answer to this question. Theological progressives, welfare liberals and social democrats, following the lead of social-Gospel preacher Walter Rauschenbusch[129], tend to interpret this saying in light of a set of assumptions about the necessary redistributive role of government[130]. Civil libertarians, following the lead of Baptist theologian and colonial founder of Providence Plantations Roger Williams[131], tend to see in this saying of Jesus an early expression of the principle of the separation of religion and state[132]. And conservative American evangelicals, tending to follow Cauvin's *Institutes*[133], focus on the 'image and inscription'

---

[129] Walter Rauschenbusch, *Christianity and the Social Crisis* (Macmillan, 1907), 182-189.

[130] Benjamin Cremer, 'Render Unto Caesar', 16 June 2024. https://benjamin-cremer.kit.com/posts/render-unto-caesar.

[131] Roger Williams, *The Bloody Tenent Yet More Bloody* (Calvert, 1652), 43, 119-122, 264.

[132] David Parsons, 'Render Unto Caesar', 11 June 2020. https://www.icej.org/blog/render-unto-caesar/.

[133] Jehan Cauvin, *The Institutes of the Christian Religion*, tr. Henry Beveridge (Calvin Translation Society, 1845), III. xix. 15.

Christ's kingly claim over Pilate

part and interpret it as an admonition to follow the law while at the same time eschewing the idolatry of Caesar[134]. All of these interpretations fall to various degrees short of the mark.

The state in Jesus's time did not have a redistributive function. The Senate in Rome, not being particularly well-known for its selfless philanthropy, had no mandate to redistribute wealth to the plebeian masses. Again, Michael Hudson's work on economic history is valuable here. The Roman state did not have a far-sighted palace-temple complex such as the Bronze Age West Asian polities had[135]. Its primary goals were expansionistic and extractive: they used their military power to seize more lands and subject-peoples, and further enrich the well-connected patrician class using the resulting war indemnities and tax receipts[136].

Likewise, the question of the separation of church and state simply wasn't relevant to the context. The temples to various deities, including Herod's Temple in Jesus's time, were not sanctuaries detached from state power, they were its instruments. Herod was a Roman client-king; how could his temple have been anything else? Jesus's answer cannot be

---

[134] R. C. Sproul, 'Render Unto Caesar', Ligonier Ministries, 20 December 2015. https://learn.ligonier.org/sermons/render-unto-caesar.

[135] Likewise, theological progressives in Western capitalist 'democracies' grievously overestimate their own governments' will to meaningfully redistribute wealth downward. – *Auth.*

[136] Hudson, *Collapse*, 13-14.

reduced to Cauvin's 'two kingdoms' doctrine (rooted in Augustine's *City of God*), nor to a proto-Jeffersonian 'wall of separation'. Such lenses presume a post-Theodosian *modus vivendi* between state and church, alien to the Pauline community's first- and second-century context of official Roman persecution!

A lexicographical approach clarifies Jesus's intent. The Greek verb ἀποδίδωμι 'to repay, to require, to restore, to make recompense' appears in this passage of Matthew (and the corresponding ones of Mark and Luke), clearly denotes economic restitution. Jesus avoids the 'trap' set by His Herodian and Pharisaical interlocutors by reframing the entire question: 'Who *owes* Caesar?'

Because the tax was payable to the Romans in coinage of Roman mint, the *question* of tax could *only* pertain to those who trafficked in Caesar's coinage. Those who owed a debt to Caesar couldn't be the labourers, tenants and slaves held in debt-bondage! (They paid 'in kind'.) By bringing Him the coin, though, the Herodians and Temple authorities are indicting themselves with the receipts of their own betrayal of the Law. They're the ones who traffic in the idolatrous *bullae* while neglecting God's command (Deut 15:1-2) to cancel debts!

On the other hand, the Septuagint text of Ezekiel uses the same term ἀποδίδωμι to clarify what is owed to God:

ὁ δὲ ἄνθρωπος ὃς ἔσται δίκαιος ὁ ποιῶν κρίμα καὶ δικαιοσύνην ἐπὶ τῶν ὀρέων οὐ φάγεται καὶ τοὺς ὀφθαλμοὺς αὐτοῦ οὐ μὴ ἐπάρῃ πρὸς τὰ ἐνθυμήματα οἴκου Ισραηλ καὶ τὴν γυναῖκα τοῦ πλησίον αὐτοῦ οὐ μὴ μιάνῃ καὶ πρὸς γυναῖκα ἐν ἀφέδρῳ οὖσαν οὐ προσεγγιεῖ καὶ ἄνθρωπον οὐ μὴ καταδυναστεύσῃ

Christ's kingly claim over Pilate

ἐνεχυρασμὸν ὀφείλοντος **ἀποδώσει** καὶ ἅρπαγμα οὐχ ἁρπᾶται τὸν ἄρτον αὐτοῦ τῷ πεινῶντι δώσει καὶ γυμνὸν περιβαλεῖ καὶ τὸ ἀργύριον αὐτοῦ ἐπὶ τόκῳ οὐ δώσει καὶ πλεονασμὸν οὐ λήμψεται καὶ ἐξ ἀδικίας ἀποστρέψει τὴν χεῖρα αὐτοῦ κρίμα δίκαιον ποιήσει ἀνὰ μέσον ἀνδρὸς καὶ ἀνὰ μέσον τοῦ πλησίον αὐτοῦ καὶ τοῖς προστάγμασίν μου πεπόρευται καὶ τὰ δικαιώματά μου πεφύλακται τοῦ ποιῆσαι αὐτά δίκαιος οὗτός ἐστιν ζωῇ ζήσεται λέγει κύριος

*If a man is righteous and does what is lawful and right—if he does not eat upon the mountains or lift up his eyes to the idols of the house of Israel, does not defile his neighbor's wife or approach a woman in her time of impurity, does not oppress any one, but **restores** to the debtor his pledge, commits no robbery, gives his bread to the hungry and covers the naked with a garment, does not lend at interest or take any increase, withholds his hand from iniquity, executes true justice between man and man, walks in my statutes, and is careful to observe my ordinances—he is righteous, he shall surely live, says the Lord God. (Eze 18:5-9)*

Jesus's audience knew this text. His command to 'render to God' was not setting out a proper function or scope of government *vis a vis* the Temple. God strikes no such bargains with pretenders and rival claimants. There is only *one Lord*—and Caesar ain't it! Caesar's little pocket-idols may let him play mafia don, but the earth and everything in it still belong to the real Boss, the real Big Cheese: 'Elōhîm. And 'Elōhîm's 'piece of the action', His 'cut', is that we release those in our debt and restore their collateral to them (Matt 18:21-35). Not that we'll ever be off the hook, but that's the only way we can hope to appeal to His mercy.

In the Houses of the Poor

They live in the vanity of their minds

This use of ἀλήθεια is also Pauline, and in this context it is aimed precisely against its own Hellenistic derivation! The most prominent repeated use of it is found in Ephesians 4:

ἐστιν **ἀλήθεια** ἐν τῷ Ἰησοῦ ἀποθέσθαι ὑμᾶς κατὰ τὴν προτέραν ἀναστροφὴν τὸν παλαιὸν ἄνθρωπον τὸν φθειρόμενον κατὰ τὰς ἐπιθυμίας τῆς ἀπάτης ἀνανεοῦσθαι δὲ τῷ πνεύματι τοῦ νοὸς ὑμῶν καὶ ἐνδύσασθαι τὸν καινὸν ἄνθρωπον τὸν κατὰ θεὸν κτισθέντα ἐν δικαιοσύνῃ καὶ ὁσιότητι τῆς **ἀληθείας** διὸ ἀποθέμενοι τὸ ψεῦδος λαλεῖτε **ἀλήθειαν** ἕκαστος μετὰ τοῦ πλησίον αὐτοῦ ὅτι ἐσμὲν ἀλλήλων μέλη

*The **truth** is in Jesus. Put off your old nature which belongs to your former manner of life and is corrupt through deceitful lusts, and be renewed in the spirit of your minds, and put on the new nature, created after the likeness of God in **true** righteousness and holiness. Therefore, putting away falsehood, let every one speak the **truth** with his neighbor, for we are members one of another. (Eph 4:21-25)*

The old, corrupt *'former manner of life'* is precisely ἐν ματαιότητι τοῦ νοὸς αὐτῶν *'in the futility of their minds'* (Eph 4:17); ἀλήθεια 'truth' is therefore contrasted with ματαιότης 'vanity'. This opposition is mirrored in another pair of opposites in the same verse: διανοίᾳ 'knowledge' and ἄγνοια 'ignorance'. This language which Paul is using here, may be referenced back to the deuterocanonical Wisdom of Solomon:

μάταιοι μὲν γὰρ πάντες ἄνθρωποι φύσει οἷς παρῆν θεοῦ **ἀγνωσία** καὶ ἐκ τῶν ὁρωμένων ἀγαθῶν οὐκ ἴσχυσαν εἰδέναι

Christ's kingly claim over Pilate

τὸν ὄντα οὔτε τοῖς ἔργοις προσέχοντες ἐπέγνωσαν τὸν τεχνίτην

*Surely **vain** are all men by nature, who are **ignorant** of God, and could not out of the good things that are seen know him that is: neither by considering the works did they acknowledge the workmaster.* (Wis 13:1, BES)

While the Wisdom of Solomon makes 'vanity' the property of the ἄνθρωποι 'human beings', it ascribes its opposite, 'truth', to the Lord, to be given out to those who trust Him: οἱ πεποιθότες ἐπ' αὐτῷ συνήσουσιν **ἀλήθειαν** '*They that put their trust in him shall understand **the truth***' (Wis 3:9). And in like fashion, διανοίᾳ 'understanding' is withheld from λαοὶ 'the people' that the seemingly-untimely death of God's prophets is to them no injury (Wis 4:14-15).

The Wisdom of Solomon is a key text for understanding Paul's critique of the Gentiles in Ephesians, precisely because it borrows Platonic and Middle Platonic terms of art in order to subvert and negate them. Both ἀλήθειαν 'truth' and νόημα 'mental object' are technical terms which occur in the *Parmenides* dialogue of Plato[137] between the eponymous thinker, Zeno and Socrates—yet such mental constructs are likened in the Wisdom of Solomon to the idols fashioned by human hands. Their opposites, 'vanity' and 'ignorance', are applied liberally to such constructs.

---

[137] Plato, *Parmenides*, 128B, 131B.

In the Houses of the Poor

The Wisdom of Solomon's polemic against Gentile 'vanity' (13:1) and 'artifice' (14:17) set the stage for Paul's inveighment against *'life in the futility of the mind'* in Ephesians 4:17. This *genre* of polemic, never directly or explicitly aimed against any particular Hellenistic philosopher, nevertheless allows Paul to circumvent the entire construct of Hellenistic dialectic by relocating ἀλήθεια ἐν τῷ Ἰησοῦ 'the truth in Christ' (Eph 4:21).

This is the lexical trajectory along which we should approach the trial, in John 18, of Jesus at the hands of Pontius Pilate: the Roman magistrate who gives voice to his era's 'take' on Sceptic and Stoic thought.

Davidic Messiah, or Gracchian tribune?

There is a brief, blackly-comedic interlude in which Jesus's Judahite custodians dither on the threshold of the governor's residence (πραιτώριον). The bleak farce of the scene derives from the fact that His captors, though they had no qualms about making a night raid across the *Wādī al-Jūz* to apprehend Jesus by stealth, and though they had no qualms about using physical violence against Him in the home of the High Priest, now suddenly don't want to cross the threshold of the governor for it would μιανθῶσιν 'defile them' (presumably on account of the idolatrous symbols of Pilate's vestiture), even though they need the governor to issue the death sentence they are pursuing. Saint John mocks their sudden squeamish punctility on cleanliness codes (John 18:28) and the fine points of Roman legal jurisdiction (18:31).

Christ's kingly claim over Pilate

The very first interrogation that Pilate makes of Jesus is whether or not He is a βασιλεὺς 'king'. This question serves a double literary purpose. The first purpose is to relate and contrast Jesus to the *məlākîm* מלכים of the Hebrew *Kətubîm*. In contrast to Saint Matthew's and Saint Luke's Gospels, Saint John lays *zero* stress on Jesus's Davidic lineage. Indeed, he even shows Jesus as *fleeing* kingship (John 6:15). And even the 'kingly' imagery of Jesus's (second, in John) entry into Jerusalem serves less to emphasise Jesus's role as king than the distinction between true and false prophecy, given Judas's earlier dispute with Jesus over the costly fragrant oil.

But the juxtaposition of Jesus's entry into Jerusalem with the raising of Lazarus seems to show the manner and nature of Jesus's kinghood quite clearly. John takes great pains in his twelfth chapter to stress that ἐμαρτύρει οὖν ὁ ὄχλος ὁ ὢν μετ' αὐτοῦ ὅτε τὸν Λάζαρον ἐφώνησεν ἐκ τοῦ μνημείου καὶ ἤγειρεν αὐτὸν ἐκ νεκρῶν '*the crowd that had been with him when he called Lazarus out of the tomb and raised him from the dead bore witness*' (John 12:17). Saint John portrays the kingship of Jesus as **tribunal**. He rides into Jerusalem exactly after, and because, he takes up the cause of the two bereaved sisters in 'the poorhouse' (*Beit 'Ānīâ* בית עניה), when they are threatened with eviction.

And this is the second literary purpose of Pilate's question. Such a spectacular rise to prominence, after a populistic miracle raising two poor women's dead brother and thus saving their tenancy! To a Roman ear, this would very much evoke the political career of Tiberius Gracchus, a century and a half prior: ἀλλ' ἄοικοι καὶ ἀνίδρυτοι μετὰ τέκνων πλανῶνται

In the Houses of the Poor

καὶ γυναικῶν '*houseless and homeless they wander about with their wives and children*'[138]. Gracchus was accused in the Roman Senate of *appetere regnum* 'pursuing kingship': the charge on which proceeded the Senatorial riot that killed him. It is just such a Gracchus that Pilate wants to know if the Judahites have delivered to him.

The confrontation between Jesus and Pilate appears in each of the Gospels (Matt 27:11-14, Mark 15:1-5, Luke 23:1-7). Yet the other three, 'synoptically', have Jesus making no reply to Pilate other than σὺ λέγεις 'you say so' or some variant thereof. And in John, too, He says it, but instead He frames it as a question: ἀπὸ σεαυτοῦ **σὺ τοῦτο λέγεις** ἢ ἄλλοι εἶπόν σοι περὶ ἐμοῦ '*Do **you say this** of yourself, or do others say it to you about me?*' (John 18:34)

We make a mistake if we make this question about us, twenty-first century Americans. When He asks whether Pilate is speaking for himself or what others told him, Jesus is asking precisely whether He is being put on trial for the **Roman** charge of *appetere regnum*, or for the **Judahite** charge of blasphemy.

---

[138] Plutarch, *Lives*, tr. Bernadette Perrin (William Heinemann, 1921), 9.5.

Christ's kingly claim over Pilate

The vanity of the second kingdom

Lanthanide metals. The question of the denarius. Deuterocanonical wisdom against *Parmenides*. Jesus as a West Asian Tiberius Gracchus. I can hear you asking me already: 'So what? *Get to the point*, Matt!'

Although Pilate is the one being challenged in literary terms, Saint John's purpose is to challenge *his audience* with the question of Jesus Christ's kingship. Is Jesus a 'rival claimant' to Caesar? Is He an insurrectionist? Is He trying to revive the fallen Hasmonean kingdom? In His appearance before Annas, it was the exclusive claims of the pro-circumciser clique and the pretensions to secret knowledge of the Hellenisers that were on trial. Here, it is contemporary configurations of *political power* and its nature that are on trial.

This is why Jesus expands His answer to Pilate in Saint John's Gospel. Jesus does not avoid the question of kingship put to Him by Pilate, but instead turns the question back on His accuser. Then it becomes Pilate's turn to evade: '*Am I a Judahite?*' (John 18:35)

Here is where we need to thread a very careful needle, because it becomes very easy to make a mistake. *Every* American who passes comment on Caesar's bust and inscription on the denarius, from Roger Williams and Thomas Jefferson down to R.C. Sproul and Benjamin Cremer, gets it grossly wrong. They all want to recognise *two Caesars*: a Caesar who gets to rule here and now in this world, and, in Jesus Christ, a Caesar who gets to rule sometime, in the sweet by-and-by. Maybe. If we let Him. All American Christians—

progressive or conservative, nationalist or libertarian—who seek to carve out a separate sphere for *their* Caesar, *their* Obama, *their* Trump, ultimately want to serve two masters (Matt 6:24).

Scripture has a term for this. It's *zānâ* זנה: harlotry.

And when Jesus answers Pilate that His kingdom is '*not of this world*', we English-speakers tend to suspect, or fancy, that He is making just such a secularist distinction. *Our* Caesar, *our* Queen Victoria, gets to rule this world however she pleases. Jesus gets to rule somewhere (or sometime) else. Yet we need to *hear* the term κόσμος as it was meant by Saint Paul and his school.

In the Septuagint text, it is actually very rare for the term κόσμος to refer to 'the final frontier'. Bill Shatner, with all due respect, is not a Greek! More often, κόσμος was used to translate '*adî* עדי 'jewellery, ornaments', whether literal anklets, headbands, rings and so on (Exo 33:5-6; Isa 3:19-26; Jer 2:32, 4:30; Eze 7:20, 16:11, 23:40), or figuratively to refer to the Sun, the Moon and the stars, the 'ornaments' of the heavens which the children of Israel were commanded not to worship (Deut 4:19, 17:3; Isa 13:10)! In an even more abstract sense, it was used to refer to the *tifā'râ* תפארה of a dignified man—his 'headpiece, crown, splendour' (Prov 17:6, 20:29).

Saint Paul's highly-technical use of the word κόσμος '*the world*', in his letters to the churches and particularly his first to that in Corinth, is rooted precisely in this Semitic sense of 'adornment, ornamentation, jewellery'—the sort of 'shiny' which is valued by kings and by which they express their favour or their own resplendence. '*The world*' is, in Saint Paul's writings, very often a stand-in for greed after material wealth

Christ's kingly claim over Pilate

and *libido dominandi* (*e.g.* 1 Cor 5:10). And he inverts the logic of '*the world*' by saying that God chooses out of it as *His* adornment, that which men despise (1 Cor 1:27-28)!

Another aspect (pun intended, as usual) of this discourse is political: all West Asian kings, all kings of the Mediterranean in fact, appealed to some 'cosmic' or astrological justification for their rule—hence the ban in Deuteronomy on the Hebrews worshipping the sun, moon and stars in place of their Creator. In like manner, Roman emperors often declared themselves (as in the *divi filius* inscription on the denarius) to be the avatars of astral deities walking on earth[139].

So Jesus, in response to Pilate's question, disavows the *tifā'râ* תפארה 'splendour' of kingship, and also the ὑπηρέται 'officers' with whose aid a king would command armies in a military struggle for power, and also the 'astral' mandate from the celestial deities. But He is not ceding any ground to Caesar. He claims kingship not for Himself but for God. Likewise, when He says His kingdom οὐκ ἔστιν ἐντεῦθεν '*is not from here*' (John 18:36), He isn't claiming God's kingship in some other 'verse, but in *this one*. His claims draw their weight, not from the stars or from Caesar's shiny hat, but from a higher authority: One Who reigns over כל העמים תחת כל־השמים '*all the peoples under the whole heaven*' (Deut 4:19).

---

[139] Shannon Grimes, 'Under a Star-Spangled Banner: Politics and Astral Religion in the Roman Empire', in *Heavenly Discourses*, ed. Nicholas Campion (Sophia Centre Press, 2016).

In the Houses of the Poor

Just as with the question of the denarius, nearly *every* modern-day American religious thinker fails the test of this *mašal*... with the noteworthy and honourable exception of Michael Hudson. There are three reasons for this. First: we have been steeped in dualistic philosophical *a prioris* which separate a 'realm of the mind' from the 'realm of stuff'. (This separation is precisely what the Wisdom of Solomon attacks.) Second: we have been too long accustomed to Christians wielding political power in a pro-creditor way that apes the pre-Christian Caesars. And third: we have a *mythos* of *bourgeois* rebellion that interprets Jesus as Paul Revere or Davy Crockett. As a result, our readings of Pilate's interrogation of Jesus tend to adopt Pilate's politics, even (and especially!) when we think they don't.

The Jesus of Saint John's Gospel subverts all expectations. He subverts His own role in the 'synoptic' Gospels, as His Davidic lineage is deliberately downplayed. Greater focus is placed on His resurrection miracle in the 'poor-house', giving His political mandate a populist, Gracchian flavour. Yet when Pilate questions Him, Jesus disavows any military plans against Rome... but also appeals to a higher authority than the stars. His kingship is ἐλήλυθα εἰς τὸν κόσμον ἵνα μαρτυρήσω τῇ ἀληθείᾳ *'coming into the world, to bear witness to the truth'* (John 18:37). And then, of course, comes Pilate's famous question: τί ἐστιν ἀλήθεια *'What is truth?'* (18:38)

The purpose of such philosophical questions—the banter of Parmenides and Zeno and Socrates—is always, *always*, to justify the *human* reference-point against the divine. We want to know where *we* get to draw the line of church-state separation. What

Christ's kingly claim over Pilate

percentage do *we* get to take? That's ματαιότης. That's *vanity*. It's the vanity of those who hand off Jesus to Pilate without crossing Pilate's threshold, so they can get to play at being pious while still wielding state power in their own interest.

Pilate suspects that he's got the Big Boss in front of him, so he can assert Rome's dominance over Jesus's *appetere regnum*. But Jesus isn't plea-bargaining with Pilate. Instead, He is issuing a warning to Caesar that God, the real Big Boss, is coming for the whole ball of wax. And Saint John himself drives the final nail into any sort of 'two kingdoms'-style accommodation with Caesar. He does this in his Apocalypse:

ἡ βασιλεία τοῦ κόσμου τοῦ κυρίου ἡμῶν **καὶ τοῦ** Χριστοῦ **αὐτοῦ** καὶ βασιλεύσει εἰς τοὺς αἰῶνας τῶν αἰώνων

*The kingdom of the world has become the kingdom of our Lord **and of his** Christ, and he shall reign for ever and ever.* (Apoc 11:15)

They made long their furrows

A clarification on John 19:9-15

When a Roman asks you where you're from...

One observation from my previous book that I made regarding Jesus's appearance at the Feast of Booths (John 7:14-53), was that the people there trying to 'grasp' Him (either physically to arrest Him, or to comprehend Him with their minds) were asking all the wrong questions. Some of them were asking, 'where is He from?' and others were asking, 'where is He going?' These approaches map to the importance various factions within the Pauline community attached to Jesus's Davidic ancestry, or else to His ultimate goal, His aim, His, as it were, philosophical τέλος. Saint John's 'farcical' chase scene at the Feast of Booths, which ends futilely, suggests that they are all asking the wrong questions. Only Nicodemus, who had come to Jesus before with questions about origins only to be answered that 'the wind blows where it wills' (John 3:8), seems to approach the point: Jesus is only to be understood by His **deeds** (7:51)[140].

So here again, we see Pilate returning to Jesus. His question 'What is truth?' (John 18:38) is met with silence. He cannot hear Christ's ἀλήθεια 'truth' because, as Pilate pertains to Caesar, his heart is already full of ματαιότης 'vanity'. He returns to

---

[140] Cooper, *Lamb*, 175-178.

They made long their furrows

Jesus after scourging and mocking Him, and asks Him, πόθεν εἶ σύ *'Where are you from?'* (19:9)

This is a callback to the *irrelevant* question of Jesus's origins, both during Nicodemus's nightly visit (John 3:1-15) and the reprise at the Feast of Booths (John 7:25-29). But in both of these prior cases, it was the leaders of the Judahites who were asking Him this question. Now we have the same question being placed by Saint John's Gospel in the mouth of a Roman functionary of Caesar.

Note what has just happened. After Christ disavows the shiny κόσμος (that is to say, the *tifā'râ* תפארה 'splendour' of kingship, John 18:36), a στέφανον ἐξ ἀκανθῶν 'crown of thorns' is set on His head (19:2). These lexemes are linked through the LXX (Prov 17:6). Christ disavows the militant ὑπηρέται 'servants' who would fight on His behalf (18:36), but then He is brought before the ὑπηρέται of the Judahites and presented to them as their king (19:6). We can't hear this in English, because 'world' and 'crown' don't map to each other, and neither do 'servants' and 'officers'. But in the Greek, Saint John is taking the literary irony and *rubbing his hearers' faces in it*. The same things which Jesus disavows for Himself, are given to Him by the Roman authorities with the intention of mocking Him.

The 'Judahite question' of Jesus's origin, in the mouth of the Roman functionary, thus cements in the hearer's mind that the Romans are the ones now making the category error about Jesus's kingly claims. Pilate and his soldiers clearly believe they are upholding Roman legitimacy against a mortal threat in the shape of a king. This is why they scourge and mock this new Tiberius Gracchus that they think they have in their power. Yet the pageantry of Roman state cruelty serves an ironic function in the text. Pilate and his functionaries are the ones who have declared a king other than Caesar. They are destroying the man *they* have proclaimed as king.

Of course Jesus doesn't answer the 'Judahite question' from Pilate (John 19:9). How can He? Pilate won't hear. In mocking Him, they are heaping up mockery for their own Caesar. Pilate confronts Jesus Christ with the power of the Roman state, which is his claim to authority: οὐκ οἶδας ὅτι **ἐξουσίαν** ἔχω ἀπολῦσαί σε καὶ **ἐξουσίαν** ἔχω σταυρῶσαί σε '*Do you not know that I have **power** to release you, and **power** to crucify you?*' (John 19:10)

Last year, I wrote an exegetical commentary on Romans 13[141], which linked exactly the ἐξουσία 'authority' (Rom 13:1-2) found here, to the *šallîṭ* שליט 'mighty, power, ruler, governor' found in Ecclesiastes 8:2-9. This exegetical link was bolstered by the fact that both ἐξουσία 'authority' and ψυχή 'soul, breath' (Ecc 7:28) / πνεῦμα 'wind, breath' (Ecc 8:8) are juxtaposed with each other in both texts. The upshot of that piece was that Saint Paul was consoling and encouraging those *suffering from persecution*, to those coerced by the arbitrary will of a king who '*does whatever he pleases*' (Ecc 8:3). Both 'the Preacher' of the *Kətūb*, and Saint Paul, are offering the wisdom that no one lives forever: אין אדם **שליט** ברוח לכלוא את־הרוח '*no man has the **power** to retain his spirit*' (Ecc 8:8); that the rulers of this world will find

---

[141] Matthew Franklin Cooper, 'On being "subject to authority"', *Skeireins*, Substack post (19 Nov 2024).

They made long their furrows

themselves 'in the dock' at a higher Court; and that even those who seem to rule here will be answerable to the God Who allowed them to have power in the first place.

Saint John is taking that selfsame teaching from Ecclesiastes, making it explicit, and placing it in the mouth of Jesus Christ. He says: οὐκ εἶχες **ἐξουσίαν** κατ' ἐμοῦ οὐδεμίαν εἰ μὴ ἦν δεδομένον σοι ἄνωθεν '*You would have no **power** over me unless it had been given you from above*' (John 19:11). It is a word of comfort and strength to those who are facing down the business end of a Roman spear for the teaching.

It is worth acknowledging that this is precisely the sort of comfort to an afflicted and persecuted church that Saint John offers in his Apocalypse. The heavenly court that is shown in the fourth and fifth chapters of the Apocalypse features four ζῷα 'living creatures' (= *nefeš ḥayyâ* נפש חיה), a parody of the West Asian astral deities or predatory symbols of imperial glory, *prostrating* themselves before the One God (Apoc 4:6-9). Again, this image is offered as comfort and encouragement (Apoc 1:4-7) to people who were faced with public mockery, torture, exile and death as a result of their opposition to Caesar and their support for the debt-relief programme and jubilee politics which are shown in the Book of Acts.

The third place of judgement 'on the Pavement'

Note here that Jesus is being judged in three places. The first place is in the High Priest's house. The second place is at the threshold of Pilate's gubernatorial residence. We ought to pay close attention to the third place of judgement. Remember that

In the Houses of the Poor

for Saint John, numerology is particularly important. Peter denies Jesus three times (John 18:17, 25, 27); and later Jesus questions Peter about his love for Him a corresponding three times (John 21:25-27) before rendering against Peter an ominous judgement about his death. Such a threefold *'āwad* عاود or 'repetition' of a particular didactic point is the Scriptural signal for a *complete* judgement, an *irrevocable* or *final* judgement.

Thus, it behooves us to pay particular attention where such an *'āwad* appears. The final place of judgement where Pilate brings Jesus is called by two names in Saint John's Gospel. One of them is Greek and the other is Hebrew. The Greek name given is λιθόστρωτος: 'the Pavement'[142]. But the Hebrew name

---

[142] In his *Exposition of the Gospel of John* (Zondervan, 1968), English Calvinist author Arthur Walkington Pink commits a striking eisegetical error, one which reveals the danger of relying on translation artefacts rather than hearing the text in its original language:

The word for 'Pavement' is found nowhere else in the New Testament... but its Hebrew equivalent occurs just once in the Old Testament, and it is evident that the Holy Spirit would have us link the two passages together. In 2Ki 16:17 we read, 'King Ahaz cut off the borders of the bases, and removed the laver from off them; and took down the sea from off the brazen oxen that were under it, and put it upon a pavement of stones.' In Ahaz's case, his act was the conclusive token of his surrender to abject apostasy. So here of Pilate coming down to the level of the apostate Jews. In the former case it was a Jewish ruler dominated by a Gentile idolater; in

They made long their furrows

given is Γαββαθα. It is noteworthy that λιθόστρωτος does not gloss any Hebrew word with the consonants *g-b* ג-ב which the

---

> the latter, a Gentile idolater dominated by Jews who had rejected their Messiah! (Pink, *Exposition*, 1038.)

This interpretation collapses under the barest scrutiny. Let this passage stand as a *šənînâ* שנינה to the dangers of relying too heavily on the King James Bible, as neither the original Hebrew text nor the Greek LXX warrant connecting these disparate passages. The alleged linkage exists solely in the English translation. Pink's approach exemplifies how translation reliance can distort rather than illuminate Scripture.

The Greek word λιθόστρωτος is not used to translate 2 Kgs 16:17's *marṣfat 'abānîm* מרצפת אבנים 'a mosaic of stones, a place with stones fitted together'. The LXX of 2 Kgs 16:17 rather uses the term βάσιν λιθίνην: literally, a 'stone walkway'. The Greek λιθόστρωτος does link to the Semitic root *r-ṣ-f* ר-צ-ף 'mosaic, tessellating stonework', but neither here, nor exclusively.

The links are rather in the Second Paralipomenon: ויכרעו אפים **ארצה** על־**הרצפה** 'they bowed down with their faces to the earth on **the pavement**' (2 Par 7:3); in the book of Esther: מטות זהב וכסף על **רצפת** בהט־ושש ודר וסחרת 'couches of gold and silver on a mosaic **pavement** of porphyry, marble, mother-of-pearl and precious stones' (Esth 1:6); and in the Song of Solomon: תוכו **רצוף** אהבה מבנות ירושלם 'it was lovingly **wrought within** by the daughters of Jerusalem' (Song 3:10).

Saint John is pointing us to a decorative mosaic of semi-precious stones at this place: a design meant to accentuate, for the purpose of literary irony, the vice-regal prestige and judicial authority of Pilate. It doesn't have anything to do with the functional cobblestone walkway that Ahaz used to remove the Temple's decorative accoutrements. – Auth.

In the Houses of the Poor

name Γαββαθα might indicate; instead, it glosses Hebrew words with the triliteral root *r-ṣ-f* ר-צ-ף. This mismatch is therefore significant, and Saint John is clearly seeking to draw our attention to it.

The Hellenised Semitic name Γαββαθα (which becomes in Classical Syriac *Gəpîpta'* ܓܦܝܦܬܐ, *Pəšiṭta* John 19:13) points to a root which in Classical Syriac is represented as *g-p-'* ܓܦܐ 'back, shoulder, flank, wing'. And wouldn't you know it! Another prominent place where this triliteral root appears in the *Pəšiṭta* New Testament is in Saint John's Apocalypse!

ܘܐܪܒܥܬܝܗܘܢ ܚܝܘܬܐ ܚܕܐ ܚܕܐ ܡܢܗܝܢ ܩܝܡܢ ܐܝܬ ܗܘܐ ܠܗ ܓܦܐ ܫܬܐ ܚܕܪܝܗ ܘܡܢ ܠܓܘ ܡܠܝܢ ܥܝܢܐ ܘܫܠܝܐ ܠܝܬ ܠܗܝܢ ܐܝܡܡܐ ܘܠܠܝܐ ܠܡܐܡܪ ܩܕܝܫ ܩܕܝܫ ܩܕܝܫ ܩܕܝܫ ܡܪܝܐ ܐܠܗܐ ܐܚܝܕ ܟܠ ܗܘ ܕܐܝܬܘܗܝ ܘܐܝܬܘܗܝ ܗܘܐ ܘܐܬܐ ܀

'And these four living-ones, each of them, had six **wings** round about; and within were full of eyes; and they rest not day and night from saying, Holy, holy, holy, Lord God Almighty, Who wast, and art, and art to come.' (*Pəšiṭta* Apoc 4:8, Etheridge)

The 'lower court' in which Jesus is displayed by Pilate before the Judahites, is thus textually linked through Saint John's own corpus, as a travesty of the true 'higher court' in which Pilate and his Caesar are made to bow before the One God. Yet this court is also linked to the apocalyptic literature of the Old Testament—the one book, in fact, which is written partly in Aramaic.

וארבע חיון רברבן סלקן מן־ימא שנין דא מן־דא׃

קדמיתא כאריה וגפין די־נשר לה חזה הוית עד די־מריטו גפיה ונטילת מן־ארעא ועל־רגלין כאנש הקימת ולבב אנש יהיב לה׃

They made long their furrows

וארוּ חיוה אחרי תנינה דמיה לדב וֹלשׂטרחד הקמת וּתלת עלעין בפמהּ בין שׁנַּהּ
וכן אמרין לה קוּמי אכלי בשׂר שׂגיא:

בּאתר דּנה חזה הוית וארוּ אחרי כּנמר ולה **גפּין** ארבע דּיעוֹף עלגּבּהּ וארבּעה
ראשׁין לחיותא ושׁלטן יהיב להּ:

בּאתר דּנה חזה הוית בּחזוי ליליא וארוּ חיוה רביעאה דּחילה ואימתני ותקיפא
יתּירא ושׁנַּין דּיפרזל להּ רברבן אכלה וּמדּקה וּשׁארא בּרגלהּ רפסה והיא משׁנּיה
מןכּלחיותא דּי קדמיהּ וקרנין עשׂר להּ:

'And four great beasts came up out of the sea, different from one another. The first was like a lion and had eagles' wings. Then as I looked its wings were plucked off, and it was lifted up from the ground and made to stand upon two feet like a man; and the mind of a man was given to it. And behold, another beast, a second one, like a bear. It was raised up on one side; it had three ribs in its mouth between its teeth; and it was told, "Arise, devour much flesh." After this I looked, and lo, another, like a leopard, with four **wings** of a bird on its **back**; and the beast had four heads; and dominion was given to it. After this I saw in the night visions, and behold, a fourth beast, terrible and dreadful and exceedingly strong; and it had great iron teeth; it devoured and broke in pieces, and stamped the residue with its feet. It was different from all the beasts that were before it; and it had ten horns.' (Dan 7:3-7)

Even in the English translation of the RSV, we should be able to see the clear textual and literary-thematic linkages between Daniel's apocalyptic vision and that of Saint John at the end of the New Testament, the use of the imagery of 'wings' on these beasts notwithstanding.

There can be no question that this is the allusion that Saint John wants us to draw. As Mār Aprahaṭ Ḥakkimā (*a.k.a.* Saint Aphraates the Sage, Farhād Dānāi) shows us in his *Demonstrations* in the early fourth century, these animal motifs

In the Houses of the Poor

are inherently political in a West Asian literary context. They represent *empire*. The lion corresponds to Babylon and Nebuchadnezzar; the bear to the Persian Empire of the Haḫāmaneši; the leopard to the Greeks under Alexander; and the ten-horned beast of Daniel's night visions to Rome[143].

The travesty under Pilate in Saint John's Gospel is a reflection of the heavenly court of his Apocalypse, which in turn is a clear adaptation of the Scriptural visions of Daniel. This is the judgement wherein the imperial 'beasts' of this world, whether the Babylonian lion or the Roman (or American!) eagle, will be subjected to the overriding judgement of the Ancient of Days and the 'one like the Son of man' (Dan 7:13) Who is given authority as His *locum tenens* on the earth.

'They made long their furrows'

The spectacle of the 'lower court' at Christ's third trial may link directly with John's Apocalypse and with the Aramaic section of the Book of Daniel. However, Saint John said Ἑβραϊστὶ. This lexeme is also to be taken as interfunctional with Hebrew. Thus, we need to take account of the relevant instances of the biliteral consonant cluster *g-b* ג-ב in Hebrew.

The Hebrew term *gab* גב refers to the 'back, shoulder', the high or elevated part of a quadrupedal animal. But by

---

[143] Mār Aprahaṭ Ḥakkimā, *The Demonstrations*, tr. Adam Lehto (Gorgias Press, 2010), V.xv-xix, 159-161.

They made long their furrows

extension it can refer to a man-made or natural geographical feature: a ridge or mountain or citadel that resembles the raised back and shoulders of a beast. So we see in Ezekiel: בבנותיך **גבך** בראש כל־דרך ורמתך עשית בכל־רחוב '*building* **your vaulted chamber** *at the head of every street, and making your lofty place in every square*' (Eze 16:31). It does not have a positive connotation when referring to something *built*! Through Ezekiel the Lord calls Jerusalem a bold-faced harlot, an adulterous wife, who advertises her shamelessness in the open and prominent places. So indeed the authorities of Herod's Jerusalem go to this vaulted chamber to importune the Caesar of Rome to rid them of their Lord's Son!

But this lexeme also links to the Psalms. Here the scourging of Jesus (John 19:1) becomes relevant:

רבת צררוני מנעורי יאמר־נא ישראל:
רבת צררוני מנעורי גם לא־יכלו לי:
על־**גבי** חרשו חרשים האריכו למעניתם:

'*Sorely they have afflicted me from my youth,*' *let Israel now say.* '*Sorely they have afflicted me from my youth, yet they have not prevailed against me. The ploughers ploughed upon* **my back,** *they made long their furrows.*' (Psalm 128:1-3)

The Greek name of the place highlighted by Saint John attests to the imperial power of Rome—the inlaid mosaics of precious stones show off Rome's imperial glory (as they did in Ahasuerus's court in Esther 1:6). But the Semitic name serves a triple purpose. It contrasts the corrupt proceedings of this 'lower court' with the inevitable 'higher court' seen in Daniel's visions reinterpreted in Saint John's Apocalypse. It also alludes to the harlotry of the Judahite authorities: their rejection of

In the Houses of the Poor

Christ held up as a mirror for their rejection of Ezekiel. And lastly, it highlights the bloody cruelty and iniquity of the judicial process. Yet the same Psalm assures the hearer that the torments of the present will not last and the persecutors will not prevail.

Crucify the messenger

A clarification on John 19:17-24

Golgotha and Galilee – around and around we go[144]

As fans of the young adult fiction novels of Madeleine L'Engle will be aware, the Greek language has two different words for time, both of which appear in Scripture. In Greek, χρόνος refers to time in sequence, of events in a particular linear order; whereas καιρός refers to what is appointed, a 'right moment'—or, as the final title in L'Engle's *Kairos* series puts it, 'an acceptable time'.

We can see the differences of usage from two passages in the Gospel of John: **τοσοῦτον χρόνον** μεθ' ὑμῶν εἰμι καὶ οὐκ ἔγνωκάς με Φίλιππε '*Have I been with you **so long**, and yet you do not know me, Philip?*' (John 14:9) And: Ὁ **καιρὸς** ὁ ἐμὸς οὔπω πάρεστιν '*My **time** has not yet come.*' (John 7:6) The first refers to a duration, and a movement between two states, from lack of knowledge to (supposed) knowledge. Jesus is talking about the length of time they had been together. The second, which Jesus utters before the Feast of Booths, refers to a ripening, a fruition, something that occurs in the fullness of time.

I point out this dichotomy in Greek because we modern 'Judaeo-Christians' carry with us a certain set of false

---

[144] Matthew Franklin Cooper, 'Golgotha and Galilee – linked at the roots', *Skeireins* (Substack post, 7 June 2025).

assumptions back into Scripture about how time in Scripture is supposed to work. Unfortunately, it looks like those of us in the West must once again lay that problem at the feet of Saint Augustine.

One of the primary problems the New Testament authors attempted to address—especially Saint Luke, who by nature of his intellectual training was acutely aware of it—was the tendency of contemporary followers of the *Torah* to want to interpret it in terms that would make it palatable or respectable among the Greco-Roman governing class; *i.e.* presenting the Law and the Prophets to them as a *historical* text[145]. The New Testament authors saw it as their project to *liberate* the teaching of the Hebrew scrolls from those like Josephus, who would make it an antiquarian interest meant to bolster particular political claims within a Roman context.

As I mentioned in my commentary on John 5[146], even Christian redactors and transmitters of Scripture were unfortunately not immune from the temptation to historicise the texts which were entrusted to them! Someone who had been given the task of transcribing Saint John, at some point, *mis*-transcribed Βηθζαθά ('the house of the olive tree', the form in which the toponym appears in the *Codex Sinaiticus*) as Βηθεσδά ('the house of mercy', 'the house of reproach',

---

[145] Fr Marc Boulos, 'A Greek tragedy takes flesh—and still dwells among us', *The Bible as Literature* podcast 543 (24 Nov 2024), https://www.youtube.com/watch?v=O7ycc6ZWaxg.

[146] Cooper, *Lamb*, 124-128.

occurring in later transcriptions of the Gospel). My interpretation of this mistranscription, is that the hand which did it was attempting to harmonise Saint John's Gospel with the toponymy of Jerusalem, the better to establish *historical grounds* for a Christian political claim to the holy places of that city. Such mishandlings of Scripture routinely result in horrific distortions of the teaching, which have century after century resulted in fanaticism and communalist violence.

A larger-scale distortion of the same kind occurs when we fix *literary* events in Scripture to discrete periods and times in human history, pillaging God's καιρός and stashing it like footpads and thieves into man's χρόνος. Bishop James Ussher's seventeenth-century claim that the events that began the Book of Genesis occurred at two in the afternoon on the twenty-third of October, 4004 BC, is only the most infamous example of a *genre* of eisegesis inaugurated by Augustine's *Civitas Dei*. Augustine, who (like Job!) asks how such evil as the Gothic sack of Rome could have befallen the Empire, takes that human perspective as the starting-point for a grand theory of history. He periodises human history into six discrete ages, each one a 'progression' from the one which preceded it, each one unfolding a further stage in God's ultimate plan.

But we are dealing with an *Asian textual tradition*. Herodotos did not write the *Torah*, the *Nəbi'îm* and the *Kətubîm*; West Asians did. Scripture's approach to history is unlike Augustine's, or James Ussher's, or Francis Fukuyama's concept of history. It is *cyclical*, not linear or progressive. The authors of Scripture came out of the same cultural context that the

Crucify the messenger

Sumerians and Akkadians did, who believed that history must always make an *amar-gi*, a return to the mother.

When a Semitic ear hears in John 19 the mention of a place called Golgotha (Γολγοθᾶ = Aram. *Gûlgaltā'* גולגלתא), they would be reminded of another toponym which is rooted in the Semitic triliteral *g-l-l* ג-ל-ל: Galilee (Γαλιλαία = Aram. *Gəlîlā'* גלילא). The recursive duplication of the root in Golgotha (a 'skull' that rolls around and around) resonates with Galilee: the 'circuit' where Jesus took His first disciples and worked His first miracles. This linguistic echo underscores the *cyclical completion* of Jesus's work in the world. The doubled root in Golgotha also alludes to the completion of His Father's purpose, in the καιρός-sense of the 'fullness of time'.

If we are following the four Evangelists, whose four books in fact all tell the same *repeated* narrative *four different times*, then, we need to put away both Augustine's thoughts about a progressive unfolding of God's will in human history, and also the thoughts of Ussher and those who followed him, that God's irruption of history can be predicted and anticipated according to human political designs. As Fr Paul Tarazi notes (and he makes his case quite convincingly!), the entire narrative 'arc' of Scripture, all of its basic premises and the Semitic vocabulary needed to interpret them, are already present between Genesis 1:1 and 2:4, with an elaboration extending from Genesis 5:1 to 6:8[147]. What follows are all variations on the basic themes already present: that God's provision has been made very good

---

[147] Fr Paul Tarazi, *Decoding Genesis 1-11* (OCABS Press, 2020), 34-35.

and sufficient for all, and human beings' attempts to limit, control and usurp that provision all end in ignominious failure. Yet human beings in their civilisations persist in making such attempts against God's provision—leading to cycles of confident rise, hubris, decadence and fall.

And what is happening here? God has sent His Son as His messenger into Galilee to do His deeds: turning water into wine, healing human beings of their illnesses and disabilities, overturning moneychangers' tables, feeding multitudes, freeing men of their debts, saving poor women from eviction, even raising the dead. And how do we human beings repay Him? We want to maintain control over *our* Temple, *our* Imperium, *our* claims on the debt-money of our fellow-servant. So we crucify God's messenger at Golgotha. Jesus shows consistently through His deeds how God's provision is very good and sufficient for us all. But, because of human beings' greed and ambition and penchant for domination of each other, we can't have nice things. There is no new thing under the sun (Eccl 1:9).

'Pilate also wrote a placard'

Prior to His execution, Jesus has a placard (τίτλος, a Greek borrowing from Latin corresponding to 'title') affixed above His cross (John 19:19). Pilate inscribes this placard in three languages—Hebrew, Latin and Greek. Such placards were not merely informational in purpose: they were punitive instruments of imperial terror, invitations to public ridicule and shame. They served to erase identity, enforce submission,

Crucify the messenger

and bolster imperial ideology. The use of such placards is not alien to modern contexts.

Between 1880 and 1945, with a reprise in the 1950s and 1960s, after losing its independence and being annexed by the Japanese Empire, Okinawa was subject to a series of particularly oppressive assimilation policies. Many of these Japanese policies, aimed at subjugated groups like Okinawans, Ainu and Koreans, were inspired by similar laws and regulations (for example, the infamous Dawes Act) deployed by the United States government against American Indians[148]. For example, children in Okinawa, forced to attend Japanese schools, would be punished for using their Lūchūan home language by having a *hōgen fuda* 方言札 'dialect placard' hung around their neck. The placard was an invitation for that student's peers to ridicule and shame them[149].

The forced conformity of Okinawa to the ideology of the Japanese Empire had appalling consequences for the island, which overlap with my own family history. My grandfather, Franklin Dero Cooper, was a US Navy hospital corpsman in the Pacific theatre of the Second World War. In his capacity as a medic, he served at Iwo Jima and at Okinawa in the fight against Japan. He never talked to me about Okinawa. I would

---

[148] Mark E. Caprio, *Japanese Assimilation Policies in Colonial Korea, 1910-1945* (University of Washington Press, 2009).

[149] Chinen Seishin, 'The Human Pavilion', in *Islands of Protest: Japanese Literature from Okinawa*, eds. Davinder L. Bhowmik and Steve Rabson (University of Hawai'i Press, 2016), 246-247, 288.

In the Houses of the Poor

only learn later, and second-hand, the extremes of brutality to which he must have borne witness at the hospital on the island, and the depth of suffering which the US Navy tasked him with healing. The civilian populace was decimated not only by the American assault, but also by the cruelty and Imperialist brainwashing of the IJA. The Japanese confiscated the starving Okinawans' food, used them as human shields against the American landing force, and in the face of loss instructed them to commit suicide *en masse* rather than surrender. The island had a civilian population of 500,000 before the Americans landed. By the end of the 82-day battle for the island, anywhere between 100,000 and 150,000 native Lūchūan Okinawans had died—a higher death toll than either army[150].

Saint John uses this word τίτλος instead of the αἰτία 'accusation' or ἐπιγραφή 'epigraph, superscription' of the other three Gospel texts to refer to the inscription above Jesus's exposed body on the Cross. Saint John's choice to call attention to it being a 'placard' places particular emphasis on the humiliation of the Saviour, and on the imperial ideology which demanded it.

The placard itself is inscribed in three languages: Hebrew, Latin and Greek (John 19:20). We can see from the examples of Okinawan schoolchildren and from residential Indian schools

---

[150] For a semi-fictionalised account of the Battle of Okinawa from an indigenous perspective, read: Shun Medoruma, 'Tree of Butterflies', in *Islands of Protest: Japanese Literature from Okinawa*, eds. Davinder L. Bhowmik and Steve Rabson (University of Hawai'i Press, 2016), 71-112.

Crucify the messenger

how language was made into a weapon of punishment against the enemies of empire. In this case, each of these three languages represents a different sort of accommodation with power. Hebrew, the language of the scrolls, is coopted by compradors in Herod's palace and in his Temple, as well as more broadly by the Judahite communities who reference themselves by blood-kinship rather than by their following of the Law. Latin is very directly the language of Rome, of Augustus Caesar's political authority, of legionary violence and legal domination. And Greek represents the Hellenistic claims to universal civilisation, to intellectual and mercantile supremacy, which undergirded the earlier Alexandrian and Seleucid states whose memory was carried forward by Rome.

The use of these languages on a placard of punishment drives home the imperial ideology that prompted this execution. But more than that, because this Scripture is written in Greek and because it is referenced to a Hebrew *corpus* through the Septuagint, the τίτλος also serves as a potent literary caution against those who would abuse Scripture—*even in its original languages*—to serve the purposes of human *imperium* against the kingdom of God.

The inscription itself is given as Ἰησοῦς ὁ Ναζωραῖος ὁ βασιλεὺς τῶν Ἰουδαίων 'Jesus of Nazareth, the king of the Jews'. All four Gospel texts contain the last four words exactly. Yet only Saint John's Gospel makes the inscription a bone of political contention between the Roman authorities and the Judahites. The Judahites, unlike in the other Gospels, object to Pilate's wording: they want it spelt out that Jesus only *spoke of Himself* as 'king of the Jews' (John 19:21). But Pilate dismisses them thus: ὃ γέγραφα γέγραφα 'what I have written, I have written' (19:22).

This tidbit of political drama, absent from the other Gospel texts, points directly to the conflicting claims between the Romans and the Judahites over whether Christ is a king—and *criticises them both*. The Judahites deny Christ's Messiahship so that they need not hear His teaching of *Torah*. And the Roman authorities assert Christ's *appetere regnum*, tantamount to calling Him a traitor and a subversive, for *exactly the same reason*. In claiming that 'Christ is king', they are simply looking for an excuse to disobey His message!

The single biggest insult to Saint John that we Orthodox Christians deal out, is to call him a 'Theologian'. There is no Christology in Saint John's Gospel. There are no Davidic claims. In Saint John's eyes, the Roman assertion of Christ's 'kingship' is a fatal error in judgement which exposes their faulty reference point[151]. Christ *does* perform populistic miracles (the feeding of multitudes, the raising of Lazarus) that directly lead, in Saint John's narrative, to Him being proclaimed as king. Yet Jesus withdraws Himself when confronted with the prospect of kingship (John 6:15), and is even 'troubled' by it (John 12:27). Rather, it is the Romans who are eager to execute a Gracchus, and the Judahites who are eager to disavow an inconvenient Messianic claimant.

---

[151] Cooper, *Lamb*, 44-45.

Crucify the messenger

Christ's kingdom is 'not from around here' (John 18:36). The question of kingship is thus a valid one, and indeed a central one to the Gospel at this point. Notice that it is the Roman governor, Pilate, who says that 'Christ is King' here. But he does this to assert *his own* authority, not that of Christ. His reference point is Caesar. The Judahites, on the other hand, deny Christ's kingship. But they do so out of fear, in order to preserve themselves from Roman persecution. Their reference point is *also* Caesar.

Jesus, Who refuses to answer the charge of His kingship, is the only one Who has the proper reference point. The Father alone is King. What matters, is whether or not we *do the work* that His Father sends us (John 9:4).

Through the eye of the needle

The incident with the Roman soldiery dividing Jesus's possessions and clothing among them and casting lots is present in each of the other Gospel texts (Matt 27:35; Luke 23:34; Mark 15:24). The description of that incident is, in the 'synoptic' telling, rather cursory: its function is only to show that the saying found in Psalm 21:19 (LXX) had been fulfilled. But Saint John goes into details.

First of all, he notes that there are four soldiers, and that they made equal divisions of His clothing, with the exception of the *kittûnā'* כתונא or χιτών 'tunic' that He wore. The RSV translates that this *kittûna'* was made 'without seam', but the actual Greek word used is ἄραφος 'without (the use of) a needle'.

In the Houses of the Poor

This text, then, connects Saint John directly with the three other Gospel authors. The 'four' soldiers should be taken to refer to Saint John himself and his three other Gospel-writing comrades. But the use of the term ἄραφος itself also refers directly back to the other Evangelists' work. The word ἄραφος is an ἅπαξ λεγόμενον—a word that appears nowhere else in Scripture. But it contains within itself the word ῥαφίς 'needle', which occurs in only three other places in the New Testament. And wouldn't you know it: those three other places are in the *other three 'synoptic' Gospels!*

The term ῥαφίς is only ever used in Scripture, in the saying of Jesus that εὐκοπώτερόν ἐστιν κάμηλον διὰ τῆς τρυμαλιᾶς τῆς **ῥαφίδος** διελθεῖν ἢ πλούσιον εἰς τὴν βασιλείαν τοῦ θεοῦ εἰσελθεῖν *'It is easier for a camel to go through the eye of a* **needle** *than for a rich man to enter the kingdom of God.'* (Matt 19:24; Mark 10:25; Luke 18:25) The 'needle' is therefore the test of whether or not a man is fit to enter the kingdom. All three of the 'synoptic' Evangelists *immediately* have the disciples remark on the impossibility of *any* man passing the test. Yet here, the four soldiers—that is to say, the literary proxies of the four Evangelists—have between them Christ's *kittûnā'*, which was made *without a needle.*

Everything that Christ has, has been taken away from Him—down to His clothes; down to His very life. He is now the poorest of the poor, condemned to die the most shameful death the Romans could devise, reserved for the scum of the earth, beneath a placard inviting mockery and ridicule. His very garment shows that He passed through the 'eye of the needle'.

Crucify the messenger

Yet Saint John is doing something else in this passage. The four soldiers do not tear the garment between them but instead cast lots for it. That means that the garment itself is preserved intact. This *kittûnā'* כתונא, which is a literary reference to the long-sleeved *kittûnā'* of the betrayed Joseph in the book of Genesis (37:3), is an image of Scripture itself. Saint John is asserting the literary unity of his own work with that of his three colleagues and with the Pauline school at large, and cautioning precisely against the scholarly impulse to 'tear the garment' between a 'synoptic' school and himself!

God's messenger, His *locum tenens*, the One through Whom the kingdom is proclaimed, has been put to death. But the message itself, woven without the use of a needle, has been kept without a tear despite the unworthiness of those who received it.

A drink at the seventh hour

The seventh jar and the test of Rebekah

A clarification on John 19:25-29 and 19:38-42

The Isaian warning of the three Marys

Mary, mother of Jesus, makes her second in-person appearance in the Gospel of Saint John at her Son's execution. Her first appearance was in the second chapter, at the wedding in Cana. Now, she appears beside two other Marys: her sister, 'of Clopas' (from Aramaic Ḥîlfa'y חילפאי 'substitute, replacement, exchange') and Mary the Magdalene (from Aramaic *Magdalā'* מגדלא 'tower, citadel'—John 19:25).

In a matrilineal society like Semitic Judaea, the three women could represent three different communities—such as those which are held together by Paul, or by Paul's teaching. Toponymically, Magdala was a city built by the Hasmoneans in the second century BC, and as such it was a symbol of Judahite power and memory[152]. And the term *ḥîlfa'y* חילפאי signifies a temporary agent, a stand-in or a substitute: to a Semitic hearer of the early Pauline community, it would have connotations of the regard in which Gentiles were held (Rom 11:26). The mother of Jesus Christ, representing the community of the Pauline teaching, would in such a literary schema represent

---

[152] Fr Cristobal Vilaroig, 'The birth of Magdala-Tarichaea', *Magdala.org*, 29 June 2020, https://www.magdala.org/journal/.

A drink at the seventh hour

the melding of the Gentile and Jewish halves under a new iteration of the textual discipline.

But before we analyse the literary function and purpose of the three Marys, though, we need to examine where these two Semitic roots, ḥ-l-f ח-ל-ף 'exchange' and g-d-l ג-ד-ל 'growth, greatness, strength', occur together in the Old Testament. The nearest and strongest linkage between them can be seen in Isaiah 9:

> וידעוּ העם כלוֹ אפרים ויוֹשב שׁמרון בגאוה וּ**בגדל** לבב לאמר:
> לבנים נפלוּ וגזית נבנה שׁקמים גדעוּ וארזים **נחליף**:
> וישׂגב יהוה את־צרי רצין עליו ואת־איביו יסכסך:

... and all the people will know, Ephraim and the inhabitants of Samaria, who say in pride and in **arrogance** *of heart: 'The bricks have fallen, but we will build with dressed stones; the sycamores have been cut down, but we will put cedars* **in their place.**' *So the Lord raises adversaries against them, and stirs up their enemies.* (Isa 9:8-10)

The two Marys beside the mother of Jesus attest *lexically*, through their bynames, to the final judgement currently being carried out from the Cross. What is at stake in this scene is the entirety of the *Torah*. Pilate and his Judahite accomplices are destroying One Whom *they believe* to be a kingly claimant. Pilate is acting in order to preserve the prestige and authority of Caesar. The Judahites are acting in order to ensure the continuity of their Temple, and the dependent position of institutional power they've accrued *under* Caesar. In the wake of the proclamation of the Law and the Prophets, both the Roman and Judahite authorities are rebuilding that which God has torn down (see Gal 2:18).

In the Houses of the Poor

The three Marys, standing together, thus form a tight allusion to one of the strongest prophetic denunciations in Isaiah of both kingdom-builders and temple-builders, even as the One that *they* have named as king—is executed at their hands. The root *f-n-h* פ-נ-ה is not etymologically linked to *g-d-l* ג-ד-ל, but they are synonyms and can be found together as such in the text (*e.g.* 2 Par 26:15). Thus: אבן מאסו הבונים היתה לראש **פנה** '*The stone that the builders rejected has become the head of the **tower***' (Psalm 117:22). The pride of the builders, of those who betray and destroy the teaching in favour of their own pet architectural and gardening projects, has yet to be humiliated. But the witness of the three Marys means that the builders are already being judged.

Yet the scene of Jesus's death is far, far richer in textual allusion. The entirety of the Gospel leads up to this point. I have not even begun to scratch the surface. '*Were every one of them to be written, I suppose that the world itself could not contain the books.*' (John 21:25)

The seventh hour and the judgement of the family

The execution of Jesus takes place at, or slightly after, the **sixth hour** (ὥρα δὲ ὡσεὶ ἕκτη) of the day (John 19:14). Looking back to the wedding of Cana, we read that Jesus told his mother that οὔπω ἥκει ἡ **ὥρα** μου '*My **hour** has not yet come*' (2:4). Likewise, we find that there are **six** stone water-jars that Jesus orders to be filled with water (2:6). The wedding at Cana and the execution of Jesus are thuswise not only *thematically*, but *lexically* linked.

A drink at the seventh hour

There is some excellent Greek Patristic exegesis on the crucifixion in the Gospel of Saint John. My remark on the linkage from the 'sixth hour' of the execution to the 'six' stone jars and Jesus's remark on His 'hour... not yet come', for example, is directly inspired by Saint John Chrysostom's 'hour' exegesis in his *Homilies*[153]! Likewise, drawing on Semitic lexical parallels, Ephraim the Syrian in his sixteenth *Hymn* on virginity connects the wedding at Cana directly to this scene at Golgotha[154].

Indeed, the Apostolic deposit over which the Orthodox Church retains a considerable degree of custody is a treasure-trove of capable and honest commentary on Scripture. We would do well to avail ourselves of it. Nonetheless: we Orthodox Christians especially need to exercise particular caution at this point, otherwise we *will* get lost and stumble. For example, we might end up following Bishop Cyril of Alexandria, who gets caught up in questionable mystical fantasies of 'the woman' as a category, or making Jesus the 'bridegroom' to all of human nature[155]! It's easy to see from such blather where Jordan Peterson comes by some of his more noteworthy Jungian and Campbellian idiocies.

---

[153] Specifically: Saint John Chrysostom, 'Homily 22' on the Gospel of John, Church Fathers translation collection, *New Advent*, https://www.newadvent.org/fathers/240122.htm.

[154] Ephrem the Syrian, 'Hymn 16' on virginity, in *Hymns*, tr. Kathleen McVay (Paulist Press, 1989), 329-332.

[155] Cyril of Alexandria, *Commentary on the Gospel of John*, vol. 1 (James Parker & Co., 1874), 155-157.

In the Houses of the Poor

Mary the mother of Jesus is a key, in fact an indispensable, personage *in the text*. And we honour her best and most properly when we credit her where she deserves credit. As Saint John (Maximovitch) of Shanghai and San Francisco put it, a teaching *'which seemingly has the aim of exalting the Mother of God, in reality completely denies all her virtues'*[156]. The blessed bishop of Shanghai was polemicising, of course, against Pope Pius IX and the Roman Catholic doctrine of the Immaculate Conception. But he speaks rightly, and what's good for the goose is also good for the gander[157]. However Orthodox he may be, Cyril's praise of 'the woman' as an archetype in such a context does no honour to *this particular* woman, who is *'blessed among women'* (Luke 1:42). So let's keep our heads out of the realm of mystical fantasies, and stick to the specific lexicographical linkages inside Saint John's text.

The text shows us that we are dealing, *not* with a Platonic archetype, but with *one specific* γύναι 'woman' who appears in both pericopes (John 2:4; 19:26). In the first instance, the mother of Jesus *takes charge* of the situation. Remember that women have status in Mosaic law as the *mothers of lineages* (Deut 7:3-4), so she is exercising matriarchal power at the

---

[156] John Maximovitch, *On the Orthodox Veneration of the Mother of God* (St Herman of Alaska Brotherhood, 2012), 54.

[157] I suspect that St. John Maximovitch would agree with me on this particular point, because he goes on precisely to attack the 'sophianist' excesses of Orthodox philosophers Solovyov and Bulgakov which conflate Mary with the Divine Sophia, and reduce her to a mystical feminine archetype! – *Auth.*

A drink at the seventh hour

wedding at Cana, first by telling Jesus what to do (2:3) and delegating her authority to Jesus by directing the servants to obey Him (2:5). Given how Jesus reacts to this, He isn't particularly happy—perhaps even a little embarrassed—by his mother's exercise of matronly privilege. But His ὥρα 'hour' has not yet come. He directs the servants, under His mother's orders, to fill the six stone jars with water (2:6-7).

At Golgotha, the situation is reversed. Even though Jesus is dying, on the Cross He is the one calling the shots. He directs His mother to take the disciple whom He loves as her son, and the disciple to take His mother as his own (John 19:26-27). If we think of this like a scene from a Martin Scorsese movie, the Don's right-hand man Giosuè got shot up by a couple of rival gangs, knows he's not gonna make it back for dinner, and now he's telling Baby Gianni to go take care of his mom. But whatever His reasons, functionally, Jesus is calling on His mother to put aside her Deuteronomical privilege and accept a lesser position in another man's household.

And His mother accepts.

ἀπ' ἐκείνης τῆς **ὥρας** ἔλαβεν ὁ μαθητὴς αὐτὴν εἰς τὰ ἴδια

*And from that **hour** the disciple took her to his own home.* (John 19:27)

Remember, this happens after 'the sixth hour' (John 19:14). Now in verse 27, there's another hour—the seventh. Here it behoves us to consider that we may be dealing not with chronological χρόνος-time, but instead with the cyclical καιρός-time, the time of fruition. *This* is Jesus's hour, and it has come (2:4).

This hour has seen the judgement of the Empire—Pilate has declared Christ as king three times (John 18:37; 19:5; 19:14) now. It has seen the judgement of the Temple, whose custodians are proven recreants who profess no king but Caesar (19:15). Now it is seeing the judgement of the last of the institutional authorities which seeks to control the teaching: *the Family*. I can foresee objections that Jesus is being a male-chauvinist jerk here, but those objections badly miss the point. Jesus is not exercising arbitrary or tyrannical power over His mother; He's making her one last dying plea. He is enjoining His mother to relinquish *her* power over Him, and she does so by joining John's household.

Mary's value is that she's the only person present at the Crucifixion who is shown to actually *obey the teaching*. And her obedience distinguishes her among the others; she alone is shown as honourable. Pilate is exposed as a traitor to Caesar; the Temple authorities are exposed as traitors to Yahweh; only Mary is shown to be faithful. Once again Saint John Maximovitch says it correctly: being '*one in spirit with Him*', Mary is the only '*one Who performed the will of God and instructed others*'[158] in it.

---

[158] Maximovitch, *Veneration*, 63.

A drink at the seventh hour

The seventh jar and Rebekah's test

I want to turn attention back to the λίθιναι ὑδρίαι ἕξ 'six stone jars' at the wedding at Cana (John 2:6). Those are important here for several reasons.

Reid Cooper, known for his studies on olivine-rich volcanic basalts originating from the Mid-Atlantic Ridge[159], remarks that the eastern Mediterranean basin is also an 'absolute mess'—in technical geological terms, of course. It's a patchwork of fragmented tectonic plates whose boundaries form one of the Earth's most seismically active systems of transform faults. At one point, however, it was home to an oceanic rift which produced large outcrops of black basalt in Asia Minor, particularly at the bases of composite volcanoes such as Mount Ararat. Fr Marc Boulos takes up this insight linguistically, and notes correctly that λίθος is homophonically linked to Λυδία 'Lydia', the basalt-producing region in Asia Minor[160]. The hardness and majestic black lustre of Lydian basalt made it suitable for extensive use in West Asian and North African stoneware, for everything from potters' wheels to statuary, from royal inscriptions (the Code of Hammurabi is inscribed on a great big block of basalt!), to, yes, *water-jars*.

---

[159] Reid Cooper and David Kohlstedt, 'Interfacial Energies in the Olivine-Basalt System', *Advances in Earth and Planetary Sciences* 12 (1982), 217-228. I am quite happy to say that I am the son of the primary author of this paper. – *Auth*.

[160] Marc Philip Boulos, *Dark Sayings* (OCABS Press, 2023), 32.

In the Houses of the Poor

The homophonic link between λίθος and Λυδία also plays an important role in the Book of Acts. A woman named Lydia appears as a seller of 'purple wares'. Not just any woman, either: she is a *matriarch*, a *materfamilias*, who hears Paul's teaching, submits to it, and is baptised *together with her household* (Acts 16:14-15). This link to matrilineal authority is something to be borne firmly in mind when reading John 2.

Now that we're a little more familiar with the materials-science of λίθιναι, let's turn to the ὑδρίαι 'jars' themselves. The Greek word ὑδρία is used in the LXX to translate the Hebrew word *kad* כד, which refers to a large earthenware jar or pail. The most prominent appearance of the *kad* in the *Torah* is in Genesis 24, wherein Abraham sends a trusted servant into Mesopotamian Harran to seek a bride for his son. The servant meets the young virgin Rebekah by her family's well, and she draws water in her *kad* to give him and his camels a drink. By this sign the servant knows Rebekah to be a woman of hospitality, suitable to be married to his master's heir. Chrysostom speaks thus of this passage:

What [Abraham's servant] says is indeed such a sign, even if he does not utter these words... He has a special reason for seeking a generous girl. Since he came from a household in which the deeds of hospitality especially flourished, he sought above all to choose a woman whose character would be compatible with his masters'... Let us not see only the fact that he asked for water, but let us consider that it shows a

A drink at the seventh hour

truly generous soul not only to give what is asked but to provide more than what is requested.[161]

Mary alone proves herself free to follow the teaching of the *Torah*, because she alone has heard the voice of Abraham's servant. Observe: the disciples have fled. The Judahite authorities Annas and Caiaphas will not hear Jesus because they're seeking in Him the imprint of a Gentile teaching that isn't there, and He is struck on the face when He answers them! Pilate cannot hear Jesus's answers to him because he deflects into absurd questions like 'what is truth?' when Truth is staring him in the face. They all mock and denounce Jesus. Only His mother obeys Him when He gives her a command: to enter into the household of His 'other disciple'.

This is the hour of judgement. The test of Rebekah lies before Jesus's mother, and the author of the text. Jesus, like Abraham's servant, is thirsty (John 19:28). What does she do? It is the 'seventh hour', the καιρός which had *not* come in Chapter 2... and here is a seventh vessel. It is not an ὑδρία or *kad* כד; it is merely a little σκεῦος, a 'bowl'. The Hebrew equivalent *kəlî* כלי is even more emphatic in its smallness: it's a jewellery-box! And what is inside is not good wine, it's not even water. It's ὄξος 'sour', the kind of watered-down and 'gone-off' wine that was given to common soldiers.

---

[161] Saint John Chrysostom, 'How to Choose a Wife', in *On Marriage and Family Life*, trs. Catherine P. Roth and David Anderson, *Popular Patristics* vol. 7 (SVS Press, 1986), 103-104.

In the Houses of the Poor

And the mother of Jesus and the disciple Jesus loved take the sour wine from the little bowl, put it in a sponge, put the sponge on the end of a stalk of hyssop, and give it to the dying man to drink (John 19:29).

Just as Rebekah had no idea who the strange man was at the well when she went out to draw water, so too neither the mother of Jesus nor the disciple nor Jesus Himself *know* that the Resurrection will occur. There is no thought of reward here. Jesus is at His last gasp. He can do no more for them. This is a test of whether these two people, faced with a broken man in need, will do for Him the teaching of the *Torah*, even with as little as a jewellery-box of sour wine and a sponge! And they do.

And how was Rebekah rewarded for showing hospitality to Abraham's servant? She was given two σκεύη 'bowls': one *kəlî* כלי of silver and one *kəlî* כלי of gold (Gen 24:53). These parallels are deliberate. We are meant to trace these links back to the *Torah*.

Let's return briefly, once again, to Acts. Our basalt-black matriarch Lydia first hears the words of Paul and obeys them (Acts 16:14). She is baptised 'together with her household', subjecting them all to the teaching and placing herself under discipline. But note: after that—she *opens her house* to Paul and Timothy and Luke (Acts 16:15)! The law of hospitality is a *universal* law, one which the Gentiles are meant to hear as well as the Judahites.

The crucifixion of Jesus in the Gospel of Saint John is the culmination, the final revelation of this law. We can see it in the tight language links between John 2 and John 19, and between both of these and Genesis 24. Salvation comes to

A drink at the seventh hour

Abraham's house through one Mesopotamian girl's *generosity to a thirsty stranger*. And salvation comes to the world through one bereaved Aramaic woman's *generosity to a dying man on a cross*.

Burying the body: parodies of generosity

The blood and water that emerge from Jesus's side after his death (John 19:34) are yet a further textual link back to the wedding at Cana, as well as back to Jesus's insistence that a man must be γεννηθῇ ἐξ ὕδατος 'born of water' in the chapter which follows (3:5). Jesus is dead, but the water of life is now present in abundance.

But then *after* Jesus is dead, two more characters show up who offer extravagant generosities to Him, when they can do Him no more good. In fact, these 'generosities' proceed from a corruption of conscience.

Joseph 'of the Heights' (Ἀριμαθαία = Aram. *Ramtā'* רמתא 'a high place') is introduced as a 'secret' disciple of Jesus on account of his fear of the Judahite authorities. But he goes and *asks Pilate* to take custody of Jesus's body. This should strike us as incongruous. If Jesus is his master, then why is Joseph appealing to the authority which killed Him? And together with him is Nicodemus, the Pharisee with a particularly ironic Greek name[162], bringing along a hundred pounds of fragrant oils and spices for Jesus's burial.

---

[162] See Cooper, *Lamb*, 71-92 (chapter 3).

In the Houses of the Poor

Notice that both of these people are marked by their reliance on the familial authority which Mary, Jesus's mother, has *just* relinquished! If the Aramaic *Ramtā'* is a reference to the *Ramâ* of Jeremiah, as stands to reason because they stem from the same Semitic triliteral root *r-m-h* ר-מ-ה, then this Joseph that appears in John 19:38 is linked lexically to Benjamin, whose home was in Ramâ. And both Joseph and Benjamin are, in Genesis, the natural sons of Rachel's womb.

קוֹל **בְּרָמָה** נִשְׁמָע נְהִי בְּכִי תַמְרוּרִים **רָחֵל** מְבַכָּה עַל־בָּנֶיהָ מֵאֲנָה לְהִנָּחֵם עַל־בָּנֶיהָ כִּי אֵינֶנּוּ

*A voice is heard **in Ramâ**, lamentation and bitter weeping. **Rachel** is weeping for her children; she refuses to be comforted for her children, because they are not.* (Jer 31:15)

The place-name Ramâ רמה is an interesting one. It serves two functions which are relevant to this pericope. As a place of 'lamentation and bitter weeping', it is the burial-place of the Prophet Samuel (1 Sam 25:1, 28:3). It also links to the Isaian warning against builders. It is the place where the Israelite king Ba'šā' begins building a fortress at Ramâ in his war against the Judahite king 'Āsā', who dismantled the fortress and used the materials to build a different fortress in the tribal territory of Benjamin (1 Kgs 15:17-22)!

As I explained in *The Lamb before Its Shearers*, Nicodemus's name is likewise linked to the *mišfaḥâ* משפחה 'family'. This term too is matrilineal in orientation, deriving from *šifḥâ* שפחה 'maid-servant, concubine'! Interestingly enough, the triliteral *š-f-h* ש-פ-ה can also function as 'high' or 'to lay bare', as it was

A drink at the seventh hour

the maid-servant's job to sweep and clean and pile and store up.

Here, then, we have two men whose names proclaim them as appealing to the familial authority. Yet Joseph 'of the Heights', in a single breath, shows that his loyalties are divided. He's a disciple of Jesus, but secretly, for fear of the Judahites. And he goes *to Pilate* to plead for Christ's body. Suddenly, *all three* of the discredited authorities—family, Empire and Temple—return in force! The Isaian warning of the three Marys against the pride of builders should now be ringing harshly in our ears.

And at Joseph's side we have Nicodemus with ὡς λίτρας ἑκατόν 'about a hundred pounds' weight' of μίγμα σμύρνης καὶ ἀλόης 'myrrh mixed with aloe' (John 19:39). The use of λίτρα and σμύρνης hearkens back functionally to Mary's gesture of gratitude to Jesus for saving her brother and her poor house (12:3), and both pericopes hearken back to the Song of Solomon:

שְׁלָחַיִךְ פַּרְדֵּס רִמּוֹנִים עִם פְּרִי מְגָדִים כְּפָרִים עִם־**נְרָדִים**:
נֵרְדְּ וְכַרְכֹּם קָנֶה וְקִנָּמוֹן עִם כָּל־עֲצֵי לְבוֹנָה **מֹר וַאֲהָלוֹת** עִם כָּל־רָאשֵׁי בְשָׂמִים:

*Your shoots are an orchard of pomegranates with all choicest fruits, henna with **nard**, **nard** and saffron, calamus and cinnamon, with all trees of frankincense, **myrrh and aloes**, with all chief spices...* (Song 4:13-14)

A young woman rubbing Jesus's feet with one pound of fragrant oil and spices is nice. It's attractive. It's sensuous. Despite the rather spicy undertones, Saint John clearly approves Mary's act as worthy. This act here is not: a leering, bearded old man dumping *a hundred pounds* of Bed Bath &

In the Houses of the Poor

Beyond on Jesus's corpse at His burial. It's *the exact opposite* of titillating. It's burlesque.

Saint John is calling our attention to the contrast here in order to highlight the *qualitative* distinction between the two displays of generosity. The mother of Jesus's selfless act of *releasing* Jesus from her matronal authority, and subsequently offering him wine when He thirsted, is the fulfilment of the *Torah* in the assembly's hearing. What Joseph and Nicodemus are doing is *outwardly* generous: giving Jesus a shiny new-hewn tomb and bathing His body in fragrances.

But their reasons are self-seeking! Joseph 'of the Heights' is acting out of self-preservation, the same motive that drove the other chief priests and Pharisees as they plotted against Jesus's life (John 11:47-48). His appeal to Pilate flatters Pilate's authority while keeping Joseph pristinely free of suspicion. The 'new tomb' provided by Joseph evokes Ba'šā' and his fruitless building project in Ramâ in 1 Kings.

And Nicodemus's perfuming of the body, which Saint John satirically couches in the sensuous language of the Song of Solomon, goes beyond gratuitous and garish display of conspicuous consumption, personal wealth and performative Judahite piety. It's *harlotry*. Look at how Saint John uses the word ὀθονίοις 'linens' here. He doesn't use the common λίνεος 'linen' (corresponding usually to Heb. *bad* בד 'white linen'), or βύσσος 'byssus, fine linen' (from Heb. *bûṣ* בוץ) or even βύσσινος 'twined linen, linen garments' (Heb. *šeš* שש 'bleached linen'). This ὀθόνιον is not a frequently-seen word in the Septuagint text. Apart from the Gospel of John, it occurs only in some

A drink at the seventh hour

redactions of the Gospel of Luke, and in the Book of Hosea, where it is used to render *fēšet* פשת 'flax':

כי זנתה אמם הבישה הורתם כי אמרה אלכה אחרי מאהבי נתני לחמי ומימי צמרי **ופשתי** שמני ושקויי:

לכן הנני־שׂך את־דרכך בסירים וגדרתי את־גדרה ונתיבותיה לא תמצא:

ורדפה את־מאהביה ולא־תשׂיג אתם ובקשתם ולא תמצא ואמרה אלכה ואשׁובה אל־אישי הראשון כי טוב לי אז מעתה:

והיא לא ידעה כי אנכי נתתי לה הדגן והתירושׁ והיצהר וכסף הרביתי לה וזהב עשׂוּ לבּעל:

לכן אשׁוּב ולקחתי דגני בעתו ותירושי במועדו והצלתי צמרי **ופשתי** לכסות את־ערותה:

> *For their mother has played the harlot; she that conceived them has acted shamefully. For she said, 'I will go after my lovers, who give me my bread and my water, my wool and **my flax**, my oil and my drink.' Therefore I will hedge up her way with thorns; and I will build a wall against her, so that she cannot find her paths. She shall pursue her lovers, but not overtake them; and she shall seek them, but shall not find them. Then she shall say, 'I will go and return to my first husband, for it was better with me then than now.' And she did not know that it was I who gave her the grain, the wine, and the oil, and who lavished upon her silver and gold which they used for Ba'al. Therefore I will take back my grain in its time, and my wine in its season; and I will take away my wool and **my flax**, which were to cover her nakedness.* (Hos 2:5-9)

The real corruption of conscience lies in this: these two Judahites are collaborating to bury the *Torah*. If both Joseph 'of the Heights' and Nicodemus were secret disciples of Jesus, then there's no way they can evade responsibility for what they're doing here. Saint John is accusing these 'secret' disciples of Christ of going after false gods, just as did the Israelites and Judahites of Hosea's time. Only the false gods to whom Joseph of Arimathea and Nicodemus are paying tribute, are Roman governance and Judahite temple authority.

The test of Rebekah is not an abstract exercise

This Johannine passage must cut American Christian consciences in particular to the quick, if we are hearing it honestly. The test of generosity and hospitality is *not* an exercise in abstraction. It has real-world, present-day consequences.

Shortly after 4 in the morning of 29 February last year, hundreds of starving Palestinians gathered along a stretch of coastal service road. They were there in the hopes of receiving basic foodstuffs from the ar-Rašid aid convoy that had arrived in Gaza City under guard by Israeli tanks. As the Palestinians approached the aid convoy, Israeli troops guarding the rear began opening fire into the crowd, murdering dozens of people and sending the rest into a panicked stampede. Aid workers who were on the scene described the Israeli troops' action as a pre-planned 'ambush' against the people who came for food. In what came to be known as *Majzarat aṭ-Ṭaḥīn* مجزرة الطحين 'the Flour Massacre', at least 118 people were killed, and over 760 people were injured. The Israeli defence ministry claimed it was acting in 'self-defence'[163].

Since the Flour Massacre, dozens of separate incidents of attacks by Israeli armed forces on Palestinian aid seekers have been documented. Over the following two weeks alone, by 12 March 2024, 400 Palestinian aid seekers were murdered by the Israeli military, to the point where aid attacks were being described as the 'new normal'[164]. The most recent such incident happened less than a week ago at the time of this writing, when at least 51 Palestinians were killed and over 200 more were injured by an Israeli attack on a line of UN trucks[165]. Israeli officials continue to insist that its military only acts against people who approach the convoys in a 'suspicious' manner, and opens fire only after giving repeated warnings.

Less than two months before the Flour Massacre, the NGO IFAIR heaped praises on the United States as 'one of the most generous countries in the world'[166]. A grotesque proportion of

---

[163] Caroline Radnofsky, Aurora Almendral and Leila Sackur, 'How did 118 people die in Gaza's Al-Rashid aid convoy violence?', *NBC News* (14 March 2024).

[164] Tarek Abu Azzoum, 'More Palestinian aid seekers killed waiting for food', *Al-Jazeera* (12 March 2024).

[165] Mohammed Jahjouh, Samy Magdy and Joseph Krauss, 'At least 51 Palestinians killed while waiting for aid trucks in Gaza, health officials say', *AP News* (17 June 2025).

[166] Tom Zeising, 'America the generous', *IFAIR.eu* (19 January 2024), https://ifair.eu/2024/01/19/america-the-generous-leading-the-world-in-charitable-giving-what-are-we-missing/.

that largesse goes toward the Israeli military. If the Flour Massacre and the aid-based killings which follow it are any measure, then God preserve the world from such 'generosity' as ours!

The measure of generosity is not in the amount given, or else Nicodemus would be the hero of the day with his hundred pounds of myrrh and aloe, and not the mother of Christ with her little *kəlî* כלי of sour wine. It is also not in the honour or prestige of the beneficiary, or else Saint John would be praising Joseph of Arimathea. The test of Mary, the test of Rebekah, is the measure of generosity. You give what you can, sincerely, because the stranger in front of you is thirsty. Not because they're from the same family as you. Not because it sheds glory on your empire. Not because it shows the virtue of your temple.

After the Crucifixion, the 'seventh hour' is always right now. When we hear the Able Herdsman's voice, even as He is laying down His life for the sheep, how do we answer Him? Do we give the thirsty water? Do we feed the hungry? Do we visit the sick? Do we seek justice for those to whom it is denied? The test of Rebekah presents itself anew to each hearer of Saint John's Gospel.

The race is not to the swift

The 'strong' disciple versus the 'weak' one

A clarification on John 20:1-9

Mary Magdalene, discoverer of the lifted stone

Mary Magdalene, the 'bitter tower', is a particularly intriguing literary character in the Gospel texts, and a particularly versatile one in terms of the allusive functions she provides to the authors of the texts. We can see this even in her function in the Gospel of Saint John. Her appearance together with Mary of Clopas (*Ḥilfa'y* חילפּאי), which is unique to John's Gospel, provides a textual allusion to Isaiah 9 and its specific proscription against the pride of builders. This allusion provides the basis for Saint John's criticism of Joseph of Arimathea and Nicodemus, whose familial pride led them to take charge of burying the body of Jesus, after the seventh hour had passed. In the process, they place themselves on the side of Empire in asking Pilate for Jesus's body, and on the side of the Temple in fearing the Judahites.

And now Mary Magdalene appears, by herself, at the tomb that Joseph of Arimathea provided (John 20:1)! Saint John's choice of word for 'tomb' is an interesting one. He does not use the standard Homeric Greek τάφος 'tomb', the word which often appears in the LXX as a translation of *qeber* קבר 'sepulchre, tomb' and which is preferred by Saint Matthew in his Gospel (Matt 23:27-29; 27:61-28:1). Rather, he uses the comparatively rarer (in the LXX) μνημεῖον, derived from the

The race is not to the swift

same Greek root μνάομαι 'to be mindful of, to remember' which furnishes us with English words like '**mnemo**nic' and 'ana**mne**sis'.

Even though both Greek words are used to translate *qeber* קבר, their functionality is slightly different. The Septuagint uses τάφος to refer in general to a burial-site, a grave where someone is buried. The μνημεῖον, by contrast, is taken to refer to a *monument* or a *mausoleum*: an edifice or stele carved and shaped by human hands to *remind* people that someone is buried here. For example:

מה־לך פה ומי לך פה כי־**חצבת** לך פה **קבר חצבי** מרום **קברו** חקקי בסלע משכן לו

τί σὺ ὧδε καὶ τί σοί ἐστιν ὧδε ὅτι **ἐλατόμησας** σεαυτῷ ὧδε **μνημεῖον** καὶ **ἐποίησας** σεαυτῷ ἐν ὑψηλῷ **μνημεῖον** καὶ ἔγραψας σεαυτῷ ἐν πέτρᾳ σκηνήν

What have you to do here and whom have you here, that you have **hewn** *here a* **tomb** *for yourself, you who* **hew** *a* **tomb** *on the height, and carve a habitation for yourself in the rock?* (Isa 22:16)

Wow. Would you look at that? Mary Magdalene is here to *remind* us of yet another Isaian passage whose purpose is to *shame the builders*, and those in particular who build *marôm* מרום 'on the heights'! This is the same Semitic consonantal pair, *r-m* ר-ם, which provides the root for the Hebrew toponym *Ramâ* רמה and the Aramaic *Ramtā'* רמתא which are Hellenised as **Arimathea**! Once again, the 'bitter tower' evokes a prophetic denunciation of those who would seek to inter the 'dead' teaching in a *qeber* קבר carved by human hands.

In the Houses of the Poor

Modern 'Judaeo-Christian' commentators do this poor lady immense injustice. As it took Roman Catholics nearly 1300 years to figure out, she is *not* a penitent harlot[167]. And as we Eastern Orthodox, to our shame, somehow *still* haven't figured out, she isn't a Roman Imperial court jestress changing the colour of eggshells[168]! No; the function of this Miriam from Magdalā' in the Gospel texts is always linked to her Hasmonean heritage, coming as she does from a Hasmonean city.

In Luke 8, she appears together with Joanna (*Yôḥānâ* יוחנה or *Yuwannā* يوَنّا, distaff equivalent of 'John') the wife of Herod's steward Ḥouza (a nominalisation of Aramaic *ḥaze'* חזא or ܣܘ 'to see, to behold', thus: 'overseer' or 'supervisor'); and with Susanna (*šūšan* שושן 'lily'). The Herodian, client-state links of Joanna are obvious; while Susanna is a symbol of heraldic trumpets or of imperial architecture, especially the capitols of pillars fashioned in Egyptian style (see 1 Kgs 7:19, 22). This triptych of women can thus be taken as a semiotic literary

---

[167] The pre-Vatican II Catholic fanfic treatment of the 'bitter tower', identifying her with the 'sinful woman' of Luke 7, originates with a 591 AD address by Pope Gregory the Dialogist, 'Homily 33' on penitence, in *XL Homiliarum in Evangelia* II (Libraria Academica Wagneriana, 1892), 264-274. It took until the Church calendar changes in 1969 for the Roman Catholic Church to realise that the Dialogist's interpretation was not, in fact, infallible.

[168] *e.g.* Abbah Raphael, 'Christ is Risen! Did you know? The red egg of Orthodox Easter', St. Barnabas Orthodox Mission Kenya (1 May 2016), https://orthodoxmissionkenya.org/christ-is-risen/.

The race is not to the swift

reference either to Davidic / Hasmonean / Herodian; or, more likely, Hasmonean / Herodian / Greco-Roman rule.

These three women of Luke 8 are characterised as having been healed of wicked spirits and infirmities. Subsequently, they accompany Jesus in His preaching and delivery of the good news of the kingdom. Obviously, they cannot perform this function if they are still tied to the dynastic lines whom they represent! Their healing and exorcism is thus innately tied to their detachment from their social roles as dynastic matriarchs.

The other consistent literary roles of Mary Magdalene in the Gospel texts are: as a witness to the Crucifixion (Matt 27:56; Mark 15:40; John 19:25); as a witness to Jesus's *absence* from the tomb (Matt 28:1; Mark 16:1; John 20:1); and as a witness to the other disciples of what she had seen (Mark 16:9-11; Luke 24:10-11; John 20:18).

Because she is so often presented to us as a witness, her role in the text is *prophetic*. She is able to see that which, for example, Judas cannot see. And she is able to hear that which the other disciples, Peter in particular, cannot hear. So, even though Mary is linked by her name to a *migdal* מגדל 'tower', and thus falls under the prophetic denunciation herself, she is nonetheless in a better position to speak than those who don't have eyes to see or ears to hear the text. We can think of her, therefore, as a kind of 'watchtower'. If Martin Scorsese were directing the Gospel of John, she would be Molly 'the Lookout'.

This prophetic role is *explicit* in John 20. Note that she comes to the tomb πρωῒ σκοτίας ἔτι οὔσης 'early, while it was still dark' (John 20:1)! This saying thematically hearkens back to the

In the Houses of the Poor

Qidrôn קִדְרוֹן of John 18:1, and lexically back to the σκοτία 'darkness' of John 1:5. Unlike Judas, and unlike the officials and servants he brought with him to arrest Jesus, Mary Magdalene *can* βλέπει 'see' in the dark. And she sees that τὸν λίθον ἠρμένον ἐκ τοῦ μνημείου 'the stone has been taken away from the tomb'.

The stone: God's overrule of human judgement

The use of λίθον 'stone' elsewhere in the Johannine text implies a place of judgement, beginning with the planned execution of the woman caught in adultery (John 8:3-7). Yet note how, after Jesus speaks, the λίθον does not judge the woman, but rather he who would throw it! There is also the λιθόστρωτος 'pavement' of John 18 which serves as the court of judgement in which Pilate condemns Christ, but again Saint John points us back through an unrelated Aramaic root to the Book of Daniel, in order to show that the actual judgement is not against Christ but against Pilate. Likewise, the six λίθιναι ὑδρίαι 'stone jars' of John 2, whose set is completed by the little σκεῦος 'bowl' or 'jewellery-box' found by the disciple and the mother of Jesus in John 19, reveal God's approbation of the mother of Jesus in the test of Rebekah even as the Roman and Judahite authorities are executing her Son.

So not only is the λίθον 'stone' a symbol of judgement! In Saint John's usage, a 'stone' is always a kind of *overrule*, an *overturning* of human judgement. Here he is following Paul's usage of λίθον in Romans 9:33, which directly alludes to the *'eben negef* אבן נגף 'stone that strikes' of Isaiah 8 and

The race is not to the swift

the *'eben bōḥan* אבן בחן 'stone that tests' of Isaiah 28. God's judgement always runs against what human beings do, or try to do, to reinforce their own political, religious, or economic power structures.

The lifting of the stone itself hearkens back to John 11. At the 'house of the poor', Jesus instructs 'them'—implied in the aorist second-person plural imperative ἄρατε and subsequently in the aorist third-person plural indicative ἦραν of the verb αἴρω 'to lift'—to lift the stone to Lazarus's tomb, despite Martha's objection that the body would stink after four days (John 11:39). Who are 'they' in this passage? There is Jesus, a singular person, giving the order. There is Martha, a singular person, resisting the order. And there is Lazarus, a singular person, who is trapped behind the stone and cannot do anything. But there are also the Judahites who make a pretense of offering condolences to Mary and Martha in the poor-house, while in fact they are trying to evict them (11:31), who come to the tomb with Jesus and Martha (11:33). It is *their* judgement which is overturned in this case. The two women's brother is alive; thus, they cannot evict the women from their house as they had planned.

Now Mary Magdalene, though she saw clearly and correctly what had been done with the stone, comes to the wrong conclusion about it. She says: **ἦραν** τὸν κύριον ἐκ τοῦ μνημείου καὶ οὐκ οἴδαμεν ποῦ ἔθηκαν αὐτόν '**They have taken** the Lord out of the tomb, and we do not know where they have laid him.' (John 20:2) This 'they' could potentially refer to Joseph of Arimathea and Nicodemus from the end of the last chapter. That would be a valid hearing from the context. But another valid reading, is

In the Houses of the Poor

that Mary Magdalene is pointing to the Roman and Judahite authorities who had Christ executed.

Regardless of which 'they' Mary Magdalene means, this usage of ἦραν 'they have taken', in connexion with the coverstone of a tomb, constitutes a direct literary echo of John 11. The Judahites' eviction of Mary and Martha from their house was *overturned* with the lifting of the stone, by Jesus's raising of Lazarus from his tomb. So here, too, the condemnation of Jesus Christ, executed as a kingly claimant and a threat to both Roman and Judahite political arrangements, is *overruled* by the *actual* King.

The race is not to the swift

Mary Magdalene *runs* to inform Peter and 'the other disciple' (Saint John; see Chapter 5 above) about what she has seen. Saint Paul uses this verb, τρέχω, and the synonymous doublet δραμών, throughout his letters in repeated reference to his own apostolic mission (1 Cor 9:24-26; Gal 2:2; Phil 2:16), and more broadly to the labours that his followers are subsequently called to do in furtherance of that mission (Gal 5:7; 2 Ths 3:1; Heb 12:1). It is not always positive, either. He warns against running κενὸν 'vainly' (Phil 2:16) and ἀδήλως 'to no purpose' (1 Cor 9:26).

It's worth taking very careful consideration of the sequence of events that follows. When Peter and John hear it, they also *run* to the tomb, but John *outruns* Peter and reaches the tomb first (John 20:4). However, although John reaches the tomb first, and stoops to look inside and see the burial linens on the

The race is not to the swift

ground, he *does not go inside* (20:5). Peter, coming up behind John, storms past him *into* the tomb and finds the linens discarded and the face-cloth lying by itself, rolled up, separately (20:6-7). Only then does John go into the tomb, sees what Peter sees, and believes (20:8).

Once again, there is the (very modern) temptation to read this passage as Saint John boasting. This is not the point. Rather, the author has laid out this sequence of events for a specific literary reason. The key to understanding this sequence lies in Saint Paul's distinction between running with a specific goal in mind, and running 'to no purpose'. The goal of 'the other disciple' is not to enter the tomb, but instead to παρακύψας 'peer inside' it. This is language that Saint Peter himself uses:

περὶ ἧς σωτηρίας ἐξεζήτησαν καὶ ἐξηραύνησαν προφῆται οἱ περὶ τῆς εἰς ὑμᾶς χάριτος προφητεύσαντες ἐραυνῶντες εἰς τίνα ἢ ποῖον καιρὸν ἐδήλου τὸ ἐν αὐτοῖς πνεῦμα Χριστοῦ προμαρτυρόμενον τὰ εἰς Χριστὸν παθήματα καὶ τὰς μετὰ ταῦτα δόξας οἷς ἀπεκαλύφθη ὅτι οὐχ ἑαυτοῖς ὑμῖν δὲ διηκόνουν αὐτά ἃ νῦν ἀνηγγέλη ὑμῖν διὰ τῶν εὐαγγελισαμένων ὑμᾶς ἐν πνεύματι ἁγίῳ ἀποσταλέντι ἀπ᾽ οὐρανοῦ εἰς ἃ ἐπιθυμοῦσιν ἄγγελοι **παρακύψαι**

The prophets who prophesied of the grace that was to be yours searched and inquired about this salvation; they inquired what person or time was indicated by the Spirit of Christ within them when predicting the sufferings of Christ and the subsequent glory. It was revealed to them that they were serving not themselves but you, in the things which have now been announced to you by those who *preached the good news to you through the Holy Spirit sent from heaven, things **into which** angels long **to look**.* (1 Pet 1:10-12)

Remember: Saint John is the 'weak' disciple, the one who needs Jesus's support and attention. What he's saying here is that even though Saint Peter is the stronger of the two of them, he has the *wrong aim*. Peter wants to go inside the tomb. Saint John beats him to the tomb because all he wants to do is to look inside.

A tomb is literally a cave: a hole in the side of a mountain. It's dark inside. This is where the pre-dawn σκοτία from when Mary Magdalene went to the tomb becomes functional again. The desire of John is to *see* in the dark, not blunder forward blindly into it, as Peter did already once in chapter 18. John's hanging back at the entrance of the tomb and going in after Peter is what allows him not only to see, but to *trust* in what he sees.

Another very clear semantic value for μνημεῖον 'tomb' is as a place where you bury dead people. When we read the Gospel of Saint John, we have to keep in mind that he is writing it to second-century communities in several cities, Ephesus chief among them, which were then under persecution from several directions. The risk of apprehension and death was a constant one for Paul's pupils and disciples. And although the purpose of both Saint John's Apocalypse and his Gospel seems to have been to provide comfort to those who are facing death for Paul's teachings, the literary character of Peter often appears as a warning against violence, rash action or precipitous pursuit of martyrdom—again, as in chapter 18. It could well be that John, in showing how he reached the tomb before Peter

The race is not to the swift

but didn't go inside, is indicating that the better course is to be ready to accept martyrdom but not to rush into it foolishly.

'For as yet they did not know...'

This passage is absolutely key not only to Saint John's Gospel but to the body of Gospel literature as a whole: οὐδέπω γὰρ ᾔδεισαν τὴν γραφὴν ὅτι δεῖ αὐτὸν ἐκ νεκρῶν ἀναστῆναι *'for as yet they did not know the scripture, that he must rise from the dead'* (John 20:9).

The Resurrection was *not* a foregone conclusion. We can't operate ontologically or theologically here: we need to deal with the *literary* reality of the text itself. We can't get suckered into the Neoplatonic, allegorical heuristics of later theologians like Origen Adamantius or Augustine of Hippo. Did Jesus *know for a fact* that His Father was going to bring Lazarus back to life? He certainly didn't behave as though He did. Even bearing in mind before everything I said in Chapter 2 about 'prophetic tears', Jesus wept at Lazarus's tomb because Lazarus was a friend, and because he was dead. In the same way, the literary characters of the Gospel—Mary Magdalene, Peter, John—have *no way to know* that the Resurrection had just happened. For all they knew, Jesus really had just gone the way of Tiberius Gracchus and Spartacus[169]. Isaiah's 'acceptable year of the

---

[169] And Ivailo, Wat Tyler, Thomas Müntzer, Emelyan Pugachev, Rosa Luxemburg, Fred Hampton and Ḥasan Naṣrallah. – *Auth.*

Lord', proclaimed in Luke 4:19, was crushed just like any other political revolt.

Even Mary Magdalene cries aloud to Peter and John not a joyful message of resurrection, but a distraught one of violation and sacrilege. Flavius Josephus himself attests that it was Roman practice in Judaea to desecrate the grave sites of executed rebels to prevent them from becoming used as recruiting-grounds for later revolts[170]. She sees the stone lifted away from the tomb, and speaks in terms of ἦραν: '**they** have taken the Lord... we do not know where **they** have laid him' (John 20:2). She fears someone broke in and stole the body. That is indeed how she reacts when Jesus Himself comes to meet her (20:13).

Unlike with Joseph of Arimathea and Nicodemus, no pejorative or denunciatory language surfaces in these first few verses of chapter 20 to bear witness against Mary, John—or even hasty Peter! Peter is doing better here than he was doing a couple of chapters ago, when he was denying Jesus three times in the household of the High Priest: he *sees* what's inside the tomb. This is *no small thing*, given how crucial a theme sight versus blindness is throughout Saint John's Gospel. (Still, what does Peter see? He sees the harlotry of Nicodemus—discarded, and the face-cloth lying separate. Nicodemus damaged only himself with his pretensions to virtue; Jesus's 'face' was not touched by it.)

---

[170] Flavius Josephus, *The Jewish War*, tr. Robert Traill (Harmondsworth, 1981), IV.vi, 83-86.

The race is not to the swift

The thought that Jesus's body had been stolen was not lack of faith on any of their parts. Just as Strider, Legolas and Gimli had no expectation that Gandalf would suddenly reappear after falling into flame and shadow in the mines of Moria, the disciples of Jesus simply had no expectation that Jesus would be raised from the dead. They are simply trying to make sense of what they saw; Saint John states this matter-of-factly, without comment.

Again, we must relate this verse to the context of a second-century hearing. Obviously, those who are attested as first suffering death proclaiming Jesus's lordship (Protodeacon Stephen, James the Just) are *not* immediately resurrected as Jesus was. Saint John offers the disciples' confusion to his hearers as comfort: *we went through this too.* We thought the fellowship was finished; we thought the whole thing had come to an end. Then Lookout Molly came running to tell us the body was gone; we didn't know what to think.

The certitude and triumphalism of later authors is something utterly alien to the Gospel texts themselves. The textual tradition taught by Paul among the scattered urban table-fellowships and transfigured Roman households to which they belonged, was something difficult for many of its hearers to grasp—even those of Judahite background who had been immersed in these texts from their youth. Saint John is assuring his hearers: I laid at the Lord's breast, ate with Him, heard His last words on the Cross—and *even I* couldn't read the signs. Don't expect to do the same yourself before the time... of which He is the only One Who knows.

Three times 'peace'

Jesus's ominous greeting to His disciples

A clarification on John 20:19-26

The persisting value of καιρός-time

Prince Nicolas Trubetskoi's 'medallion' interpretive method and functionalist, formal-structural literary analysis may have been used first and most prominently for Russian literature. And indeed, Trubetskoi's primary points of reference were the old Russian *Chronicles* and Dostoevsky's novels. Yet those novels and those *Chronicles* were literary products of specific times and places. No less are the Hebrew scrolls and the Greek books of the Pauline school the literary products of specific times and places. And if a critical method is valid for one, it is worth scientifically assaying if it produces valid results for another!

The authors of the Hebrew scrolls were neither British science fiction authors, nor German idealist philosophers. They did not understand time as an 'arrow'. Even in translation, even the barest and most naïve reading of Ecclesiastes should provide a solid underscore to the notion that the authors of the Hebrew text understood time as *cyclical*. Indeed, the relation between the scrolls shows that its authors understood time the same way that ancient Iranians, Indians and Chinese did, and not as *linear* and *teleological*, the way British Whig historians, German Hegelians and orthodox Marxists think of it.

Three times 'peace'

There is, however, one important *caveat* to make. That's the same *caveat* that Michael Hudson puts forward in his in-the-works trilogy on ancient West Asian economics. In the Hebrew view, the invisible and undepictable 'Elōhîm, Who sits just 'offscreen', gets a great big red 'reset' button which He is entitled to push when human beings get too far out of hand. This is the point of the *dərôr* דרור in Leviticus 25, which in its connotation of the 'free flow' of water, and the direct lexical reference to the *šûb* שוב 'return' of men to the land, is tied directly to the Genesis account of the flood and its aftermath (Gen 8:3-9).

As Hudson tells it, the 'clean slate' proclamation in Bronze Age West Asia was a royal prerogative, a wiping out of agrarian debts that was meant to 'reset' an economy that had grown unbalanced in creditors' favour. This allowed Bronze Age farmer-soldiers to be at least somewhat assured that a state of dependency and unfreedom at a creditor's hands was never permanent. They would be restored to their customary lands when the next king came to power[171]. The innovation of the Hebrew authorial school which wrote Leviticus and Deuteronomy, and the books of Isaiah and Jeremiah, was to take this proclamatory power out of the hands of earthly kings, who could (and did!) abuse and undermine its intent, and place it in the hands of an invisible, inscrutable, and therefore incorruptible, God of gods.

---

[171] *e.g.* Hudson, *Philosophy*, 51.

In the Houses of the Poor

The three Hebrew bodies of text each have, and have between them, definite shapes and reliefs to the fields of their 'medallions'. The first five books of the *Torah* establish the pattern. Human history is allowed to cycle through phases of gathering and scattering: of rise, *hubris* and fall of palaces, temples, cities and civilisations—until such time as God sees fit to intervene, in His own καιρός (= Heb. *'êt* עֵת 'season, due time, opportunity'), which cannot be predicted or planned for. The rise and fall of the Cainite and Noahide civilisations in the first eleven chapters of Genesis is the template on which the story of the Israelite civilisation proceeds.

If the *Torah* gives us an impression of the cyclical, organicist historiosophy of Oswald Spengler, Constantine Leont'ev and Nicolas Danilevsky, who each independently proposed a 'life cycle' of civilisations, that is probably no accident. But the *Torah* does not propose it as a 'natural' cycle, like the change in seasons. The *Torah* also gives us the conditions on which God's judgement, His pressing of the 'reset' button, can be forestalled. These are the books of the Law, given in rudimentary form in Exodus, and in expanded form in Leviticus, Numbers and Deuteronomy. We can appeal to God to delay or withhold His judgement through *obedience* to His Law. That is: we can refrain from idolatry (not worshipping people or places or ideas or things); we can set aside a time to hear His words; we can honour the people that give birth to us and raise us; and we can extend hospitality or at least refrain from injuring or dishonouring our neighbours.

However, even the people to whom this Law is given do not obey it! The *Torah* furnishes the basic conceit from which the

Three times 'peace'

other two bodies of scrolls proceed. The *Nəbî'îm*, the prophets, are sent among the people to warn them of the impending divine 'reset', which the people deserve for having failed to follow His Law, in the hopes of restoring the people to obedience and thus saving them from the wrath to come. (Ironically, the only people which *genuinely listens* to a Hebrew *nabî'*, and lastingly changes its behaviour *en masse* in accordance with God's Law, are a *foreign* people: the Assyrians of Nīnəwē in the Book of Jonah. And Jonah gets mad at them for it!)

And what happens when the people continue to disobey God's Law is the province of the *Kətubîm*, the writings. There are two divisions among the writings. The first are the 'historical' *Kətubîm*: a historical-fictional treatment of the rise, hubris and fall of the kingdoms of Israel and Judah—which ends in the exile in Babylon. And the second are the 'wisdom' *Kətubîm*, in which the interpretive framework of all three scrolls is put forward in the form of *mašalîm* משלים: 'likenesses' or 'bywords'.

The model of χρόνος-time versus καιρός-time which we see in the Greek Scriptures produced by the Pauline school, including the Gospel of Saint John, operates from the same set of assumptions as the Hebrew Scriptures. They are indeed part of the *same literary tradition*.

Saint Paul's 'grace' and 'peace'

In his podcast *A Light to the Nations*, in a homily on the sixth chapter of the Gospel of Luke, Fr. Fred Shaheen of Saint

In the Houses of the Poor

Matthew Orthodox Church in North Royalton, Ohio expands on the Tarazian insight that Saint Paul begins nearly all of his letters with χάρις ὑμῖν καὶ εἰρήνη 'grace to you and peace' (*e.g.* Rom 1:7; 1 Cor 1:2; Gal 1:3; Phil 1:2…) and ends his letters only with χάρις 'grace' (*e.g.* Rom 16:24; 1 Cor 16:23; Gal 6:18; Phil 4:23…)[172]. The χάρις of God is the freely-given starting-point, the 'point A' of each of the letters of Paul over which we have no control; and the εἰρήνη of God is the ending-point, the 'point Z'… over which we *also* have no control. The pedagogy of the Pauline teaching begins with the given 'grace' of God, and exposits a universal expansion of the *Torah* which we are meant to follow to 'point Z'. Yet each of the Pauline letters ends *only* with the χάρις, which is an invitation to put the lesson within that letter into practice. If the ending were εἰρήνη, that would mean that everything has been said and done, God's judgement had been delivered, and nothing more could be put into practice.

On its surface, this would seem to be a repudiation of the Hebrew Scriptures' cyclical understanding of time. For there to be pedagogy, there has to be progression: benchmarks, formative assessments, a learning target. Yet the cyclical structure of the letters, beginning with 'grace to you and peace' but ending only with 'grace', indicates that only the first part of the lesson is ever given. The second part of the lesson is left

---

[172] Fr Fred Shaheen, 'From A to Z', *A Light to the Nations* podcast 51 (28 February 2025), EphesusSchool.org. https://alighttothenations.transistor.fm/episodes/a-to-z.

Three times 'peace'

to the hearer: ὥσπερ διέταξα... οὕτως καὶ ὑμεῖς ποιήσατε 'as I directed... so you also are to do' (1 Cor 16:1; cf. Luke 10:37). Paul *never* gives the summative assessment, the final exam, because that's *not* his job: ἑκάστου τὸ ἔργον φανερὸν γενήσεται ἡ γὰρ ἡμέρα δηλώσει 'each man's work will become manifest; for the Day will disclose it' (1 Cor 3:13)!

This is, in fact, no different at all from the cyclical history exposited in the *Torah*! Paul has not deviated or innovated anything away from the Hebrew scrolls; he is merely proclaiming the same teaching to a different audience. The χάρις of God to the people of Ephesus, or Corinth, or Philippi, or Galatia, is the same 'grace' which is allotted to Cain, and the same grace that is allotted to Noah, to Abraham, and to David. And that is the grace of *instruction*. The God of the text gives each of these heads-of-household, each of these patriarchs, a set of classroom rules, a course syllabus and a list of assignments: in short, He gives each of them a *Torah*. And then occasionally he sends a teaching assistant, a *nabî'*, into the classroom to check in on the students' progress and to warn them that there will be an exam that they need to be ready for.

But in each case, when the exam comes, they are never ready. Cain's children become so horrendous in their mistreatment of each other that God wipes them all out in a flood. Noah's children erect the Tower of Babel, from which God scatters them over the face of the earth. Abraham's children sell one of their own brothers—the one 'good' brother, in fact—into slavery, and God delivers them over to slavery in Egypt. And David's children become debauched landlords and idolatrous worshippers of the gods of their wives. God at last tires of getting them to behave, and sends them into Babylon.

In the Houses of the Poor

The idea of that human history consists of a series of 'dispensations' or 'covenants' that progress from one state of human maturity to another is a later imposition of historicist logic onto the text. A *bərît* ברית is simply a 'treaty, pledge, pact, arrangement' brokered between two human agents or between God and a human being. God does not replace a *bərît* with another until humans break it by failing to hold up their end: that's the function. Thus, the succession of *bərîtôt* is not 'progress'. The development of a 'dispensational' approach to Scripture *among Christians*, very likely arose in response to the claims of Flavius Josephus and others that the Hebrew writings provided them with a historical claim to honour and political status within the Roman political structure.

So, as Fr Marc Boulos is fond of saying: Paul's letters are not 'good news' to the nations, they're just 'news'[173]. The news is, because of Jesus, executed on a charge of *appetere regnum* for preaching the 'acceptable year', *all* nations have now received the χάρις 'grace' that was given to David. You're all enrolled in the class now. Pass/fail. No add/drop. Good luck! Here's the syllabus.

Having Saint Paul for a TA does not invalidate that syllabus. History—*at least from a human perspective!*—is still cyclical, and its logic now carries forward universally. Sorry, Josephus: the 'good news' of Christ is not going to save your Temple! And

---

[173] Fr Marc Boulos, 'Thorny trees are not for normie trees', *The Bible as Literature* podcast 539 (25 Oct 2024), https://www.youtube.com/watch?v=1IkUbPW2w0U.

Three times 'peace'

sorry, Augustus: He's not going to save your Empire! The difference is that, as far as Paul is concerned, *we've already gotten the warnings* that we need. Why should Saint Paul need to say over again, what was already said by Ezekiel, by Isaiah, by Jeremiah? The instruction is the 'grace', but we aren't going to get check-ups and reminders from the nəbî'îm anymore. As far as Paul was concerned, the last of these was Saint John the Forerunner[174]. We need to be ready for God's εἰρήνη whenever He declares it.

The ominous sound of Jesus's 'peace'

Jesus comes among the disciples, into the place where τῶν θυρῶν κεκλεισμένων 'the doors were shut' (John 20:19). As I mention in *The Lamb before Its Shearers*, the Greek θύρα 'door' (pronounced THEE-rah) can, and in some places should, be read as a cross-lingual pun for *Torah* תורה. The link between 'the door' and 'the instruction' or 'the scroll' of the Law is made functionally explicit at several points in the prophetic and wisdom writings (*e.g.* Prov 8:32-36, Jer 36:23-24, Eze 44:2-9). It is most certainly meant that way in John 10! Jesus is the Able Herdsman who enters the sheepfold by means of the *Torah*, by submission and obedience to the teaching of the One God. All others who approach the sheepfold, by means other than the

---

[174] Obviously, it would be a different tale for a people who had not received this 'grace' in the first place. There was still room for one more *nabiyy* نبي, it seems, among the Arabs. The witness of Paul to the Roman Empire does not preclude the witness of Muḥammad. – *Auth.*

teaching, are thieves. And by that example Jesus *is* the door, the *Torah*[175].

Let's look again at the verb here: εἰσέρχομαι 'to come in'. It's a compound verb, like the German *hereinkommen*. Jesus says ὁ δὲ **εἰσερχόμενος** διὰ τῆς θύρας ποιμήν ἐστιν τῶν προβάτων '*but **he who enters** by the door is a shepherd of the sheep*' (John 10:2)—it's a participle nominalisation of the verb. And here we see **ἦλθεν** ὁ Ἰησοῦς καὶ ἔστη **εἰς** τὸ μέσον '*Jesus **came** and stood **among** them*' (John 20:19). Someone who is dealing with the translation alone, might miss this, but it's a play on the same verb. Of course the Able Herdsman came in by the doors even though they were shut!

We should not attribute Jesus's 'sudden' appearance to supernatural means, or to some ontological Neoplatonic transfiguration of the flesh. That isn't the point of the text. The usage of θύρα / θύρας / θυρῶν in these passages is functional and *mašal*-ic. He who enters by the door is the shepherd, and Jesus *is* the door. What meaning would it have for Him to have the doors be 'shut' on Him?

Yet now we come to the reason that the doors were shut in the first place. They were shut, διὰ τὸν φόβον τῶν Ἰουδαίων '*for fear of the Jews*' (John 20:19). This same phrase, in the exact same words, appears in John 19:38 to describe the attitude of Joseph of Arimathea and Nicodemus. Saint John's usage of this phrase there was entirely pejorative. The men who came to

---

[175] Cooper, *Lamb*, 238.

Three times 'peace'

bury Jesus were doing so entirely out of self-preservation, and out of a desire to appear righteous in the eyes of the Roman and Judahite Temple authorities. These same authorities, too, are portrayed as fearful (John 12:42-43). Now the other disciples of Jesus are found in the exact same fear, not having believed the words of Lookout Molly (who in this instance is a model of hearing and obedience!), and are huddled behind shut doors.

So when we hear Jesus say εἰρήνη ὑμῖν 'peace be unto you', *three times* in the twentieth chapter of the Gospel of Saint John (20:19, 21, 26), we need to be hearing it the same way Saint Paul meant it in his letters.

Εἰρήνη ὑμῖν—Time's up.

Εἰρήνη ὑμῖν—Pencils down.

Εἰρήνη ὑμῖν—Turn in your papers.

Threefold repetition connotes *judgement*: irreversible and final. In the canonical format of the Greek Scriptures, Saint John's Gospel is the *final* Gospel. It is the *end* of the instruction to the disciples. And when they are found, it is in the same state of mind and in the same condition of fearful disobedience as that which characterised Joseph of Arimathea and Nicodemus!

Red Alert! Warp core breach! The *Enterprise*-D saucer section has lost helm control. It's going down into the atmosphere of Veridian III—which is about to explode from a sun going nova.

And our reaction to Jesus's return should be exactly the same as Cmdr Data's: 'Oh, *shit!*'[176]

Is there hope after this judgement?

This moment at the end of the Gospel of Saint John is ominous. Much like Jesus's appearance at the Feast of Booths in Chapter 7, this passage has an eschatological function. Just as John (the Forerunner) is not That One but is rather a witness to Him (John 1:7-8); so the last Gospel bearing the name of John is not That Day, but rather is a witness to That Day. Just as the *Enterprise*-D crew lives to see three more movies and a sequel TV show, all thanks to an eight-dimensional space-wizardry plot device and a well-timed cameo by Bill Shatner, so too the disciples of Jesus live to be *sent out* into the world, with *this book* in hand that witnesses against them... or, more precisely, uses their example as a cautionary tale.

Jesus's admonition to His disciple Thomas, who did not believe even the other disciples about His return (who, in turn, did not believe Mary Magdalene when she told them—Thomas is not unique; his failure is the same as the other disciples' failure), and to whom He delivers the final εἰρήνη, is precisely that μακάριοι οἱ μὴ ἰδόντες καὶ πιστεύσαντες *'blessed are those who have not seen and yet believe'* (John 20:29). This admonition speaks precisely to those to whom the book is addressed. And what follows is the author 'breaking the fourth wall' and

---

[176] David Carson, *Star Trek: Generations* (Paramount Pictures, 1994).

Three times 'peace'

addressing the audience: ταῦτα δὲ γέγραπται ἵνα **πιστεύσητε** '*but these are written so that **you may believe***' (John 20:31).

Full circle, back to Galilee

A clarification on John 21:1-11

Gone fishin'...?

Kayano Shigeru (1926-2006), the foremost Ainu rights and environmental protection activist in Japan as well as social-democratic member of the Diet during the 1990s and early 2000s, in his autobiography *Our Land Was a Forest*, describes the traditional life of the indigenous Ainu people of Nibutani on the island of Hokkaidō. In his description of the seasonal rhythm of this life, he touches on the types of fish—trout and salmon in particular—that were harvested by the Ainu for their sustenance at different times of year, as well as on the methods used by the Ainu for this harvest. He writes:

> *For salmon fishing, we used nets and hooks. The net, made of a heavy-duty cotton thread, was approximately 1.3 by 2.7 metres. A 3-centimetre-wide, 2.1-metre-long stick was tied to each end of the net. Four men boarded two dugout canoes, and while one in each manoeuvred the canoe, the other held one stick of the net. Rowing downstream so that the canoes formed an inverted V-shape, they let the net float in the water. When salmon entered the V, the men moved their canoes together and, wringing the net as they pulled it up, caught the fish in what was now like a hammock. This was one of several fishing methods and was called* yasi *(scooping).*

> *My father, Kaizawa Seitarō, was very fond of salmon fishing—or perhaps he was simply desperate to catch salmon because his family could not survive without them. When he caught the first salmon of the year, he placed it on a cutting board at the master's seat to the*

> side of the fireplace, with the salmon's head pointing toward the fire and its belly toward the left of the fireplace. Sitting to the right of the fireplace, my father bowed ceremonially to the salmon and said in Ainu, "Thank you for honouring us with your presence at our house today."[177]

This is the style of subsistence fishing that we should be thinking about when we hear about 'fishermen' in ta Vivlía. We should not be thinking about recreational sport anglers, or upper middle-class families in Minnesota who take a trailer out on the lake and go ice-fishing in January. Still less should we be thinking about fishing fleets or commercial fisheries in the North Atlantic. Saint Peter's and Saint Andrew's families would have been similarly dependent on his catch, to Kaizawa Seitarō and his family in Nibutani. A good catch could mean prosperity, and better money in the pocket than would go to a landless agricultural labourer for the same day's work; but a poor catch could mean starvation.

When the Japanese under the Meiji Emperor moved into Hokkaidō in force, they imposed laws and taxes that harshly proscribed traditional Ainu fishing practices and robbed them of their livelihood. The Ainu were forced by legal compulsion and economic necessity to move into Japanese-run camps and cities, and take menial jobs that supported their colonisers. In a similar way, the imperial Roman state imposed itself on

---

[177] Kayano Shigeru, *Our Land Was a Forest*, trs. Kyōko Selden and Lili Selden (Westview Press, 1994), 19.

In the Houses of the Poor

traditional fishermen in Syria and Judaea, in order to conscript them and fund their construction projects.

The return of Jesus from the dead in the previous chapter, and the pronouncement of the threefold εἰρήνη, seems to have had an anticlimactic result. The adverse judgement on the disciples has not interrupted their lives. They still have to eat. This is why Peter, Thomas, Nathanael, James and John *'and two others of his disciples'* (John 21:2) went out at night on their boat, *'but that night they caught nothing'* (John 21:3).

The other purpose this episode serves is as a *cyclical* reference internal to the text. It is again noteworthy that Nathanael is the only disciple here whose place of origin is mentioned explicitly[178], and it also happens to be the place where the 'action' is: τῆς Γαλιλαίας 'in Galilee' (where the Sea of Tiberias is located). The mention of these specific disciples, Andrew, Peter and Nathanael, in this order, with the explicit reference to Galilee, is a direct and unavoidable reference back to the *beginning* of Jesus's teaching in this Gospel (John 1:35-2:1).

The prophetic function of ἁλιεύς

The word ἁλιεύς, in Greek, derives from ἅλς 'salt, brine, sea', and is an occupational or associative noun, to the effect of 'seaman, someone who works on the sea'. In the LXX, it

---

[178] Cooper, *Lamb*, 149-172.

Full circle, back to Galilee

translates Semitic triliterals derived from the consonant pair *d-g* ד-ג 'fish': Hebrew *dayyāg* דיג, or Aramaic *dawwāg* דוג 'fisherman'. The geminated consonant in the middle (on a *faʿʿāl* فعال grammatical pattern) generally indicates productive occupation, as is still common in Arabic: like *Ḥaddād* حداد 'smith' from *ḥadīd* حديد 'iron'; or *Dallāl* دلال 'auctioneer, broker' from *dalla* دل 'to advertise'; or *Ḥabbāz* خباز 'baker' from *ḥubz* خبز 'bread'.

The function of 'fisherman' appears in several places in the Hebrew texts. In Job, it appears in God's speech to Job out of the whirlwind, daring him to put a *ṣilṣal dāgîm* צלצל דגים 'fisherman's spear' through the head of Leviathan, knowing such a task to be beyond the scope of anyone who is not God (Job 41:7). But in the prophetic writings, the 'fishermen' are *always* associated with the fulfilment of a prophetic warning or promise.

In the vision of Ezekiel of the mighty life-giving water that flows from the eastern threshold of the Temple, the *dawwāgîm* דוגים will spread their nets along what was once the Dead Sea, but which is now teeming with all kinds of fish (Eze 47:10). In Isaiah, the *dayyāgîm* דיגים of the Nile are made to lament, as their waters dry up in response to God's punishment of Egypt's idolatry and reliance on wicked, exploitative counsellors (Isa 19:8). But the most relevant reference for the present passage in Saint John's Gospel is the one from Jeremiah, because it uses the verbal form *dîg* דיג 'to fish, to go fishing', which is what Saint Peter proposes to do in John 21:3. The relevant function is again one of *judgement*:

הנני שלח לדיגים רבים נאם־יהוה ודיגום ואחרי־כן אשלח לרבים צידים וצדום מעל כל־הר ומעל כל־גבעה ומנקיקי הסלעים

In the Houses of the Poor

> Behold, I am sending for many **fishers**, says the Lord, and they shall **catch them**; and afterwards I will send for many hunters, and they shall hunt them from every mountain and every hill, and out of the clefts of the rocks. (Jer 16:16)

The fishermen are semiotically linked to Egypt through Isaiah; and the hunters are a classic image for Babylon (think: Gilgamesh as the hunter-hero). The idea is not, as the section-header writers for the RSV translation of Jeremiah interpret it, a 'restoration' of Israel. Jeremiah is proclaiming *ḥarb* חרב: the destruction, between Egypt and Babylon, of the ambitions of humans for kingship.

The function of ἁλιεύς / *dayyāg* דיג in the prophetic books is important for the same reason as the modern-day analogue of the Ainu subsistence salmon-fishermen. American Judaeo-Christianism has inherited a soft, fluffy *bourgeois* image of the 'fishers of men', filtered through generations of missionaries and church leaders. That's an image we need to get rid of if we want to make sense of the last chapter in Saint John's Gospel. This is not a 'gathering' of people. The disciples are clearly not yet ready to fulfil that prophetic function. Instead, this is the chastisement and disciplining of *Peter*... and by extension the rest of the disciples with him.

The (repeated) reeducation of Peter

The disciples, led by Peter on this fishing trip, are coming back from an unsuccessful catch; thus, their survival is in question. When Jesus, who appears on the shore, calls out to them to ask them for fish, they are unable to extend hospitality

Full circle, back to Galilee

to Him (John 21:5); thus, their honour is in question. Peter is being brought back to the beginning of the Gospel, to Galilee, for a chance to *redo* that which he did incorrectly the first time.

Fr Paul Tarazi points out one way in which Peter is being given a 'do-over'. He points to the repeated use of the Greek verb ἑλκύω 'to drag, to draw off' in this passage, and contrasts it with prior uses in the same text:

> *Recalling once again that Galatians 2:11-14 is the background for the Gospels' portrayal of Peter's denials, it is only fitting that his reinstatement would likewise be in the context of a meal and that he would be offered once again a chance to endorse the mission to the Gentiles. The latter is represented by Jesus' command to cast the net on the other side—the 'right' side of the boat. In effect Peter is told to do the opposite of what he did at the time of Jesus's betrayal, when he cut off the slave's 'right' ear. The parallel between the two passages is confirmed by the presence of the verb* helkyō *(draw, pull away) in both* [John 18:10 and 21:6, 11]*...*
>
> *Since* helkyō *occurs twice more in John, in the sense of drawing people to the Father (6:44) and to Jesus (12:32), the message is clear: it is Peter's latter action of drawing the net, not drawing the sword, that reflects Jesus's will. The net should be cast in the open sea representing the Roman Empire at large, which is peopled by Gentiles as well as Jews.*[179]

---

[179] Fr Paul Tarazi, *The New Testament: Introduction – Johannine Writings* (St. Vladimir's Seminary Press, 2004), 260.

In the Houses of the Poor

Jesus's instruction to Peter to 'draw' the net on the 'right' side of the boat, however, is only the first of several ways He has to correct him. The occurrence of the verb διαζώννυμι 'to bind, to gird on' likewise directs our gaze back in the text to the Last Supper, at which Jesus 'girded on' the λέντιον 'handkerchief, linen cloth' to serve the disciples by washing their feet (John 13:4-5; see Chapter 4). Here too, Peter made two missteps, both out of a failure to hear his Teacher's lesson: vacillating comically between social discomfort at being served by his Teacher in such a way; and obsequious desire to ingratiate himself. Here it is Peter who 'girds on' his ἐπενδύτην 'upper garment' at once, for he had been γυμνός 'naked', and ἔβαλεν ἑαυτὸν flings himself into the sea to swim over to Jesus (21:7).

But these three Greek lexemes occurring together, διαζώννυμι and γυμνός and βάλλω, points to one specific place in the Septuagint: the prophecy, following the judgement against Samaria as 'Āholâ אהלה (= 'her tent'), against Jerusalem as 'Āholîbâ אהליבה (= 'a tent in her'). The Lord informs Ezekiel that Jerusalem had lusted after the images of the ἐζωσμένους (= ḥagôrê חגורי) 'girded' Chaldeans, and brought them to her as her lovers. Therefore He will bring down the same judgement upon Jerusalem as He had upon Samaria, and deliver her into their hands, and they will βαλοῦσιν (= yāsîmû ישימו) 'fling' themselves upon her from every side, and uncover her γυμνὴ (= 'ervat ערות) 'nakedness' (Eze 23:11-30).

In Ezekiel's prophecy, it is the things that Jerusalem most desires—political prestige, represented by the vermillion of the Chaldeans' clothes; priestly authority, represented by the

Full circle, back to Galilee

girdles on the Chaldeans' belts; and military power, represented by the turbans on the Chaldeans' heads, so that they 'look like officers'—that undo and ruin her. The allusion in John 21:7 to Ezekiel's indictment of the two kingdoms tells us that Peter suffers from the same problem. This is why he abandons the boat as it is coming to shore: Peter's desire is not for the teaching, but instead for an ισμός, an ideology. Peter is obsessed with master-servitor roles, and also with ingratiating himself, which is why he acts like a buffoon while Jesus is washing his feet in John 13.

Peter, having abandoned the boat, is forced to swim to shore. John takes care to mention that the boat is πηχῶν διακοσίων 'a hundred cubits' offshore. Interestingly, this is exactly the length of the court for the Tent of Meeting (Exo 27:18). And the disciples are behind him in the boat, dragging a δίκτυον 'net' (see Exo 27:4—such a 'net' was part of the Tent of Meeting by design) full of fish. The boat which Peter has just abandoned is a double allusion to the Lord's Tent. This shows us that Peter's is *not* the Lord's Tent, but rather ʾāholâ אהלה 'her tent', the tent of the harlot, or worse, in ʾāholîbâ אהליבה 'a tent in her'. One has to take this as a caustic criticism of Peter's embrace of the Judaisers within the Pauline community, and in fact his abandonment of the Pauline teaching.

Thus Jesus has to stage yet another 'do-over' for Peter. This happens with the ἀνθρακιά 'charcoal fire' which is already prepared with fish and bread—it stands to reason, provided by Jesus Himself, or by the Father. The ὀψάριον... καὶ ἄρτον 'fish and bread' on the fire allude back to the feeding of the multitudes (John 6:9-11). And the ἀνθρακιά, of course, refers to

Peter's threefold denial of Jesus in the house of the High Priest (John 18:17-27).

I argue in *Lamb* that the 'five' loaves of bread in John 6 firstly represent the Law—the *Torah*, the first five books—but also that they represent the *universality* of that Law, indicating the four cardinal directions plus the centre[180]. Furthermore, I argue that the 'two' fish in John 6 form a *taijitu* 太极图 representing the Gentiles and the Jews[181]. The fact that Jesus brings Peter before a charcoal fire with the *universal* food, representing the Gentiles and the Jews, onto it, is the strongest possible Johannine rebuke of Peter's betrayal of the Pauline table-fellowship and his denial of the *Torah* to the Gentiles.

After this, Peter is the one who is sent back to the boat to haul up the net, which contains 153 fish (John 21:11). Tarazi, who is careful to make note of Johannine numerology, argues persuasively that this number 153 is a reference to the *hamôn gôyim* המון גוים 'multitude of nations' in Genesis 17: the numeric values of these eight Hebrew letters add together to make 160. The seven disciples who are present in the boat when the fish are taken aboard can be subtracted from this to make 153[182]. The implication is that the disciples are meant to go out as 'fishermen' of the *sum total* of human beings, to *all* the nations, and not just to the Judahites.

---

[180] Cooper, *Lamb*, 151-152.
[181] Cooper, *Lamb*, 159.
[182] Tarazi, *Johannine*, 262.

Full circle, back to Galilee

John 21 revisits three of Peter's failures: his status-mongering at the washing of the disciples' feet (John 13:5-10); his cutting off the right ear of the slave named 'king' (John 18:10-11); and his threefold denial of Jesus (John 18:17-27). Yet each of Jesus's answers to each of these failures resonates with the *same central point*: the Pauline teaching is meant *for all peoples* to hear and obey, not only for Jews. Saint John is hitting Saint Peter over the head again and again with this same teaching in order to get it into his head.

Fish to the fire

One further point: the fish are being brought to the charcoal fire. If the 153 'fish' together with the disciples are *hamôn gôyim* המון גוים 'the multitude of nations', it does *not* make for a comfortable analogy. We are being brought to the same judgement that Saint Peter is—and in fact, Peter is the one bringing us to that judgement! This makes sense particularly if we consider the *dayyāgîm* דיגים of Jeremiah 16 as being the operative reference.

The test of Saint Peter is implicit in the semiotics of the net and the boat, and is explicitly referenced to Ezekiel 23 by the Greek verbiage Saint John chooses in the seventh verse. The test is of *whose 'tent' he is in*. Is he in the Lord's Tent of Meeting, or is he in the tent of the harlot? And we see he is in front of a 'charcoal fire' like the one he warmed himself by in the courtyard of the High Priest: the moment when he denied Jesus.

In the Houses of the Poor

If this is the test of Peter, and Peter is the one hauling us in his net to the judgement, then the same question which is put to him will be asked to each of us in the *hamôn gôyim*. Are we inside the hundred-cubit yard of the Lord's tent? That is, are we seated in the presence of the One God 'Elōhîm, hearing His commands *and doing them*? Or are we in the tent of some other authority, or rather allowing some other authority to pitch their tent in us? Are we hearing Jesus's command, through the seven disciples, to love our '152' neighbours (that is to say, *all of them*)? Or are we closing our ears to that command, and coming up with some excuse to deny Him?

Closing remarks of a Gothic disciple

A final clarification on John 21:21-25

Not the first barbarian to read John

Ephesus, the Greek city-state of the Ionian coast where Saint John lived in his mature years, was destroyed by the Gothic people in 269 AD, with the Temple to Artemis there being the highest-profile loss. This is how the sixth-century Byzantium-dwelling Gothic historian Jordanes describes the destruction of Ephesus:

> *While he was given over to luxurious living of every sort, Respa, Veduc and Thuruar, leaders of the Goths, took ship and sailed across the strait of the Hellespont to Asia. There they laid waste many populous cities and set fire to the renowned temple of Diana at Ephesus, which, as we said before, the Amazons built... even to-day, though it is happily situated near the royal city, it still shows some traces of its ruin as a witness to posterity.*[183]

What Jordanes recounts here is a historical fact. The sack of Ephesus actually happened. The ruins of the Temple of Artemis are still there. They can be visited. The Goths had better-known exploits, to be sure: the battle of Adrianople under Fritigern in

---

[183] Jordanes, *The Origin and Deeds of the Goths*, tr. Charles C. Mierow (Arepo, 2011), 58, xx.107.

Closing remarks of a Gothic disciple

378 AD, for example, or the sack of Rome under Alaric's Visigoths in 410 AD. These events are also historical facts.

I brought up these events in Chapter 1, and I brought Ephesus up again in Chapter 10. Why do I do so? In the 16th century, Austrian courtier Wolfgang Lazius portrayed the Goths as bold adventurers and unifiers of Europe: the predecessors and prototypes, in fact, of the Habsburgs he served[184]. Am I, like him, seeking to place my Gothic ancestors on such a pedestal? Am I hailing the Goths as great leaders, mighty warriors, brave men of stout spirit and heroic prowess, exemplars of an indomitable fighting spirit? Am I attempting to honour their legacy and use them as a tangible, historical inspiration on which to build new empires, or revitalise an old one?

Or, conversely, am I leveraging my modern perspective and cultural moment in order to condemn them? British historian Edward Gibbon once famously excoriated my ancient forebears as *'rude savages of the Baltic'*, *'destitute of a taste for the elegant arts'*[185]. Am I, like him, casting the Goths as wicked vandals? Am I invoking them as evil oppressors to be erased? In the style of a virtue-hoarding [186] professional-managerial class self-

---

[184] Wolfram, *Goths*, 2.

[185] Edward Gibbon, *The Decline and Fall of the Roman Empire* vol. 1 (T. Miller, 1820), 434.

[186] To understand what I'm getting at here, please read Catherine Liu, *Virtue Hoarders: the Case against the Professional Managerial Class* (University of Minnesota Press, 2021).

promoter, am I seeking to burnish 'woke', 'anti-racist' and 'culturally-aware' *bona fides* at the expense of my own patrimony?

The Goths who destroyed Ephesus were human beings. In their basic nature and inclinations they were no different, no better and no worse, than the Greek and Jewish residents of the city they sacked and destroyed. They are kin to me by blood, so I give them the *kabod* כבד they are due. But to idolise them as heroes, as *gibborîm* גברים, would be *zənût* זנות 'idolatry, harlotry'. Note how the Judahites in John 8:41 pridefully boast in their ancestry that they ἐκ πορνείας οὐ γεγεννήμεθα 'are not born of fornication', even though Jeremiah has already prophesied against them, 'fathers and sons together', that that is indeed exactly what they are (Jer 13:13-15, 27)! Note that the word translated as πορνεία in the LXX is precisely this *zənût* זנות.

Conversely, to ontologise my Gothic ancestors' villainy in order to boast in my own generation's righteousness would be *mərî* מרי 'rebellion'. I am a child of the Gothic 'household', and the relationships within a household are not unimportant in Scripture. Saint Paul warns against husbands πικραίνεσθε 'growing bitter' against their wives, with this warning extending to children and parents both (Col 3:18-21). This same verb is carried from Paul's writings into the Johannine literature through the Apocalypse: the trumpet of the third angel whose falling star ἐπικράνθησαν 'embitters' a third of the waters and causes many human beings to die (Apoc 8:11). The same Greek root, though inflected as παραπικραίνω, is used to translate in Ezekiel the *mərî* מרי 'rebellious' house of Jerusalem (Eze 2:5-8).

Closing remarks of a Gothic disciple

At this point, I think, the *mašal* משל I am making should be clear. It should be obvious that I am not writing for an audience of 16th century Austrian proto-nationalists or 19th century British Whigs. I am writing for 21st century Americans (and possibly Britons) who are caught in a similar kind of trap. Now that the old Cold War liberalism of Jean Bethke Elshtain is in hospice care, her ideology's bastards have control over the two default settings of American Christendom at this point: the open harlotry of the Christian nationalists, and the insipid posturing of the pronouns-and-rainbow-flag culture guerrillas.

Getting back to the Goths. I do not think for a moment that my late-antique ancestors were any better than the Romans or the Greeks. We had our idolaters, too, like Athanaric. And our vaunted 'rebel', Fritigern, was driven by a desire to ingratiate himself with Emperor Valens in his embrace of Arianism. Yet at least one of the Goths was listening to the Gospel of John. The author of the *Skeireins*, whoever he was (or they were, as it may have been a collective effort), was clearly inspired, and deeply so, by the man whose hometown his forebears had destroyed. Knut Schäferdiek's assertion that this is the work of Bishop Theodore of Heraclea in Gothic translation[187] oversteps a bit, I think. But his critical analysis and linguistic reasoning is in my opinion well-argued: that the commentary reflects Bishop Theodore's exegetical style, authorial voice and outlook.

The *Skeireins* author read the Gospel of Saint John and was impressed by the text's insistence on **obedient *praxis***, by its

---

[187] Schäferdiek, 'Fragmente'.

emphasis on the **universality** of the teaching, by its **opposition to identity politics**, and by its assertion of God's **sufficiency**. The *Skeireins* author, facing an audience of Arians, made a startling and even prophetic claim for Christ's *functional* Godhood in His obedient subordination. In so doing, the *Skeireins* author indicts *both* his pagan countrymen seeking to assert their particularity, and his Arian brethren who are busily sucking up to the Roman Emperor.

The *Skeireins*, for all that it consists only of eight scraps of palimpsest in a Vatican library vault, is nonetheless comfort to me that I am not the first barbarian to read the Gospel of Saint John. It is my profound hope that I will not be the last, either. I do not say this out of pride, or out of a mistaken estimation of the legacy that my own work will leave. I say it in a very real awe and fear of the Day of the Lord, into which the Lord's Prayer asks Him not to lead us.

A word to Gen Z from a Gothic millennial

The last chapter of Saint John's Gospel ends with Jesus asking Peter three times if he loves Him. Peter protests each time that he does love Jesus. But Jesus answers him with the phrase: βόσκε τὰ ἀρνία μου '*feed my lambs*' (John 21:15); ποίμαινε τὰ πρόβατά μου '*herd my sheep*' (John 21:16); and βόσκε τὰ πρόβατά μου '*feed my sheep*' (John 21:17). The pastoralist imagery here is profound. In a footnote to *The Lamb before Its Shearers*, I remarked that this scene, with Jesus interrogating Peter

Closing remarks of a Gothic disciple

repeatedly over his love for Him, is ominously similar to the interrogation of the traitorous Žamuḫa by the Great Khan[188], and the Khan's threefold offer of forgiveness and friendship to his former sworn brother as recounted in *The Secret History of the Mongols*. Even Jesus's prophetic 'sentence' upon Peter explaining how he is to die (John 21:18) seemingly anticipates the bloodless method by which Žamuḫa was executed: by having his spine broken[189].

Actually, what's happening in these verses is much more interesting than that. The judgement on Peter, that *'when you were young, you girded yourself* [ἐζώννυες σεαυτὸν] *and walked where you would; but when you are old, you will stretch out your hands, and another will gird you* [ἄλλος σε ζώσει] *and carry you where you do not wish to go'* (John 21:18), is an emasculation. Remember from John 13, and from Chapter 4 in this book, that to ζώννυμι 'gird oneself up' (= Heb. *'ēzār* אזר; *ḥāgar* חגר) is to be a man. This verb only ever applies to *men*. So in Peter's 'sentencing' under the judgement of the text, Jesus is taking away Peter's masculinity and giving it to someone else, who will use it for a purpose that Peter will not like. For Peter, such a judgement must be devastating, given the degree to which we see in the text that he values his status, his martial prowess (with the sword), and his belonging among the soldiers and the officials in the courtyard of the High Priest.

---

[188] Cooper, *Lamb*, 35n-36n.

[189] Urgunge Onon, *The Secret History of the Mongols: the Life and Times of Chinggis Khan* (Routledge Curzon, 2001), 186-190.

In the Houses of the Poor

O my younger brothers of Gen Z, open your ears to a word from your Gothic millennial elder brother. There are ways, divers and sundry, to chase status, prestige and power in America. Each one of them is as futile as the next, but don't let that stop you! There are still so many establishment think-tanks you can join, so you can fight the 'commies' and 'rooskies' and 'mullahs' from behind a screen in a suburban northern Virginia cubicle. If that doesn't appeal to you, then you can join a prayer circle of plaid flannel-wearing hipster-beards transplanted from said Virginia suburbs to an astroturf Appalachian startup mission, and help 'Daddy' send the 'illegals' packing. Or you can dye your hair, get your nose pierced, name-tag your preferred pronouns to a suitably androgynous outfit, and start mansplaining to a bunch of your like-minded peers in a rented library conference room about how their language is 'problematic' and 'ableist'. But no matter how you choose to assert your masculinity in postmodern America: ***you are not exempt*** from Peter's judgement. Like Žamuḫa when his tribesmen sell him out to the Great Khan, ***you are screwed***.

Now, there are two ways you can respond to that. You can reject the judgement. You can listen to the elders who are being paid (by Olin, by Heritage, by Brookings, by Soros) to lie to you. You can double down on one of your preferred methods of self-assertion, and ride it to the dead end of your choice. Or you can accept the fact that you are screwed. Hear the judgement again, start over, submit to the teaching and start loving your fellow fish in Peter's net, because you're no better off than they are. As Jesus says: ἀκολούθει μοι '*take my road*'

Closing remarks of a Gothic disciple

(John 21:19)! Who knows? Maybe in the end, His judgement will be better than, deep down, you fear it is.

Of course, Peter himself does not seem to take the hint, at all. Nor does he take the pronouncement of judgement graciously. He still asks the question of his Lord: κύριε οὗτος δὲ τί *'Lord, what about this man?'* (John 21:21) He asks this, as though he thinks the 'other disciple' also deserves judgement. And Jesus's answer to him is downright chilling: τί πρὸς σέ *'what is that to you?'* (John 21:22)

Deflating the disciples' λόγος

When Saint John refers to himself, or tells of his own actions in the book bearing his name, and particularly in places where he enjoys a seeming position of privilege (like at the Last Supper), we tend to assume that he's boasting, or that he's placing himself above the other disciples[190]. One assertion I make repeatedly throughout this book is that when we think John is boasting in one of these self-references, it's because we are either ignoring the original Greek or reading it with a corrupted conscience. Up to this point I've had varying levels of textual evidence for that assertion. But here at the very end of his Gospel, Saint John knocks us over the head with it and spells it out for us plainly. From this I can only assume that even when he wrote it, in his own time and among his own

---

[190] For one example: Beardan Coleman, 'Scripture's only recorded foot race', blog post (The King's College, 29 March 2016).

audience, Saint John was already dealing with people who misunderstood and misheard him. And he anticipated that people would continue to mishear him as long as his work was read aloud.

Jesus's full answer to Peter is: ἐὰν αὐτὸν θέλω μένειν ἕως ἔρχομαι τί πρὸς σέ σύ μοι ἀκολούθει '*If it is my will that he remain until I come, what is that to you? Follow me!*' (John 21:22) And Saint John immediately follows that up with: ἐξῆλθεν οὖν οὗτος ὁ λόγος εἰς τοὺς ἀδελφοὺς ὅτι ὁ μαθητὴς ἐκεῖνος οὐκ ἀποθνῄσκει '*The saying spread abroad among the brethren that this disciple was not to die*' (John 21:23), which he goes on to explain *in the text* as a clear mishearing of what Jesus said.

In this passage, Jesus is *not* exempting Saint John from judgement. He is merely telling Peter that Saint John's judgement is *not his business.* Jesus's exclamation about John is hyperbole, to the effect of: '**even if** *I should keep him alive until I come back...*' But the punchline is: '*why should you care [what judgement I pass on him]*'? *You* take my road, *yourself. You* obey the teaching. Yet when the disciples hear it, they start saying amongst themselves that John must be privileged, that he alone must be chosen to live until Jesus returns in glory! Saint John himself is telling his hearers directly that this is the *wrong* takeaway. You can almost *feel* the frustration Saint John has with his second-century AD hearers when he writes οὐκ εἶπεν δὲ αὐτῷ ὁ Ἰησοῦς '*yet Jesus did not say to him...*'!

I have also made it a point, going back to the beginning of *The Lamb before Its Shearers*, that when Saint John uses the word λόγος, it is *not* the philosophical λόγος of the Greeks. Instead, it is referring to a particular 'saying', a citation from the *Torah* in

Closing remarks of a Gothic disciple

particular. But here, notice that the human λόγος of the disciples is in fact a *negative* thing. It's gossip; it's hearsay; it's rumour. This 'saying' of the brethren is *incorrect* and John has to finally set the record straight: 'I'm not immortal! I'm not privileged! I'm not exempt from judgement! All He said was that my salvation was *none of your business!*'

The λόγος that begins the Gospel of Saint John is the λόγος ἦν πρὸς τὸν θεόν '*the word* [that] *was with God*', the word which was life and light to men. Yet at the very end of the same Gospel, at last, we have the philosophical, Platonic λόγος of man. They say that *John* will not die: this is a wilful error that John himself, ὁ γράψας ταῦτα '*who wrote these things*' (John 21:24) has to correct! Despite Jesus in their midst, the disciples are still ἐν τῇ σκοτίᾳ '*in the dark*' and οὐ κατέλαβεν '*don't have a clue*' (John 1:5)!

'What is that to you?'

The universal human response to being placed under scrutiny, it seems, is to baulk the scrutiny by looking for someone else to compare oneself to. What Saint Peter does to Saint John in the last few verses of this Gospel, is something that the Orthodox Church Fathers warn against with insistent frequency. Saint Paisios the Athonite was famous for saying this:

In the Houses of the Poor

One who justifies himself with excuses makes no progress in the spiritual life, nor can he find any inner peace... There is no stronger barrier to the grace of God than excuses![191]

Saint Paisios comes by such a saying honestly. Such sayings are commonly found in the *Apophthegmata*. Abba Poemen the Shepherd, one of the highest-regarded of the Desert Fathers of Egyptian Scetis, said:

A man may seem to be silent, but if his heart is condemning others he is babbling ceaselessly. But there may be another who talks from morning till night and yet he is truly silent; that is, he says nothing that is not profitable.[192]

In another famous anecdote from the *Apophthegmata*, Abba Moses the Robber refuses to condemn another monk in Scetis who committed a crime.

A brother at Scetis committed a fault. A council was called to which Abba Moses was invited, but he refused to go to it. Then the priest sent someone to say to him, 'Come, for everyone is waiting for you.' So he got up and went. He took a leaking jug, filled it with water and carried it with him. The others came out to meet him and said to him, 'What is this, Father?' The old man said to them, 'My sins run out behind me, and I do not see them, and today I am coming to judge the

---

[191] Jeremy McKemy, 'Judging ourselves and others', *Orthodox Road* (16 October 2014).

[192] Benedicta Ward, tr., *The Sayings of the Desert Fathers* (Cistercian Publications, 1975), 171.

Closing remarks of a Gothic disciple

errors of another.' When they heard that they said no more to the brother but forgave him.[193]

It is an unfortunate aspect of modern Orthodox Christian intellectual life in the West, that we do not consider the entire life situation of the monastics who produced these sayings. The Orthodox *ressourcement* of the Desert Fathers and of the Patristics in general, puts a great deal of emphasis on the Fathers' ascetic disciplines and their prayer rules. It has now gotten to the point where there is a cottage industry, a glut, even, of Orthodox books and pamphlets on how to structure your prayers and fasting in the mode of the Desert Fathers. But these books, almost to a one, ignore the importance of hearing the Scriptures read aloud, and of studying the Scriptures in the original language.

Asceticism is only the smaller part of how these monks lived. Far more important than the asceticism or the prayer rules, in the lives of the Egyptian monks, were their exercise of hospitality to visitors[194]; and their physical work, which included weaving sandals and baskets to be sold to meet the dietary and living needs of the brothers as well as their philanthropic giving. Sister Benedicta Ward notes that their most important prayer practice was their *daily hearing of the Scriptures*, often for as many hours as they worked in the day. Every monk would recite from the rest of *ta Vivlía* on Saturdays and Sundays. The 'Jesus Prayer' was meant for the monastic

---

[193] Ward, *Sayings*, 139.
[194] Ward, *Sayings*, xxiv-xxv.

disciple to fill the time between hearing the Psalms. It was secondary in importance to the Psalms themselves[195]. And because the monks were Copts, Syriacs and Greeks, we may take it as read that they were hearing the Psalms either in the Septuagint Greek or in an Aramaic *targum*.

It is in *this context* that we need to understand the sayings about not making excuses and not condemning others. The point is not that you make yourself humbler, more contrite, further advanced in the spiritual life on the path to *theosis*. The point is in fact much simpler: *if you are talking*, then *you are not hearing the text*. And if you are talking about the failures of someone else, then you are *certainly* not paying due attention to where *you* are found, by the text!

Jesus's τί πρὸς σέ in answer to Peter reflects precisely this insight. Jesus has to repeat Himself to Peter—ἀκολούθει μοι (21:19) and then, more emphatically, σύ μοι ἀκολούθει (21:22)—because Peter *was not hearing Him*. And John's punchline is: *no one else* was hearing Jesus either! That's why they all thought Jesus was talking about John not dying until He came again, rather than telling Peter off for ignoring His command!

---

[195] Ward, *Sayings*, xxvi.

Closing remarks of a Gothic disciple

The grace of the next cycle

ἔστιν δὲ καὶ ἄλλα πολλὰ ἃ ἐποίησεν ὁ Ἰησοῦς ἅτινα ἐὰν γράφηται καθ' ἕν οὐδ' αὐτὸν οἶμαι τὸν κόσμον χωρῆσαι τὰ γραφόμενα βιβλία

But there are also many other things which Jesus did; were every one of them to be written, I suppose that the world itself could not contain the books that would be written. (John 21:25)

These two books, *The Lamb before Its Shearers* and *In the Houses of the Poor*, are meant to be read together. Together they form a single commentary on the Gospel of Saint John in the style of, and with the inspiration of, the fourth-century Gothic *Skeireins* text. Thematically they diverge somewhat, though they are tied together by a common focus.

The former book, *The Lamb before Its Shearers*, carefully follows the *Skeireins* passage for passage, making direct quotes from the Gothic commentary where appropriate. The themes of that book: light versus darkness, hearing versus willful non-hearing—all follow directly from the Gospel text. However, *Lamb* is also much more closely and urgently tied to the events of its time, namely the still-ongoing Israeli genocide against the Palestinians of Gaza. *The Lamb before Its Shearers* traces how the Johannine Gospel text systematically dismantles human claims to philosophical and theological wisdom, as well as political claims to power. In Saint John's account, Jesus demolishes the political claims exercised through familial belonging (the first meeting with Nicodemus); through doctrinal 'closeness' to God (John the Forerunner's arbitration of the dispute among his followers); or through legal correctness (the healing at the House of the Olive). We are thus left, in the first ten chapters of Saint John's Gospel, following a Teacher who rejects worldly kingship after the feeding of the multitudes, who refuses and even mocks the question of His origins and His destination at the Feast of Booths, and who ruthlessly deflates the identity politics of his Judahite interlocutors at the healing of the man born blind.

The present book, *In the Houses of the Poor*, can no longer follow the *Skeireins* text, but continues along the path it points to in its reading of the Gospel of Saint John. Greater attention must necessarily be paid here to the historical and political context of the world of the literary text. The Teacher performs another 'populistic' miracle: raising Lazarus from the dead and thus saving his two sisters from eviction. This time, He is dragged along the path that leads to kingship... and His death. Saint John's prior work, deconstructing all political and cultural and religious claims to authority, returns here with a vengeance as he applies that deconstruction specifically to the Roman and Judahite authorities in their treatment of Jesus before and after His arrest. Jesus is arrested on a charge of seeking kingship, highlighting the irony that both Pilate and the High Priest are actually guilty of the crime they accuse Him of! They seek to enthrone *themselves* as gods, as they judge Him guilty and condemn Him to death.

Saint John's 'BS-question' *voir dire* of his hearers in Chapter 7 is his first attempt to delink us from our Messianic and philosophical assumptions. Another attempt is made in Chapter 9 and Chapter 10, where Jesus argues that an Abrahamic bloodline is not sufficient to make you a 'son' of the

Closing remarks of a Gothic disciple

teaching. Jesus's Davidic lineage should thus be *removed* from our consideration when the question of His kingship arises at His trial in Chapters 18 and 19. And Jesus's 'so-you-say' ambivalence as to the question of His kingship, is meant to get hearers to recognise the pitfalls of both *political idolatry* (that is, harlotry) and *political rebellion* (that is, contumely).

Pilate is the one who proclaims 'Christ is King'. But he does so *not* out of loyalty to Jesus, but out of loyalty to Augustus. He is a harlot who proclaims one master while serving another. The Judahite authorities are the ones who answer back to him 'No kings (but Caesar)'. They are ungrateful, spoiled, bitter, perverse children who detest the God who brought them out of exile. Such is the judgement of the text on the executioners of Jesus.

Mary, the mother of Jesus, is the only one who comes off clearly justified in the text's eyes. She *relinquishes* her creditor-claims over Jesus as His mother and enters the household of the 'other disciple'. She hears the command from the Cross, and she does it. Thus at the seventh hour, the hour of judgement, when she is confronted with a dying man who is thirsty, she is able to give Him a drink from the seventh jar of wine.

Apart from the mother of Jesus, and possibly Mary Magdalene, no one else in the text seems to get the message. Joseph of Arimathea and Nicodemus make clowns of themselves in their deference to Pilate and the Judahite authorities over the burial of Jesus. The disciples are found cowering in fear, not having believed the words of Mary Magdalene, when Jesus returns. And Peter finds he has to answer for all of the times he failed to hear and do his Teacher's teaching.

As for us who hear the text? We have the grace of the next cycle of history. We have the text, from the hands of those whom the text judges. Let them hear, as have ears to hear. And let them do, as have hands to do the work.

Acknowledgements

In the name of God our heavenly Father, my heartfelt gratitude goes out to my family: to **the *Skeireins* author**; to my grandfather, **CPO Franklin Dero Cooper**; and to my father, **Dr Reid Franklin Cooper**.

For encouraging my work, and for putting my words to paper, I am much obliged to **Fr Paul Nadim Tarazi**; to **Fr Timothy Lowe**; and to **Fr Marc Boulos**.

I incline my ear to the prophetic utterance of **Fr Paul Abernathy**; of **June Morits**; and of **Madeleine L'Engle**.

www.ingramcontent.com/pod-product-compliance
Lightning Source LLC
Chambersburg PA
CBHW040309170426
43195CB00020B/2898